A TREATISE

UPON

CABLE OR ROPE TRACTION.

Frontispiece: Fig. 41.]

THE GEARY STREET CABLE TRAMWAY, SAN FRANCISCO, CAL., U.S.A.

A TREATISE

UPON

CABLE OR ROPE TRACTION,

AS APPLIED TO THE WORKING OF

STREET AND OTHER RAILWAYS,

(Revised and Enlarged from " Engineering.")

BY

J. BUCKNALL SMITH, C.E.

(AUTHOR OF "RAILWAY TRAFFIC AND SAFETY APPLIANCES," &C.)

Late of Chief Engineer's Department, The Cable Tramways Corporation;
Late Constructing Engineer to the Highgate Cable Tramway;
Consulting Engineer (for Cable Traction) to the Lisbon Tramways Co., &c. &c.

SECOND EDITION

With Additional Material by
GEORGE W. HILTON, M.C.E.R.A.

(AUTHOR OF "THE CABLE CAR IN AMERICA", &C.)

Late Acting Curator of Rail Transportation, The Smithsonian Institution;
Late Historian of the Chicago Cable Railways;
Professor of Economics, University of California, Los Angeles, &c. &c.

Owlswick Press: Philadelphia

1977

iv

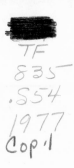

Manufactured in the United States of America.
Published by
the Owlswick Press
Box 8243, Philadelphia PA 19101.

This book was first published in 1887
by *Engineering* of London
and by John Wiley & Sons of New York.
This edition contains a new preface and notes
by George W. Hilton.

International Standard Book Number 0-913896-08-X
Library of Congress Catalog Card Number 76-53131

THIS WORK IS DEDICATED

BY

THE AUTHOR

TO

WILLIAM MUNTON BULLIVANT, ESQ.,

AS A

TRIBUTE OF RESPECT AND RECOGNITION OF HIS ABILITY AND ENTERPRISE
SHOWN IN CONNECTION WITH THE
INTRODUCTION AND ESTABLISHMENT OF CABLE TRACTION
FOR TRAMWAY WORKING IN
GREAT BRITAIN.

THE SECOND EDITION
IS DEDICATED TO

OWEN DAVIES

(1910-1968)

FROM WHOM THE ORIGINAL WAS PURCHASED IN 1947

HIS LIFE WAS A MONUMENT TO THE SERVICES OF THE SPECIALIZED
BOOKSELLER TO THE PRESERVATION AND DISSEMINATION OF KNOWLEDGE.

CONTENTS.

CHAPTER V.

CABLE TRACTION IN EUROPE AND AUSTRALIA.

CHAPTER VI.

THE COST OF CONSTRUCTING AND WORKING THE SYSTEM.

CHAPTER VII.

CONSIDERATIONS IN TRAMWAY WORKING.

CHAPTER VIII.

THE MANUFACTURE OF WIRE AND WIRE ROPES, AND THEIR APPLICATIONS.

APPENDIX.

LIST OF ILLUSTRATIONS.

PREFACE

TO THE SECOND EDITION.

———•———

PRESENTED here is a unique volume: the only book on the cable car published during the period in which cable traction was economic in rivalry to the horse car and the electric streetcar. The book is the effort of a British engineer to provide an exposition of what was mainly an American innovation. As such, the book is to some extent an historical treatise, partly an exposition of cable technology, and in large measure a tract — a frank work of advocacy of cable traction as the best available technology for British street railway service.

The author, John Bucknall Smith, was an obscure figure — as obscure, alas, as only a John Smith can be. He was born on March 25, 1856, as Arthur John Smith at 4 Stafford Terrace, Loughborough Road, Brixton, in South London. His parents were Arthur Smith, a stone and slate merchant, and the former Mary Anne Eliza Smythe. Early in life the young man dropped "Arthur" and adopted the middle name "Bucknall," which he used for the rest of his life. He signed himself "C.E." or "Civil Engineer" throughout his lifetime, but he was never a member of the Institution of Civil Engineers. Similarly, he appears never to have taken a degree in engineering at one of the major universities, but he practiced before either licensure or academic engineering degrees were widespread.

From his book we know that during the 1880's he was in professional practice in London, where he became engineer in charge of construction for the Highgate Cable Tramway, the first British cable line built with American patents. He was an engineer for the Cable Tramways Corporation, the British licensee of the patent trust which the American developers of the cable car had formed in a semi-successful effort at monopoly. As such, he consulted on construction of cable tramlines in Lisbon.

Smith was a frequent author for *Engineering*, the journal in which the present volume appeared serially before publication as a book. Not all of his contributions were signed; "Railway Traffic and Safety Appliances," the work cited on the title page of this book, for example, was an unsigned article which appeared in volume XLIV of *Engineering* in 1887, pages 87-89. What was to become Smith's one claim to lasting notice, *A Treatise upon Cable or Rope Traction as applied to the Working of Street and Other Railways*, appeared serially in *Engineering* between 1884 and 1886.* The serial version, revised and updated, provided about the first 130 pages of the book; much of the rest came from some related articles in *Engineering*.** Interestingly, the serial version is signed J. Bucknall-Smith, but the hyphen had dropped from his name by the time the book appeared in mid-1887.

Smith continued his enquiries into wire manufacture, which dominate the later portions of the present volume, and began a separate series of articles on the subject, published in *The Engineer* beginning in March 1889. These, too, were published as a book by *Engineering* in 1891 under the title *A Treatise upon Wire, Its Manufacture and Uses, Embracing Comprehensive Descriptions of the Constructions and Applications of Wire Ropes*. The identification of the author on the title page adds to our knowledge only that he had written an article, "The Diamond Industry of South Africa." One wonders whether by 1891 Smith was already losing interest in his earlier volume, for its title is erroneously listed among his

---

* *Engineering*, XXXVIII (1884), 354-355, 424-426, 444-445, 469-470, 561-564; XXXIX (1885), 26-28, 157-159, 255-257, 307-310, 415-418, 642-644; XL (1885) 270-271; XLI (1886), 561-562, 588-590, 596; XLII (1886), 2-4, 254-255, 624-627, 649-650.

** Unsigned articles, presumably by Smith, "Messrs. Bullivant and Co.'s Wire Rope Works," XXXVIII (1884), 515-517; "Messrs. Bullivant and Co.'s New Wire Rope Works," XLIII (1887), 214-215; "Messrs. Cradock and Co.'s Wire and Wire Rope Works," XLIII (1887), 344, 365-367, 374; and "The City and Southwark Subway: Mr. J.H. Greathead Engineer" (possibly by Greathead rather than Smith), XLIII (1887), 305-306, 355-357.

publications as *Cable Traction as applied to the Working of Rail and Tramways.*

After the publication of his second book, Smith fades almost completely from the historical record. Only some communications to professional journals break an otherwise complete obscurity which lasted to his death. He died in rented quarters at 43A Brunswick Road in the seaside retirement community of Hove, Sussex, on July 27, 1926. Apart from small bequests to his landlady and her daughter, he left his estate to the Chelsea Hospital for Women and the Brompton Hospital for Consumption and Chest Diseases, probably the hospitals in which his parents died. I could find no evidence of his ever having married. He was buried in the Hove Cemetery on July 29, 1926, beneath a tombstone reading "Arthur John Bucknall Smith." No obituary of him appeared in any professional journal.

Either Smith was an extraordinarily self-effacing man, or he made no effort at documenting himself in the belief that he was no longer of interest to society. That view, though erroneous, may be forgiven him, for he had identified himself with something that had proved exceptionally short-lived. As Smith's account demonstrates, cable traction by endless wire ropes was shown to be economic in San Francisco in 1873, but for nearly a decade the development was thought to be unique to San Francisco because of the city's straight streets, steep gradients and mild climate. Charles B. Holmes' installation of the technology on the Chicago City Railway in January 1882 demonstrated the economy of cable traction in cities with ordinarily harsh American winters. For six years, cable traction was the most economic technology available to American street railway operators, though the heavy investment of about $175,000 per mile of double track limited application almost entirely to major routes.

The American engineer Frank J. Sprague perfected the electric streetcar in installations in St. Joseph, Missouri, in September 1887 and Richmond, Virginia, in February 1888. Sprague's improvements reversed the situation that the cable car had been more economic than existing electric streetcars. Sprague's electric installations proved capable of providing the service with about a seventh of the investment of cable systems at half the variable cost. This advantage was not entirely realized until introduction of the General Electric Type-K controller and Westinghouse Number 3 motor in 1893. Between 1888 and 1893, the electric car and cable car were in rivalry, with the cable car being considered superior for heavily travelled routes by a dwindling number of engineers and street railway managers. Development in 1895 of the underground conduit for pick-up of electric power on lines where overhead wires were prohibited ended any attractions of cable traction for new installation. American street railways disinvested in cable systems until by 1913 none remained except for a small number of lines which climbed heavy grades in Seattle, Tacoma and San Francisco. Similarly, lines on steep grades in Dunedin, New Zealand, survived until 1957.

Smith dated his book (p. viii) April 1887, some five months before Sprague's installation in St. Joseph. An autographed copy in the possession of Victor Goldberg of London is signed June 27, 1887, probably within a few days of the publication date. Consequently, the book is a product of the period in which the cable car was still superior to the electric car. This fact is intrinsic to the strengths and weaknesses of the book. Smith lumped the electric car with the compressed air motor as "expensive or unreliable" and "generally unsuitable for street purposes." Not a single electric installation of Daft, Van Depoele or any other pre-Sprague engineer of electric cars had ever replaced a cable line; Smith could not reasonably have been expected to anticipate Sprague's great improvement.

Notably, the polemical character of the book is stronger, fresher, and more enthusiastic than it would have been even a short time later. By 1888, Smith would have had to admit a role for electric cars on routes of intermediate traffic density, or in flat cities. The decision of the City of London & Southwark Subway Company in mid-1888 to electrify the tube under the Thames, which Smith describes at length as a major cable project, could only have shaken his conviction badly. As the book stands, however, Smith's argument of the superiority of cable traction to its alternatives provides a superb insight into the thinking of cable advocates in their short period of hegemony. Thus, Smith's timing increased the value of his book as a primary source on the history of the cable car. C.B. Fairchild in his *Street Railways* of 1892 and several authors in articles considered the relative economy of electric and cable cars after 1888.

Similarly, Smith's unalloyed advocacy of the cable car caused him to enquire at great length into the historical origins of the invention. By present standards, the strongest feature of the work is the account of the historical development of cable traction in Chapters I and II. One presumes that Smith's enthusiasm for cable traction would have given him an antiquarian interest in its origins in any case, but the existence of an American patent trust with an English licensee made the question of the degree of novelty in the San Francisco installations extremely important for any operator who was considering a cable system. Although Smith had been an engineer for the British licensee, he considered the controversy upon patent rights unfortunate, described it as a "patent mania which has beset the development of the system," and remained aloof from the question of the patent trust's rights. Indeed, implicitly his text is an overpowering demonstration of the lack of novelty in the San Francisco innovation. Smith showed clearly that every important element in the system was present either in patents or in British and American installations before Andrew S. Hallidie's Clay Street Hill Railroad of 1873. Further, he noted that Hallidie had bought his franchise from Benjamin H. Brooks, who had failed to finance a similar installation. Somewhat better in the serial version than in the book, Smith demonstrated that the mechanical ingenuity in the system was the work of the German engineer William E. Eppelsheimer, who served as draftsman, rather than of Hallidie himself. Smith demonstrated so completely that Hallidie, who was at best the entrepreneur of the first commerically successful American cable installation, was not (in a mechanical sense) the inventor of cable traction that one wonders why Hallidie could have been looked on as the inventor for so long.

The date at which Smith completed his book also influences his exposition of cable technology and operating practice. Internal evidence suggests that Smith updated the serial version to approximately the end of 1886. By that time only some 62 miles of cable line had been built in America. Most

American mileage was built during the period of rivalry between cable and electric traction between 1888 and 1893. Mileage peaked at 305 in 1893; thus, some four-fifths of mileage came after Smith's book appeared. By the time Smith wrote, all of the major elements in cable traction were in existence: the iron-and-concrete conduit; the let-go curve and the pull curve; grips of the bottom, side and top types; and cable of both the ordinary and Lang-lay variety. By the early 1890's somewhat greater variety of each would have been available, however. On the other hand, it is doubtful that the draftsmanship or literary exposition of cable traction could have been improved upon. Smith had a Victorian style which was by no means economical of words, but he brought through his descriptions an understanding of the internal workings of the cable railway system with a precision and clarity that can hardly be overpraised. The drawings — presumably by the drafting staff of *Engineering* — are meticulous and esthetically satisfying, a perfect complement to the text.

The principal benefit of additional observation would inevitably have been expansion of Smith's meager list of the disattractions of cable traction on page 132. The *Street Railway Journal* and the lesser trade publications of the day paid attention extensively to the operating experience and relative cost of cable systems during the rivalry with electric streetcars of 1888-1893, bringing forth a great deal of information which was not available when Smith wrote. For example, on page 119 Smith noted that about half the power in the system is spent in moving the cable, but he concluded that this was not a disattraction in comparison with the steam locomotives which he considered the only economic rivals to the cable car. By 1893 he would probably have learned that most cable systems spent 50 to 70 per cent of energy on moving the cable, and that electric cars, where the power was transmitted without friction, had no analogous waste of energy.

Similarly, Smith stated on page 40 that slots on the pioneer Clay Street Hill Railroad had never been known to be clogged. Had he waited for the spread of cable traction to more cities with severe climates, he would have observed a chronic problem, especially in St. Paul and Portland, of slots closing from the pressure of ice formation in the ground along the conduits.

Smith's least defensible judgment was that the cable car had good control properties. On pages 42 and 63 he dwelt on the precision of control of cable cars. Actually, the worst single feature of cable traction was that a car might become uncontrollable in any of several ways. Because the vehicle's progress did not depend upon adhesion between the wheel and the surface on which it ran, a car could ascend a grade as steep as 28.5 per cent, far steeper than the maximum grade on which its brakes could hold it. Accordingly, dropping the cable on an up grade, or attempting to proceed down a major grade without the cable in the grip were potential sources of severe accidents. Smith cited one such occurrence on the Highgate Hill line, page 103, but accepted the official explanation of the accident as failure of the gripman to observe the company's rules.

Worst of all, cable traction presented an ever-present danger of a loose strand coming up from the cable, becoming enmeshed in the grip mechanism, and causing the car to proceed uncontrollable at the speed of the cable. Managements of street railways and municipal officials, as well, devoted more time and attention to this danger than to any other risk in cable traction. Smith, however, never mentioned the problem, even though it was well known by the mid-1880's.

The necessity of reworking the serial version in *Engineering* into the book version gave Smith an opportunity for modification of his judgments on the basis of emerging knowledge which the American systems were generating. There is a slight indication that Smith was coming to realize that he was overstating the attractions of the control of cable cars: the serial version in its discussion of the Sutter Street line in San Francisco describes "the perfect control of the cable cars," but in the book, page 42, Smith substituted "excellent" for "perfect."

In general I have attempted to note changes of this character, which may show a modification of Smith's opinions. On page 36, for example, Smith showed a complete reversal in judgment. The serial version read "The amount of wear and tear inflicted upon the cables by the nipping action of the car grippers is also not of a serious nature," but the final text recognized that this wear and tear "is sometimes considerable." A notable example occurs in the list of attractions of cable traction on page 131, where rephrasing of point 12 reversed the meaning completely without changing a word. "The system can be practically worked in any climate" became "The system can be worked in (practically) any climate."

I have also attempted to note changes which seem to me to reduce the historical usefulness of the work. For whatever reason, Smith removed several passages on the identity of the individuals responsible for advances. The most important of these is attribution of Hallidie's grip to William E. Eppelsheimer on page 33. Simple rephrasings for stylistic improvement, or changes in reference from "earlier articles" to "earlier portions of this book," and the like, I have not attempted to footnote. Similarly, I have not noted changes in the order of presentation of material at several points. In general, I have tried to let the book stand on its own considerable merits as a document of its time rather than to attempt to update it in footnotes into a general history of cable traction. Readers seeking the later history are referred to my *The Cable Car in America*, published by Howell-North Books, Berkeley, California, in 1971.

Smith's book was not a success in disseminating cable tramways in Britain; only Edinburgh ever had a comprehensive system. London had two isolated lines, the Highgate installation which Smith described, and a later line climbing Brixton Hill. Birmingham had a single line, and the Midland resort town of Matlock another. The Glasgow Subway which Smith noted as projected was built, but Liverpool backed off from building a cable street railway after an experimental installation. Bradford, Bristol and Newcastle also made serious enquiries into cable traction, but decided against the investment. Douglas, on the Isle of Man, had a difficult installation on a mildly hilly but extremely curvaceous route. Edinburgh's system of some 24 miles was brought forth by a combination of the municipal government's unwillingness to allow overhead wires on Princes Street, and fairly universal gradients rising or falling from Princes Street to the residential areas beyond. The individual lines in the other cities were efforts to deal with isolated grades or especially undulating streets. A 21-year franchise period was an inhibition against installing a technology with so much irrecoverable capital. In general, British tramway operators moved directly from horse cars to electric cars — no doubt to their retrospective relief.

There was, at minimum, enough cable traction in Britain to produce a number of historians or enthusiasts. Of these Victor Goldberg, J.H. Price, and Charles Lee were very kind in helping my editorial efforts directly. F.K. Pearson should be cited for his extensive historical research on the Douglas cable line. Among the Americans, John H. White, Jr., Addison H. Laflin, Jr., and David Myrick were most helpful. Finally, I particularly appreciated the spontaneous enthusiasm of David J. Williams III and George H. Scithers of Owlswick Press at the prospect of bringing this fine book before the public once more.

The edition at hand is a photographic reprint of the original with the addition of text and notes. In the interest of avoiding pull-outs, the plate on the Chicago City Railway at page 83 has been reproduced as a series of pages, and both the illustrations of a wire rope-closing machine at page 154 and of the Clifton Colliery rope haulage at page 159 have been slightly reduced. The reader should note that the numbering of plates on the list of illustrations on pages xi and xii does not square with the numbers on the illustrations themselves. The original index in all its fine Victorian irrationality has been retained in the belief that historical preservation in this instance is more important than having a useful index.

GEORGE W. HILTON

University of California
Los Angeles
October 1, 1976

PREFACE

TO THE FIRST EDITION.

————•◦•————

Tramways are now a widely adopted and thoroughly approved means of public locomotion, and the technical considerations involved in their construction and economical working have engrossed the study and attention of many able engineers for some years past. Upwards of twelve and a half millions sterling have now been expended upon the tramways of this kingdom alone, and, therefore, if only from a financial point of view, they are worthy of attention. The good service afforded by tramways in this country will be understood, when we realise that about 3 per cent. of the entire population is carried daily by this means of transport, at an average fare of less than three halfpence per person ; in some cities upwards of 20 per cent. of the population travels daily on street railroads. That animal power for working tramcars is most unsuitable, and that some form of mechanical traction ought to be substituted for the same, is now generally admitted by those acquainted with the subject. About an average of 77 per cent. of the gross receipts is consumed by working tramways with horses or mules, which in a large measure explains the fact, that while their earning capacity compares so favourably with that of railways, the working expenses are much heavier.

The chief object of this volume is to describe the application and development of a comparatively novel system of mechanical traction for street and other railways, known as the "*Endless Cable Haulage System*," which possesses features of peculiar merit. This system was first introduced during 1873 for working street railways, in San Francisco, Cal., U.S.A., where it has since achieved a marked mechanical and financial success.

Similar applications of the system have since been made and largely extended in various other cities of the United States; in New Zealand; in Australia; and other countries, with corresponding success. In 1883, a cable line was built up Highgate Hill, London, and at present similar works are in course of construction in London, Edinburgh, and Birmingham.

It is not intended in the following pages to advocate an universal application of the system, and any comparisons with other existing means of traction are wholly impartial, and made with the object of placing before the reader the relative merits of the system at issue.

The closing chapter of this volume is devoted to a short treatise upon the manufacture of wire and wire ropes, with examples of their various uses.

The writer has chiefly confined his descriptions and comments to systems of haulage and manufactures, or details relating thereto, with which he has been personally associated or acquainted both at home and abroad.

In conclusion, the Author has to acknowledge assistance received from the Editors of "ENGINEERING," from Engineers, Manufacturers, and Municipal Authorities in this and other countries; also his indebtedness to mining data, established long before " cable traction" was applied to street tramway working.

J. BUCKNALL SMITH.

113, CANNON STREET, LONDON, E.C.,
    April, 1887.

STREET AND OTHER CABLE RAILWAYS.

INTRODUCTION.

" TRAMWAYS " is the recognised, but wholly indefensible term applied in this country to street railways, which form carriage or car ways of comparatively low tractive resistance, so constructed and laid, as not to practically interfere with ordinary vehicular and foot traffic common to public thoroughfares.

The modern tramway was first employed in the United States, at New York, as early as 1832. The system was, however, not successfully introduced or accepted until about 1852, from which date tramways were rapidly extended within the States to great advantage.

In 1860 the first type of street railroad was introduced in this country, and laid on the macadamised roads of Birkenhead, according to Mr. G. F. Train's invention or design. The following year the system obtained a temporary footing within the suburbs of London. However, from inconveniences experienced, these lines had to be speedily removed, and had it not been for timely improvements, the system would have been probably extinguished for years. As it was, tramway schemes were long looked upon with grave antipathy and apprehension. The English were found to be more cautious and exacting than the Americans. However, in 1865, a "non-obstructive" street railway was exhibited at Liverpool, but although hailed by some supporters with great enthusiasm this design was also abandoned.

Notwithstanding these troubles, arising from defective schemes and details, combined with encumbrances caused by a timid and fastidious community, the principle of street tramways obtained a firmer footing about three years later.

Nearly thirty years have passed away since Mr. Train first introduced the modern system of street tramways into this country, and although his enterprise was summarily arrested by opposition created by prejudice and by the shortcomings which attend all new schemes, the system was successfully revived in 1868, when the first Act of Parliament was obtained for a system of horse tramways in Liverpool. The subsequent rapid development of horse street railroads in the United Kingdom, as also in Europe and other parts of the civilised world, is familiar to most readers, but few years of practical operation had elapsed ere engineers, impressed with the unsuitability of animal traction, were busily engaged in designing special steam locomotives and other motors for tramway purposes. In 1875 powers were granted authorising the use of steam or mechanical power upon street tramways. The marked tardiness with which horses have been and are being superseded by mechanical power for the arduous purpose of hauling our street tramcars, is more the result of certain inefficiencies in the various motors offered in the market than from any inherent unsuitability in the employment of mechanical power itself. It is, however, fair to admit that in some cases the want of efficiency is not so much attributable to the engines as to the nature of the conditions and types of permanent ways, &c., which may be quite unfit for such purposes. However, there are now many examples where locomotives are being used on appropriate roads with favourable results. On the other hand, whilst thus duly recognising in certain suitable instances the superiority of such motors over animal power, it is nevertheless incontrovertibly clear that there are many streets, in densely populated districts, in which the passage of steam engines will never be permitted.

It should not be disregarded that there are now other tramway engines in the market than those actuated by steam, as, for example, compressed air and electric motors, &c., and which are free from many of the substantially founded objections to the use of steam, but as **Note 2** yet these have proved in practice to be expensive or unreliable. Later on some analytical and comparative statements will be given and considered, for the purpose of forming some comparative estimates of the value of various systems used or proposed, for the propulsion or haulage of street tramcars. But for the present we will confine our attention to a comparatively new method of mechanically working street and other railways, and by what is known as the "*Cable System of Traction.*"

The mere idea of a "cable tramway," or in other words a tramway on which the cars are drawn or hauled by means of a cable or rope receiving its motion from a stationary and distant source of power, contains in itself no remarkable novelty as many must be aware. Cable traction has been successfully employed upon certain railways and in mines for many years past. But the specific adaptation of the principle to street railways has involved much ingenuity.

It may be remembered by some readers that this system of tramway working was first placed before the British public in a tangible form in October, 1882, or immediately after the necessary Parliamentary powers had been obtained for the construction and operation of the first cable line in England, viz., that at Highgate Hill, extending from the Archway Tavern, Upper Holloway, to Southwood Lane, Hornsey.

There can be little doubt in the minds of those acquainted with the subject, that the successful conversion (in January, 1882) of the State street horse tramway, Chicago, U.S.A., to the "cable system" of traction afforded, in a great measure, the requisite impetus for the introduction of the system into this country. The early Californian cable roads had the unquestionable advantage of an excellent and uniform climate, whereas the Chicago installation was subject to most variable weather and extreme temperatures, thus placing it under trying and crucial conditions, and somewhat similar to the possible requirements it might be called upon to withstand in the erratic meteorological variations of a British climate. At the present stage it will suffice to add that the Chicago cable lines appear a great success, and the same remark may be applied to the " Highgate Hill cable line," London, which was opened to the public on the 29th of May, 1884, and has been in satisfactory operation ever since. There is, incontestably, one peculiar practical advantage of the system in question over others at present before the public, viz., its capability of economically working steep grades. In fact, the only system that can possibly aspire to anything like reasonable competition in such cases would be the old and cumbersome rack-and-pinion roads. From the capabilities of the " cable system," it is now quite feasible to effect tramway communication in the most hilly districts which hitherto have been considered as inaccessible. At the same time the system is thoroughly applicable to the economical working of tramways constructed on level ground, and as most completely exemplified in Chicago.

In many respects the " Cable system " offers important advantages : *e.g.*, by reducing the working and maintaining expenses of tramways ; by avoiding dirt, smoke, sparks and steam, in public streets ; as also by obviating the cruelty to horses, so unsuitably employed, &c. The last-named benefit has secured for the system the warm approval and support of the " Royal Society for the Prevention of Cruelty to Animals ;" but, of course, other mechanical systems of traction could boast of the same benevolent objects. It seems certainly a cruel fact, that the working lives of tram horses average only $4\frac{1}{2}$ years, and that annually about 5000 horses are crippled, used up, or destroyed, by the tramways of this country alone. Further, a method of working that absorbs about 77 per cent. of the gross receipts can hardly be urged as a very remunerative achievement.

However, it is not proposed to consider ethical recommendations,

Note 3

which may constitute valuable ornaments to a prospectus, but to confine attention as closely as possible to purely technical matters, for in practice we may rest assured that the public and companies, however professedly humane, will still continue to use animal power so long as it suits their convenience or their pockets. Therefore, before the plea for consideration for the horses can receive much practical attention, it rests with the ingenuity of engineers to devise and establish a mechanical system of locomotion that will afford the travelling public the same, if not better, comfort and accommodation than heretofore, and an equal degree of safety in transit at the same rate of fares. At the same time any such proposed scheme should show a distinct remunerative advantage to the shareholders, and be reasonably free from the numerous objections commonly raised by municipal or local authorities, and the anti-tramway world. Then we may reasonably expect to find the employment of horse-power to be speedily recognised as an element of barbarism. Now, the cable system, when and where judiciously applied, *i.e.*, under befitting circumstances with regard to traffic and the route, certainly appears to be a wide step in the right direction, although it would not be for one moment believed that a system which is claimed to possess so many paramount advantages, could be absolutely free from some defects or objections, especially when one appreciates the great variance of opinion that must exist upon such subjects, combined with the prejudices of vested interests. However, later on, the applications, construction, and operation of the system in question, will be sufficiently described and illustrated, so as to afford a fair basis for technical investigations and criticism, but before proceeding to consider the cable tramway systems of to-day, a brief retrospective glance at their general history and development will be instructive.

For carrying out the above objects, it seems appropriate to subdivide the subject at issue into the seven following sections or chapters:—

1. Preliminary remarks upon cable or rope traction schemes which have technical bearing, &c., *e.g.*, mining and railway haulage, &c.

2. The history and development of *street cable tramways* proper, including descriptions of the principal features of the construction and operation of the Clay-street line; Sutter-street line; California-street line; Geary-street line; Union and Presidio line; Market-street line; &c., all within the city of Francisco, Cal., U.S.A.

3. The conversion of the Chicago horse lines to the cable system; the Renz Park and Columbia Avenue trial section, Philadelphia; and other later projects; the introduction of the system into the State of New York; the Brooklyn Bridge cable line; cable tramways in Kansas City, Cincinnati, St. Louis, &c.

4. The introduction and development of the cable system in the colony of New Zealand.

5. Descriptions and illustrations explaining the construction and operation of the first cable line in Europe, viz., Highgate Hill tramway, London ; also similar works progressing at Birmingham, Edinburgh, and London, &c. ; introduction of the system into Australia, &c.

6. Technical examinations of the system, with its costs of construction and working, &c.

7. Financial analyses concerning the system, with remarks and comparisons respecting this and other systems of tramway working at present in use, and concluding remarks relative to cable traction and its latest applications, &c., also respecting the manufacture of wire ropes, &c.

From the foregoing synopsis it will be understood, that if all the technical details relating to cable traction were to be thoroughly considered, the available limits of this work would be largely exceeded, so that it will be necessary to treat some branches with as much brevity as consistent with the importance of the subject.

In engaging with the first portion of the subject before us, it is proposed to briefly consider some of the earliest applications of cable traction or hauling, as more especially exemplified in the mining industries of this country. At first sight, the direct applications of wire cables for hauling purposes may appear to many to be of a very limited character ; but their value for such purposes was appreciated in this and other countries long before the locomotive was invented, and as a matter of fact has been more extensively taken advantage of for surmounting steep gradients than any other system.

On the 14th of May, 1875, ENGINEERING described the wire-rope haulage system as applied to street tramways in San Francisco, and remarked that it was "especially adapted to localities where the gradients are such as to render it difficult to employ horses, and where interference with the existing traffic cannot be permitted." This journal then gave an account (with illustrations) of an installation, explaining the manner in which the rope was driven, the method of attaching the cars to same, and the precautions taken to insure safety to the passengers, &c. Since then, by actual experience at San Francisco, the system has been found to work tramway traffic so cheaply, that some tramway companies earn from 10 to 25 per cent. upon the capital expended.

The mention of cable traction will naturally recall to the minds of many, the numerous ingenious devices and improvements made in cable haulage for colliery purposes, and which were in a great measure promoted and stimulated by the unparalleled depression experienced in the coal trade some years ago.

Ropes, metallic cables, bands, and chains have been used for years past in a variety of ways, for haulage purposes, with satisfactory results, and in many cases the lines thus worked have been of considerable length and with trying grades and curves, whilst the traffic or loads in some instances were very heavy. Latterly, in collieries, the tractive agents chiefly employed have been cables, constructed of iron or steel wires, and the great improvements made of recent years in their manufacture have done much towards developing the uses of cable traction and " telo-dynamic " transmission of power.

It will be recognised, later on, that the functions and conditions of these cable lines, were and are, in many cases, analogous (if not identical) with those of the street cable tramways of to-day, and therefore by briefly examining some of the performances of the former, it will serve as an appropriate introduction to the considerations and study of the later system.

CHAPTER I.

MINING AND RAILWAY ROPE-HAULAGE.

CABLE haulage in mines may be classified under three heads, viz., the "tail rope," the "endless chain," and the "endless rope" systems. The first of these may be briefly dismissed as having but little connection with our subject; therefore it is sufficient for the present to remark that it requires more machinery, cable, and power to operate it than the other two systems, and is devoid of certain essential features to be found in the "*endless rope or cable system.*" Later, however, we shall have occasion to refer to a modification of this method, and which for many years was in use on the old Blackwall Railway. The second or "endless chain system" has also no direct interest for us; it being a primitive method of haulage peculiar to mining operations, where it has certain economical advantages. The third, or "endless rope" system, which performs similar functions, has, however, a very important bearing upon the subjects we are about considering.

This system may be briefly described as depending on the employment of an endless hemp or metallic rope, which passes over large terminal pulleys and around a driving drum connected with a suitable motor, supported upon small rollers placed at suitable intervals in the space between the terminal pulleys. A continuous and uniform motion is imparted to this rope by means of the driving drum or clip pulley, round which it is passed. This system is generally applied to work trucks or wagons over double, or up-and-down roads, but in exceptional circumstances it has been employed for operating single roads, with suitable intermediate passing places. A train of trucks is commonly headed by a "conductor's wagon," provided with a gripping appliance for catching hold of the rope which travels between the rails, and which can be released at will; the same wagon is also equipped with suitable braking appliances. In this manner an intermittent motion may be imparted to the wagons from a continuously travelling rope or cable. It is obviously necessary that the cable should be maintained at a uniform tension, otherwise it would be frequently thrown off the various pulleys. This is usually prevented by mounting the terminal pulleys upon travelling carriages provided with tail weights. Again, auxiliary adjusting sheaves or pulleys are also frequently provided, and over these the cable is passed, so that by moving them further from each other, they are caused to draw in any undue slack.

A good modern example of the application of the endless cable system of haulage to mining purposes may be seen in operation at the Clifton Colliery, Nottingham. According to this system, the saving by the employment of endless cables over animal power is stated to be 1117*l.* per annum. The cables are run at 1½ miles per hour, delivering about three tons of coal per minute. The calculated cost of the ropes, per ton per mile, is about .22d.; similarly, pulleys, .05d.; coal, .23d.; repairs to boilers and engines, .03d.; wages, 1.1d. In this system of haulage, Lang's patent wire ropes (manufactured by Messrs. Cradock and Co.) are employed with very satisfactory results. This type of rope appears peculiarly suitable for traction purposes, and at the close of this treatise, its manufacture and merits are explained, and also further references made to the system working at this and other mines

Another interesting example may be seen at the Cadzow Colliery, N.B., where some ingenious haulage plant by Messrs. Grant and Richie, of Kilmarnock, is in daily operation. The cost of repairs of the engines and hauling apparatus is only about $\frac{1}{80}$th of a penny per ton per mile. In this system 840 tons of coal are delivered per day, and the cost per ton per mile for the different items is as follows: Ropes, .16d.; coals, .13d.; labour, 1.2d., or a total actual cost of working of 1.78d. per ton per mile.

Wire ropes have been used in mines for about fifty years past, and their invention and introduction are to be chiefly traced to Messrs. A. Smith and Newall, in about 1830 to 1835. On the Continent, wire ropes have been used in the mines of Saxony since 1834, and more than twenty-five years ago cable haulage with intermittent acting grippers carried by auxiliary cars, was employed in the Kirkwood Colliery, near Airdrie, Scotland.

Space will not permit, referring in detail to the various arrangements of machinery and apparatus employed in such systems of haulage, but those desirous of further information on the subject should consult the following publications: " L'Emploi des Machines dans l'intérieur des Mines," by A. Devillez, a report published in 1863 ; the " Transactions of the North of England Institute of Mining Engineers " (especially about 1867, which contain able and exhaustive reports on cable haulage by a specially appointed committee) ; "Mining Machinery," by G. André, &c.

The endless cable system of traction undoubtedly possesses special advantages for dealing with variable distributed loads and irregular traffic, and therefore it is well adapted for application to the working of passenger tramways. The system is, however, unsuitable where complex iunctions or branch lines are required.

Cables now used in mining haulage, are mostly manufactured of steel wires, and are usually from 2 in. to 3 in. in circumference. The average lives of these cables may vary from eighteen months to over five years, with an average performance of, say, about 600 tons carried per day, at a cost of about 2d. per ton per mile. Under some favourable circumstances about 68 per cent. of the driving power employed, has been usefully utilised. These ropes or cables are frequently driven by large sheaves or pulleys having V-shaped circumferential grooves. The necessary driving adhesion is sometimes obtained by only a half-turn of the ropes. Such driving pulleys have been found to work and wear well, and only require to have their grooves occasionally re-turned.

The tail rope system already referred to, can be advantageously applied in dealing with concentrated loads, and may be, in some cases, preferred for passenger tramways in which the two termini are the only sources of traffic. It appears, however, certain that the wear and tear of a cable is greater by this method, the relative excess as compared with the endless cable system being apparently about as 15 to 12; further, the power cannot be so economically utilised, and the respective ratios of the consumption of fuel are approximately as 30 to 13. The speeds at which endless cables have been thus usefully employed, average from two to five miles per hour, and the ascertained loss by friction of the machinery and pulleys, has frequently amounted to from 45 to 50 per cent. of the driving power expended; the latter is, however, greatly dependent upon the grades and curves of the line to be worked.

As incorrect comparisons have been made regarding the analogy of the modern cable system of street tramways with the Blackwall Railway of 1840, it will repay us to take a cursory glance at this old and ingenious scheme, and which has an interesting and instructive bearing upon the subject. The original Blackwall Railway, which was sanctioned by Parliament in 1836, and successfully opened to the public four years later, was a scheme of Messrs. Stephenson and Bidder (afterwards engineers to the line) for effecting a railway communication between the Minories and Blackwall, by means of a system practically similar to the tail rope system of haulage before described. This consisted in the employment of cables, which were attached to a train whilst their other ends went to the termini of the line, where they were attached to drums and alternately wound and unwound. Now the arrangement on the Blackwall Railway differed so far, that an open cable was employed, to which an alternating motion was imparted as above described, whilst the carriages were connected to it by gripping appliances, which could be set in action and released as desired. Further than providing means of allowing intermittent motion of the vehicles on the road, independent of the motion of the cable, it has no strict analogy as a system to that which we are about to especially consider.

However, the long experience obtained upon that line affords some interesting and practical data. The system was adopted on account of the frequent stoppages required between the termini, which were only about $3\frac{3}{4}$ miles apart, with five intermediate stations. The line was constructed upon a series of brickwork arches, which had a gradual rise of 65 ft. towards the London terminus; the smallest curve had a radius of 3000 ft. The gauge of the track was 5 ft., and the time occupied in transit between the termini was about thirteen minutes. The Minories Station was at that time the only railway terminus in London. The first hauling rope employed was constructed of hemp, with 4 in. lays, and was about $5\frac{1}{2}$ in. in circumference; it was alternately wound up and paid out by terminal drums, 23 ft. in diameter, and 3 ft. 8 in. wide; it was supported at intervals of 35 ft. by pulleys, 3 ft. in diameter, by 7 in. wide. On the curves the guiding pulleys were arranged so as to permit of 3 in. vertical and 6 in. horizontal deviation. These pulleys were mounted in horizontal bearings, but were constructed with a taper of 6 in. in their breadth. Angularly placed pulleys were afterwards tried on the curved portions of the line.

The terminal hauling drums were alternately driven at a speed of forty revolutions per minute by engines of 224 nominal horse-power at the Minories, and by others of 140 nominal horse-power at the Blackwall end of the line, the circumferential velocity being equal to about twenty-five miles per hour. Duplicate engines and boilers were provided at each end which were worked every alternate six weeks. Shortly after the line had been opened, a tendency was discovered in the rope to continually twist, and it ultimately became frequently ruptured. Subsequently a rope was tried from which the tar had been previously expelled by pressure, but this experiment gave no satisfaction. Sometimes, when these cables parted, the consequences were serious, as the tensile strain upon them, combined with their natural elasticity, caused the severed ends to recoil violently to a considerable distance, and on more than one occasion a portion of the road, or the pulleys, were torn up or deranged. In one instance the rupture of such a rope caused the dislocation of a part of the coping of the Limehouse Bridge. Breakdowns became at last so common that the engineers resolved to try metallic cables, composed of six wire strands laid round a hempen core, and weighing about 10 lbs. per fathom. This experiment was attended with a satisfactory result, and the life of the new cables was extended to nine and twelve months, whereas the hempen rope commonly broke about once a month. Wire ropes of $3\frac{5}{8}$ in. circumference, composed of six strands of six wires each, and weighing about $6\frac{1}{2}$ lb. per yard, were found to answer fairly well, although trouble was still given by the tendency of the cables to twist. Intermediate swivels were next introduced, with some beneficial results, for the purpose of overcoming this difficulty. Then troubles arose from the noise made by the pulleys and working parts, and a leather packing was tried upon them, while the cable was also served with spun yarn. Although the line was an expensive undertaking, and had involved the expenditure of about 650,000*l.*, the traffic attained was of a heavy, and, for a long time, of a remunerative character.

The number of cars in a train varied from six to twenty-six, and the loads carried averaged from 100 to 200 tons, whereas locomotives had only been able to draw from one-half to a fourth of such a load. The first-class carriages were constructed to carry forty, and the third-class seventy persons ; all were provided with two lever brakes, a coupling-up contrivance, and the rope-gripping apparatus. The trains performed from fifty to fifty-eight journeys per day, according to the season of the year, or in other words the rope travelled about 300 miles per day. The trains were controlled by opening the grips at the successive stations, and releasing one or more cars ; these were subsequently re-attached to the rope for the return trip.

After the extension in 1841, there were six stations on the system between the termini : Poplar, West India Docks, Limehouse, Stepney, Shadwell, and Cannon-street ; of these the first five ultimately communicated with the Fenchurch-street terminus ; and four, viz., Minories, Cannon-street, Shadwell, and Stepney, with the Blackwall terminus. There was a descending gradient from Blackwall to Poplar, and from Fenchurch-street to the Minories ; the trains travelling these portions of their journey by gravitation, and being attached to the rope at Poplar and the Minories respectively. The first carriage connected with the rope was carried over the whole line, and the intermediate traffic was worked by carriages detached for each station. When all the rope was coiled upon one drum the engines were stopped, and the various cars at the different successive stations re-attached ; the rope was then again set in motion in the reverse direction, simultaneously starting the carriages situated at different parts of the line. The several carriages during their return trip were thus separated by intervals, corresponding to the distance between the different stations from which they started ; and on reaching the stations (Minories and Poplar respectively) at which the hauling machinery was situated, they were released from the rope, and travelled on by momentum to the termini. The line being in duplicate throughout, up and down trains used to depart simultaneously from the Minories and Blackwall termini. The extension of the line from the Minories Station to Fenchurch-street was constructed in 1841, at a further cost of about 30,000*l.* However, for effectually working traffic between intermediate stations the system was inappropriate, and such service was necessarily very limited. During the year of 1844, upwards of 2,500,000 passengers were carried over the line, and two thirds of this traffic was derived from the intermediate stations.

Had locomotives then been sufficiently economical in their working, they would have doubtless been more suitable. But as it was, the estimated saving by the use of the rope system appeared to show about 150,000*l.* in the constructional expenditure, and 12,000*l.* per annum in working and maintaining expenses. However, we shall find that the application of the endless cable system we have in view, affords very different examples of the means of dealing with distributed traffic.

The fares of the Blackwall Railway were at the rate of 1.7d. per mile first-class, and 1.1d. per mile third-class, and the average receipts reached about 100*l.* per day. The total working expenses were from about 14d. to 18d. per car mile, or about 6s. per train. The total tonnage moved or carried over the line daily was about 7000 tons. The consumption of fuel for the engines was about 12 tons per day of fourteen hours, involving an annual cost of about 3500*l.* Grease consumed for lubricating purposes was also a considerable item, and amounted to 80 lbs. and upwards per week. Upon the whole, it was not a satisfactory solution of a cable haulage problem, and it would have probably succeeded much better had the endless cable system been used as then employed at the Euston terminus of the London and Birmingham Railway, which line had a rise of 80 ft. in the mile, and was worked at the rate of twenty miles per hour.

The cable haulage system of the Blackwall Railway was dispensed with in about 1848, not so much on account of any inherent unsuitability, as from recent improvements made in locomotives, and also from the construction of other railway systems in connection with the line, which necessitated a common method of working. It was unquestionably an expensive system, necessitating the use of elaborate engines and apparatus at both ends of the line, whilst the severe strains inflicted upon the ropes were of a destructive character.

There are numerous other instructive examples of cable traction as applied to the working of railways, &c., both at home and abroad, which space will not permit us to discuss. As, for example, from about 1834 on the Canterbury and Whitstable Railway; the Sunderland Railway; at Edge Hill, Liverpool; on the Edinburgh and Glasgow Railway, in the Edinburgh and Newhaven Tunnel; the Oldham incline; the Gloucester and Birmingham incline; the Hopton incline on the High Peak Railway; the North-Eastern Railway Companies' inclines, &c. Further, there are those of Ceylon, Croix-Rousse, Düsseldorf and Elberfeld, Schaffhausen, Bern, Lausanne and Ouchy, Leopoldsberg and Vienna, Buda and Offen, the New York Elevated Railroad, Pittsburg, U.S.A., Cincinnati, U.S.A., the San Paulo Mountain Railway, Brazil; at Hong-Kong, &c. Again, there are the gravitation and hydrostatic cable elevators at Niagara, U.S.A.; Lisbon; Scarborough, &c. Accounts of many of these lines may be found upon reference to the Proceedings of the Institution 'of Civil Engineers. In 1844 there were thirty-seven miles of wire rope used on the Durham and Sunderland Railway. At the beginning of 1873, Mr. E. Wright, of Birmingham, made a new wire rope for Edge Hill, on the London and North-Western Railway, of nearly four miles, in one length, or rather over 6500 yards. This rope was $5\frac{1}{2}$ in. in circumference and weighed over 34 tons.

Data connected with the lives of wire cables, as above employed, are of such vital interest to our subject, that it may not be superfluous to devote a few words to the San Paulo Railway above mentioned. Here metallic cables have been successfully employed for many years past, in assisting the traffic of a main line of railway over a vast mountain chain, with an elevation of 2500 ft. The lives of the early cables used upon this line averaged about two years, after having hauled some 300,000 tons. These cables were composed of steel strands, giving an aggregate of forty-two wires of No. 10 gauge, with a diameter of $1\frac{1}{4}$ in., and a breaking strain of about 35 tons.

This cable railway has now been working for about eighteen years, and according to information furnished by the engineer of the line, during this period, both passenger and goods traffic has been regularly conducted without any serious accident or delay. The lives of the cables are now doubled, and at present last for about four years, or after having run about 25,000 to 30,000 miles. This improvement appears in a measure attributable to the substitution of driving pulleys for the grooved drums originally employed. The traffic on this railway varies from 600 to 800 tons per day. But two to even four years would appear to be no remarkable durability for cables thus employed, for in 1870 Sir J. Coode laid before the Institution of C.E. examples of some metallic cables, used by himself for similar purposes, which had lasted in reliable working order for about eight years, or after having hauled 1,600,000 tons of traffic. These cables consisted of six iron strands, composed of six wires each, wound round a hempen core, so as to give a circumferential measuremennt of $4\frac{7}{8}$ in., and were painted at requisite periods with a mixture of raw linseed oil and Stockholm tar, and further, were also " served " with fine iron wire to prevent external injury.

It appears now generally admitted that the cable system of working inclines from about 1 in 25, is more economical than the use of loco-motives, leaving, of course, horses altogether out of the question.

The foregoing remarks upon various cable haulage schemes, are given in order to record data regarding the known capabilities of metallic or wire ropes, when properly constructed and attended to. An erroneous notion may exist in the minds of some persons that the weakness of such systems is in the liability of the ropes to become suddenly ruptured.

Such notions have been proved by practice to be unfounded, and indeed it would be difficult to cite a case in which a good wire rope, properly used and looked to, has suddenly given way. Upon examination, wire ropes usually give ample signs of approaching weakness by external indications of wear. The data and examples already given, regarding the safe and efficient transport of minerals, goods, and passengers by the use of wire ropes or cables, should develop confidence in their more extended application.

A few lines may, not inconsistently, be devoted to aërial or overhead wire tramways or transports, and which under some conditions have fulfilled requirements which prior to their introduction were impossible. Various kinds of these tramways are now at work in different parts of the world, in lengths varying from a quarter of a mile to ten miles, and carrying loads from $\frac{1}{2}$ cwt. to 6 cwt. on inclines as steep as 1 in 3. The names of Messrs. Hodgson and Carrington will be familiar to many, as having made a speciality of this method of transport with considerable success. The system may be generally described as consisting in the employment of an endless cable, supported upon suitable intermediate and overhead supports, and driven by an engine imparting motion to a drum, similar to cases of mining haulage already mentioned. The buckets or receptacles which carry the loads are hung and carried along such endless running cable, from one terminus to another. Each of these buckets carries from 1 cwt. to 4 cwt., and can deliver at a terminus at the rate of about 200 buckets per hour; thus the carrying capacity of a line may vary from, say, 10 to 500 tons per day. Gradients and curves are readily worked by this system of transport, and the delivery may be almost continuous. The peculiar suitability or adaptability of the system for crossing mountainous or irregular country will be apparent upon glancing at the accompanying plate, which gives an example of the method as applied to a mining industry upon the coast of Norway. In this instance the steel wire cables make one clear span of 750 yards without support, and are placed at about an angle of 45 deg., the speed at which the ore buckets are hauled being about fifteen miles per hour. The advantages and capabilities of the system may be summarised as follows : —

It avoids the expense of cuttings and embankments.

No bridges are required over rivers and ravines.

Lines can be constructed and worked on hilly ground almost as cheaply as on plains, and on inclines impracticable to ordinary railroads.

The cost is in proportion to the work required.

It occupies scarcely any land.

It is not affected by floods or snow.

It can be readily moved from place to place.

It can be used for the transmission of power at the same time as goods.

Wire Rope Transport for Mining Purposes.

The cost of these tramways, varies from about 300*l*. to 600*l*. per mile. About 150 miles of this system are in operation in various parts of the world, Spain and Mauritius enjoying a large proportion of such mileage. The system may be modified to meet requirements, *e.g.*, by single running ropes; double fixed ropes and gravitation working; single fixed ropes; double fixed ropes and power working, &c. Transporting materials, produce, or goods, according to this system, costs about 2d. per ton, but varies according to circumstances.

From that which has been already stated respecting the success that attended the working performances of early cable railways, &c., it will be apparent that the various inventors of more recent date who sought to apply the principle of rope haulage to street tramways, have been far from working in the dark, but had indeed a substantial basis to work upon, and could turn to a large and valuable amount of prior experience to guide them.

Before proceeding to consider in detail the various applications in practice of cable haulage for tramways proper, we will briefly review in chronological order some of the earlier schemes and inventions relating to the subject.

From the particulars previously given regarding cable haulage by stationary engines in mines and upon railways, it may have been seen that the endless cable system, with its necessary tension apparatus and operating appliances, was in practical use upwards of forty years ago, whilst the means of imparting (from the continuous movement thus obtained) an intermittent motion to vehicles, by means of suitable gripping gear carried on separate or special cars, was well known and employed about twenty-five years back. From the earliest proposed adaptations of cable haulage to the working of tramways upon streets, it will be apparent that it must have been recognised that the tractive agency selected would have to be so applied and operated as not to interfere with the practical efficiency of the road surfaces, or with the vehicular and foot traffic for which they had been originally constructed. This was obviously the chief problem that presented itself for solution.

As early as 1812, Messrs. W. and E. Chapman proposed to employ a fixed cable or chain upon roads or streets for the purpose of propelling cars thereon, by winding or hauling upon the same from the platforms of the cars, and about 1824 other similar schemes were enrolled at the British and United States Patent Offices. Amongst the latter was one by a W. James, who proposed to employ a travelling chain for the haulage of carriages upon highways, the chain being operated within a tunnel or channel provided in the rails. In 1829 an endless cable traction scheme, actuated by a stationary source of power, was propounded by a M. Dick. Nine years later a W. J. Curtis applied for the protection of certain improvements in machinery for facilitating transport upon railways, and amongst his numerous suggestions relating to rope or cable haulage, is an interesting description of an independent "leading car" provided with a cable-gripping apparatus fitted with vertically moving clamping jaws, for imparting intermittent motion to a train upon rails from a continuously moving "ground rope." It is further mentioned, that "at first the rope slides through the clamps and thus prevents concussion, but as the train gets into motion the sliding becomes less and less until the train attains the full velocity of the rope." This is precisely the action common to the cable-gripping appliances of to-day.

In 1845, W. Brandling proposed to employ a rope or cable system of traction for street tramways. In order to avoid any interference with street surfaces, he proposed to arrange the hauling rope so as to work within a box or channel constructed in combination with the track. A prong-shaped gripping apparatus was to be operated from each car on the line, in such a manner as to be capable of picking up or dropping the motion of the travelling rope. This appears to be the first example of the proposed employment of a constantly running cable within a longitudinally slotted underground tube or channel.

In March, 1858, E. S. Gardiner, of Philadelphia, U.S.A., directed his attention to the subject and gave a very able solution of the problem. His invention consisted in the employment of a continuous underground tube or tunnel (between the rails), having a narrow longitudinal slot throughout its length, at the level of the road—practically a similar arrangement to the continuous slotted ground or track tubes proposed and used in atmospheric railways many years before. Within this tube he proposed to mount a series of suitable supporting and guiding pulleys, so that a travelling cable could be employed within it for the purpose of hauling the cars along the track, without impeding the passage of other vehicles upon the road. The narrow slot or aperture running axially through the tubes or tunnels, and in such a manner as to penetrate the street as above referred to, was to allow the passage of the cable-gripping appliances, which were to be operated from the cars in such a manner as to permit of the latter participating in the motion of the cable when required. No particular gripping apparatus was especially described.

It does not appear that Gardiner ever pursued his ingenious invention, but it is only fair to recognise that all cable haulage schemes at present in use for street tramways, have been constructed in accordance with the principles laid down by him.

Reverting to the subject of slotted underground track tubes for atmospheric railways, and practically presenting the solution and requirements of cable tramway street tubes, it may be mentioned, that such constructions were copiously described as early as 1840.

In the following year, Messrs. Foster and Brown, of the United States, proposed to employ an overhead endless travelling rope for working street tramway traffic. A suitable gripping appliance was devised for operating above the cars so as to catch or release the cable at pleasure.

In 1860, W. Greaves proposed to lay down a tube between the rails of a street tramway for the purpose of receiving a haulage rope, suitable means being provided on the cars for attaching and detaching them. This arrangement of rope-haulage was stated to be peculiarly advantageous for " working street tramway traffic in towns, busy districts, and on turnpike roads." A subsidiary arrangement is also mentioned, in which the haulage rope is caused to travel in hollow longitudinal sleepers in connection with the track, instead of in a special slotted central tube.

In 1864, P. W. Barlow described an endless cable traction system, to be worked by stationary hydraulic power, and stated to be particularly suitable for working traffic in tunnels or subways.

In 1866, C. F. Harvey, U.S.A., proposed a cable scheme consisting in the employment of collars or ferrules upon an underground travelling rope, so as to engage with gripping forks or claws, to be lowered from the cars on the track. The cable in this case was to be worked in an open channel.

Three years later, G. F. Beauregard, of New Orleans, U.S.A., followed upon the lines proposed by Foster and Brown, and previously mentioned, namely, elevated cable traction systems, for which he devised an ingenious cable grip or catch, for passing and clearing the overhead pulleys, by arranging the supporting arm and operating parts *out* of the vertical plane of the cable and gripping jaws. This arrangement of gripping apparatus was for dealing with cases in which the supporting pulleys were situated between the hauling rope and the vehicles on the line.

Subsequently, Hyde, Monkton, Hawthorn, and others, patented certain devices connected with street cable traction, but they worked chiefly in somewhat impracticable directions, and appeared to be unaware of, or to disregard, the useful hints afforded by Gardiner many years previously.

In 1872, Abel Thompson published an account of his improvements in " Street Railways," and in which a description of an underground slotted track tube is given, constructed in an identical manner to the modern cable tramways tubes, before referred to.

During 1871 and 1872, A. S. Hallidie, of San Francisco, proposed arrangements for street cable haulage, and to his energy much praise is due. It is also worthy of notice that overhead and other cable transporting devices, were at this time coming extensively into use. Of such may be mentioned the application by the Ebertradt and Aurora Company, Nevada, U.S.A. ; the sugar-cane transports in Brazil and Peru ; the salt mine, wire rope railways of the Indian Government in the Punjaub; the British War Office's line for carrying casks of gunpowder at Purfleet ; in Bohemia, for transporting fireclay ; in the mining industries of the Spanish Government at the Asturias Mountains, &c.

Subsequently, Mr. Hallidie succeeded in getting cable haulage applied to the working of street tramways in San Francisco, where many of the gradients are too severe to be economically worked by horses or locomotives. This arrangement consisted in the employment of a continuously moving endless wire rope, carried within a longitudinally slotted tube, arranged below the surface of the street and between the tram rails. The travelling cable was maintained in its proper position by passing over and under suitable pulleys mounted within the tube, and received its requisite motion from a stationary engine situated at one terminus of the line, or at a suitable intermediate position, the power being transmitted from the motor used, to the endles rope by means of a grip pulley or driving drum. The uniform motion thus imparted to the cable beneath the road, was intermittently communicated to the cars on the line, through the intervention of suitable gripping appliances, attached to the cars by steel bars or plates, capable of passing through the slot in the upper part of the cable tube. About the same date (1872) that street cable traction was being introduced into California, U.S.A., a Captain J. Roberts, of Seaford, Sussex, applied for a British patent for certain improvements in the construction and operation of street tramways. The object of his invention was also to dispense with the use of horses upon tramways, and consisted in the employment of an endless travelling rope within a longitudinally slotted tube, arranged between the tracks and below the road surface. The endless travelling cable for hauling the cars upon the rails was not, however, carried by pulleys within the tube, but was buoyed up by floats attached thereto, which were intended to lie upon the surface of the water with which the tube was to be filled. This inventor describes the essence of his invention, as consisting in the employment of water within the underground slotted cable tube for the purpose of supporting and guiding the cable in the manner above mentioned, the idea being that there would be almost entire absence of friction and constant lubrication of the moving parts. Receiving and circulating tanks were proposed at the termini of the line, but how the system could be applied to the working of gradients is not apparent.

The interest attached to this impracticable suggestion is the following : The system proposed by Captain Roberts was devised for the purpose of extending a north metropolitan system of tramways up

Highgate Hill, from the Archway to Hornsey ; and the Patentee, with
this view, offered his invention to the London General Omnibus Company, Messrs. Hunt and Sacre, engineers, and others, who, however,
declined to entertain the project. Ten years later, the first cable
traction system in Europe was installed at Highgate, by the Steep-
Grade Tramways and Works Company, Limited.

It may be mentioned that a simple cable-gripping device is also
described in Roberts's specification, with vertically operating jaws in
connection with suitable shank plates for working through the narrow
slot in the cable tube.

From the foregoing information, we may find publications, prior
to 1873, of the system as now used; and the method of haulage
in mining industries twenty-five years ago.

Those desirous of learning more definite particulars relating to this
section of the subject, can see detail-descriptions of all the before
quoted examples, and numerous others, at the Public Library of the
British Patent Office.

CHAPTER II.

STREET CABLE TRAMWAYS IN CAL., U.S.A.

THE project for establishing cable tramway communication in San Francisco was not allowed to repose, and ultimately Mr. Hallidie succeeded in interesting some friends in the matter, and in obtaining a practical trial. For some time, however, he met with more obstacles than encouragement, and, in fact, the scheme was somewhat ridiculed, and regarded as being visionary and impracticable.

Ultimately, however, he succeeded in obtaining the co-operation of Messrs. Britton, Davis and Moffit, &c., who assisted in providing the required funds. The franchise for the line was then acquired from a Mr. Brooks, who originally intended to attempt some cable haulage scheme in the city. The public was also invited to assist, and a prospectus inviting subscriptions was issued in June, 1872. Some property owners in the neighbourhood of the projected line made promises, as numerous as vague, regarding future assistance, if the scheme succeeded, but anything like definite encouragement, in the event of a success, took more the form of a gratuitous sum than an investment. California-street was the first proposed site for a trial, but the route ultimately selected for this experimental line was Clay-street, a busy central street in the city of San Francisco, only 49 ft. wide between the houses.

The highest part of the line was to be about 300 ft. above the level of the lower or Kearny-street terminus, and its entire horizontal length was 2800 ft., or about 5600 ft. of single line. The transverse intersecting streets, which occurred about every 412 ft., were at right angles, and cut the grades of Clay-street with level crossings. The steepest gradient on the line was about 1 in 6.

The proposals contained in the original prospectus were that the line should run between Kearny and Jones-streets. The hours of traffic were to be from 7 A.M. to 11 P.M., the rate travelled being from five to six miles per hour, the trip thus occupying about six minutes. Horses were to be attached to the cars upon their arrival at the summit of the hill, where an extension was to be worked by a horse system. The promoters stated that they considered a ten-minute service of cars would be sufficient at first, and further mentioned that it was hardly to be expected that the line would pay upon the proposed capital, but that

Note 4

Note 5

the ultimate benefit would rest with the property owners and residents upon the hill. A guarantee of 45,000 dols. (about 9000*l.*) was asked as being necessary, before the construction of the line could be commenced. The projectors undertook to have the line built and opened for traffic within six months.

The prospectus was supplemented by a report, giving a detailed estimate for the work proposed, accompanied by some notes regarding the probable traffic.

The total cost of the scheme was estimated at 100,000 dols. (about 20,000*l.*) including the entire track, tube, steel wire rope, engines, tension appliances, pulleys, rolling stock, grippers, twenty horses, buildings and tools, &c. A detailed account of the actual expenditure incurred will be given later on, but at present it will suffice to state that the construction and equipment cost within the above estimate. The monthly running expenses of the road, with adequate allowances for depreciation, wear and tear, &c., were estimated in the said report at about 3000 dols., about 600*l.* Ultimately a donation of about 40,000 dols. was subscribed by the interested property holders in support of the line.

The population of San Francisco was then about 180,000, and the proportion that travelled daily by different horse tramways in the city amounted to about 28 per cent. The number of inhabitants that resided in the district of the proposed Clay-street line, was estimated at about 12,000, and by reasonable deductions from the average workings of the other tramway companies over level ground, it was to be fairly expected that the daily transport of passengers would exceed 3300, which at 5-cent fares (2½d.) would produce a daily revenue or gross profit of about 165 dols., or 33*l.*, or, say, about 230*l.* per week, or 920*l.* per month, which would leave a net profit of 320*l.* per month, after the allowances for working expenses, interest, and depreciation. Assuming the receipts to have given a profit of only 200*l.* per month, then the line would have paid 12 per cent. interest upon the estimated capital required. Facts since prove that the estimates were realised and indeed exceeded, the line having at times earned over 35 per cent. upon the capital expended, minus the above-mentioned donation. The rapidity with which this line was subsequently constructed is worthy of remark, and reflects great credit on all concerned. The terms of the franchise only allowed two months for the completion of the entire work ; the ground was broken early on the 2nd day of June, 1873, and the first trial trip made on the line by the first day of the August following. It must not be imagined that the promoters were permitted to place any rough or inefficient system of public traction in the streets of this city. On the contrary, considerable strictness and vigilance were exercised with regard to the construction, operation, and fares.

The plans submitted to the authorities were to comply with the following conditions, viz.: That the road should not present more impediments to ordinary traffic than the usual and existing horse lines ; that the rope should be arranged and operated below the street surface in such a manner as to in no way interfere with vehicular or foot traffic ; that the cars could be promptly started, stopped, or controlled upon any part of the line ; that no engine or motor should be used on or under the street that could frighten horses or endanger lives. The speed of travelling was not to be less than three or more than eight miles per hour. Further, the single passenger fares for the entire distance were not to exceed 5 cents.

Embarking upon such a restricted and more or less speculative undertaking, it was obviously of prime importance to carry out this experimental line at as low a cost as possibly consistent with adequate efficiency. In fact, the line was chiefly for demonstrative purposes, and little thought was bestowed upon its ornamental aspect. It will therefore be readily understood that some features of the construction bore somewhat primitive aspects ; as, for example, the wooden offices and engine-house, with its metal chimney shaft, &c.—in fact, wood was liberally used throughout the whole work. Before more minutely describing the construction and operation of the Clay-street cable road, some interesting particulars connected with its public opening may be briefly narrated.

Note 6

It was about 4 o'clock A.M. on the morning of the 1st of August, 1873, that the first trial trip was run upon the Clay-street line. The morning was dull and foggy, consequently the rails were slippery from the atmospheric moisture. The haulage rope or cable was set in motion by the stationary engine, and appeared to run satisfactorily through the slotted track tube in which it was mounted on suitable pulleys. A "dummy" or independent carriage to which the cable-gripping apparatus, brake gear, and other mechanical operating and controlling mechanism was attached was then brought out, and the "gripper" duly lowered into the cable tube. Ropes were next attached to the frame of the "dummy" in order to safely test the action and efficiency of the brakes upon such a severe incline. The result was, that they were found to be inadequate to the requirements. The probability of the cars precipitously rushing down this declivitous line, if the grippers should happen to slip upon the moving cable, was not remote, although at this early hour there were no vehicles, horses, or foot-passengers to collide with in such event. The above-mentioned deficiency was far from conducive to confidence, and the driver deputed to take the first car down succumbed to cogent scepticism regarding the reliability of the scheme and his personal safety. Subsequently the descending trip was performed with safety and comfort and without any interruptions.

Note 7

On the way down, stoppages at the crossing streets were tried by releasing and regaining the underground travelling cable, with satisfactory results. At the lower terminus the " dummy " was reversed and the up trip tried with similar success. A further trial was made at about three o'clock in the afternoon with a dummy and ordinary car connected, when the down trip was effected with similar satisfaction, but a slight hitch took place on the up or return journey owing to some slight derangement of the cable-gripping appliance and the interruptions occasioned by the enormous concourse of people that had assembled to witness the experiments. The first disorder was soon remedied and the trip resumed, but the public continued to persistently besiege the cars, and the " dummy " was taken possession of by some sixty persons who crowded into and about it in order to get a free ride at their own risk.

About half way up the hill, or between Stockton and Mason-streets, where there is a severe change in the grade, the crowded cars came to a standstill owing to the slipping of the freshly tarred cable upon the driving drum or pulley in the engine-room. However, this difficulty was speedily neutralised by the administration of some sawdust and a slight increase in the tension of the cable, and the trip was then satisfactorily completed.

As in all new devices or schemes, there were numerous small alterations and adjustments necessary before the road worked thoroughly well.

It was soon, however, apparent that this small experimental line was an unquestionable success, and would be, probably, the pioneer of many other similar schemes. The line with its extension has now been in successful mechanical and financial operation for upwards of thirteen years.

We will now turn our attention to the construction and mode of operating this cable line laid on Clay-street, San Francisco, U.S.A. Fig. 1 of the illustrations represents a longitudinal section of Clay-street

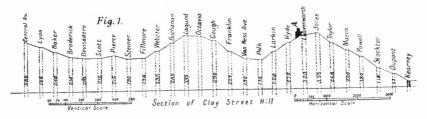

Fig. 1.

Section of Clay Street Hill

Vertical Scale

Horizontal Scale

Hill, over a part of which the line passes; Figs. 2 to 5 are diagrams illustrating the mode of working the endless cable; Fig. 6 is a perspective view of a typical permanent way and tube suitable for cable

traction upon street tramways, and is introduced for explanatory purposes; Figs. 7 and 8 are transverse and longitudinal sections of the
permanent way and cable tube, as originally constructed upon the Clay-
street line; Fig. 9 is a longitudinal section of the permanent way taken

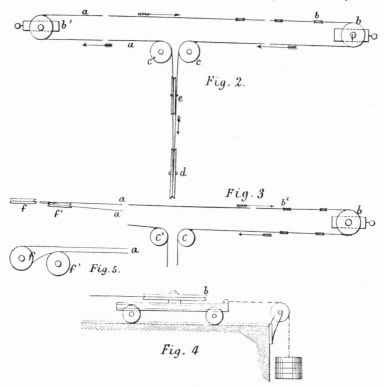

Fig. 2.

Fig. 3

Fig. 5.

Fig. 4

through the cable tube, with a "dummy" and ordinary car in place
provided with the gripping apparatus; Fig. 10 is a transverse section
taken through the permanent way and "dummy" car; Fig. 11 is a
diagram illustrating the early construction of the dummy or independent
carriage provided with cable-gripping and brake apparatus, as originally
used upon the line; Figs. 12 and 13 are respectively a perspective
elevation of the cable-gripping apparatus, with its appendages, and a
similar view of a detached portion of the same to an enlarged scale, for
the purpose of more clearly illustrating the construction and mode of
operation.

Referring to the longitudinal section illustrated in Fig. 1, it will be
seen that the engine-house, car depôt, and company's offices A, are
situated at Leavenworth-street. The differences in level on this original
portion of the line are as follows: Between Kearny and Dupont-streets,
45 ft. ; Dupont and Stockton-streets, 45 ft. ; Stockton and Powell-

streets, 62 ft. ; Powell and Mason-streets, 42 ft. ; Mason and Taylor-streets, 48 ft. ; Taylor and Jones-streets, 67 ft. ; Jones and Leavenworth-streets, 15 ft. ; the average grade throughout being about 580 ft. per

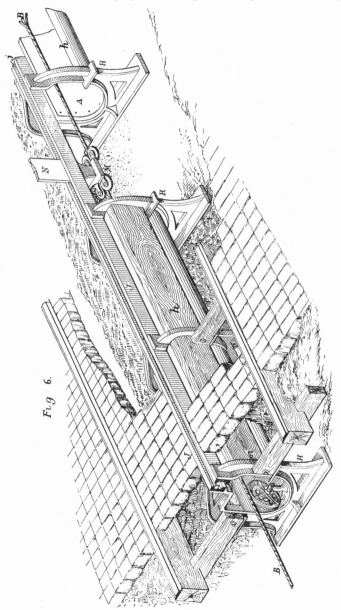

mile. From these figures it is apparent that the gradients throughout the line are of an exceptionally steep character, especially between Taylor

and Jones-streets, where the gradient exceeds 1 in 6. The line runs
at right angles to the above-mentioned streets, which are from about
45 ft. to 70 ft. wide. Clay-street itself is only 49 ft. wide from house
to house, and between the sidewalks are laid two gas services, one

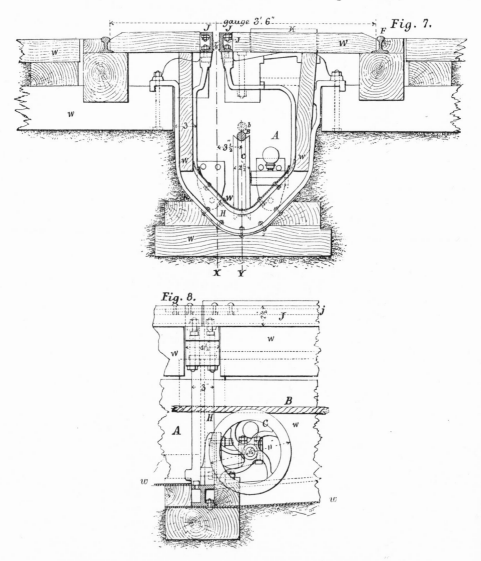

water main, a sewer and several water cisterns, all of which had to be
avoided in laying out the line, which necessarily interfered with a
greater depth from the street surface than an ordinary tramway ; the
districts adjoining the line are densely populated.

Referring to the method of working such a line, a, Fig. 2, represents the endless rope, which may be caused to travel at any desired speed,

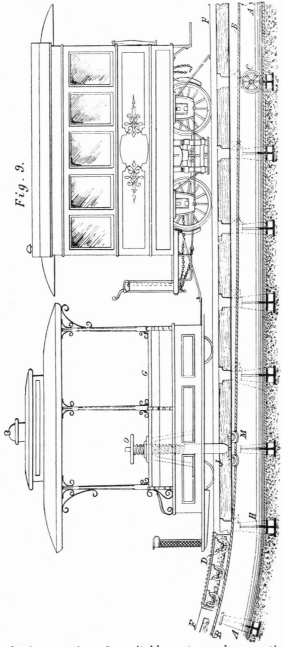

Fig. 9.

through the intervention of a suitable motor and supporting pulleys. In the diagram the cable a is represented as passing round horizontal terminal pulleys b b^1, mounted upon tension carriages with counter-weights (as shown in the enlarged view, Fig. 4), thence round a horizontal pulley c, to a vertical grooved pulley or clip drum d, connected with a suitable motor, from which the cable receives its motion.

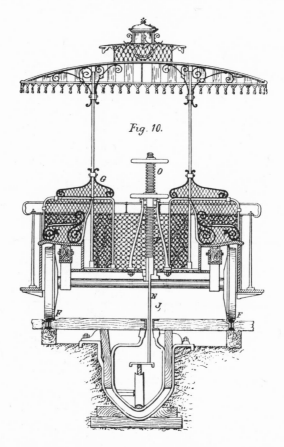

Fig. 10.

This portion of the rope is thus hauled in the direction represented by the arrows. The other portion passes round the pulley e in a similar manner to a tackle sheave, so that by shifting its axis farther from the drum d, it may be caused to take up any undue slack in the cable. On

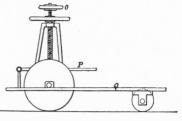

Fig. 11.

the continued outward passage of the cable it passes over another horizontal pulley c^1, and thence away towards one of the terminal pulleys b, thus completing its circuit. The distance between the terminal pulleys b b^1 must obviously vary with the length of line, and the cable is supported at convenient intermediate intervals by small rollers or vertical pulleys. It will be readily understood that the arrangements of the various supporting and guiding pulleys can be modified without departing from the general principle. For example, some of the pulleys

Fig. 12.

may be mounted in an angular position to meet certain requirements, whilst the terminal pulleys may be fixed or movable, in horizontal or vertical planes according to circumstances, the latter disposition being shown in Figs. 3 and 5. It will be easily seen that when a line is short and upon level ground, the terminal pulleys may be mounted on fixed bearings, and the necessary tension apparatus provided in the engine-house, which may be situated at any convenient part of the line, although preferably at one end. The termini of cable lines should be located upon ground as nearly level as possible, and where this is not possible it is usually advisable to build up the ground or to erect a level car platform for the lower terminus. In cases where one or both the termini are situated on a slope, it is more convenient to arrange the terminal pulleys as indicated at $f f^1$ in Figs. 3 and 5, because with vertical pulleys the returning portion of the cable is more rapidly brought within reach of the cars than with horizontal ones.

At the termini, the large compensating sheaves (Fig. 4) are placed in rectangular pits built beneath the roadway the cable tubes A passing into them. If the engine-house is located in an intermediate position on the line, the cable is conducted from the track to the driving and tension machinery and back by means of pulleys, as shown at c c^1, Fig. 2, and which are placed below the surface. When, however, the engine-house is situated at either end of the line, the last-mentioned arrangement is unnecessary. Fig. 6 shows a manner in which the reception of the travelling cable can be arranged so as to secure it from derangement, and to provide an uninterrupted means of communication with the cars to be propelled, and also to avoid all interference with the ordinary street traffic. A portion of the endless cable is shown at B travelling along the slotted tube A, in which it is supported at intervals by the pulleys C. The cable tubes must, of course, extend between the rails for the entire distance of the line, one for the up, and another for the down track.

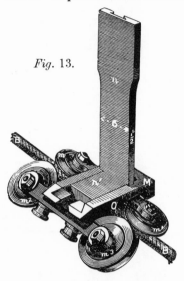

Fig. 13.

It will be seen that the cable tube may be formed of intermediate frames H, which support paralled beams J, in such a manner as to leave a narrow slot j, through which the shank N of the gripping apparatus M (worked from the cars) may freely pass, and yet at the same time the beams are sufficiently near together to prevent the wheels of any vehicles getting into the tube. The spaces between the tube frames may be filled in with earth or concrete against the retaining boards or plates h, whilst the surface of the permanent way may be formed of macadam, asphalte, stone-setts, or other suitable material. It is obvious that the gripping apparatus must be opened and the cable released at the termini of a line, as well as at the machinery pits opposite the engine-house, and where the cable is diverted from the track as already described, and illustrated in Fig. 2.

Returning to the actual construction and operation of the Clay-street Hill cable tramway, Figs. 7 and 8 represent respectively a transverse and longitudinal section of the permanent way and cable tube as originally designed and laid in August, 1873. It will be seen that wood was liberally used in the construction for the reasons already mentioned. The slotted tube A, placed centrally between the rails, was formed of the cast-iron frames H, placed about 5 ft. apart; these carried the parallel beams J, leaving the intermediate slot j, through which the cable gripper passed into the interior of the tube; C is a grooved pulley about 11 in. in diameter for supporting the cable B; these pulleys were placed along the whole length of the tube A at intervals of about 40 ft. The continuity of the tube was secured by the side-planks W, and the bottom plates w placed between the frame H as shown, and against them the earth was refilled. The continuous slot *j*, which was only seven-eighths of an inch wide, was placed on one side, whilst the cable B and its supporting pulleys C were mounted in the centre of the tube. This was done principally to accommodate the type of gripping apparatus employed, and which is shown in Figs. 12 and 13, but it also served to prevent some amount of dirt and wet falling upon the cable and pulleys. The internal dimensions of the tube A were about 12 in. by 15 in., or about 22 in. in total depth from the top of the slot or street surface. The total depth of the excavated trench was about 29 in. Fig. 9 shows a longitudinal section of the permanent way and cable tube to a smaller scale, as well as a dummy coupled with an ordinary tramcar. In this view the endless cable B is represented as running along the tube A in a plane parallel to the street surface, and supported at intervals by the small pulleys C. At any part of the line where there is a sudden change in the grade, the depression pulleys D are employed, in order to keep the endless cable clear of the top of the tube, but such a provision is only necessary in cases where the changes of grades are so marked as to produce great irregularity in the surface of the road to be traversed. In the case of Clay-street Hill, as well as in many other of the streets in the city of San Francisco, this characteristic will be readily appreciated, when it is remembered that the transverse intersecting streets, which occur about every 412 ft., cut the grades of the through streets running east and west, with level crossings. It was owing to the existence of these irregularities in the contour of the ground of Clay-street Hill, that the " *dummy car* " was first employed. As previously described, this vehicle consists simply of a short independent car, of any convenient design, provided for carrying the cable-gripping apparatus, and the necessary brake appliances.

In this arrangement, where there is any sudden change in the grade of a line, the short leading car or dummy G, with its gripping apparatus O in communication with the cable B, can more readily accommodate itself to a change of level than a larger and heavier car suitable for carrying passengers. Other objections to placing the grippers in the passenger cars were, that it would occupy valuable room, and would destroy the symmetry of their construction. The look-out of the man in charge would also be interfered with in an inclosed car, and if it were prolonged, an unnecessary dead weight must be carried, unless the gripper was removed, which would create delay and annoyance to passengers. For these reasons an auxiliary carriage was designed to carry the grip, and to be so connected with a passenger car that it could be easily uncoupled when necessary. Only men of quick perception and intelligence were employed in the capacity of drivers. These dummies were very different-looking machines when first constructed to those at present in use, and for some time much trouble was

experienced in making the dummies perform their work in a satisfactory
manner.   At first they sometimes jumped the track, and gave other
trouble, but by experimenting they have been brought down to work
satisfactorily.   Experience has shown, however, that in many cases the
uses of depression pulleys and dummy cars are quite unnecessary.

Fig. 10 shows, in cross-section, a more recent design of dummy car,
and of a pattern very popular at present in San Francisco, but the type
of dummy originally used upon the Clay-street line is represented by
Fig. 11 ; it consisted simply of a primitive truck or frame Q, upon
which the cable-gripping apparatus O was mounted, whilst a brake
strap, operated by a lever p, was applied to the front axle for the
purpose of retarding or stopping its motion.   These dummies were only
intended to accommodate the one person who was placed in charge of
the gripper or driving mechanism, whereas those subsequently constructed were fitted with seats, so as to be capable of accommodating
from fourteen to eighteen passengers, and weighed about 2200 lbs. each.
These cars, which are all provided with efficient brake appliances, are
much in favour for passenger traffic in the summer.   The cable-gripping
apparatus O carried by these dummy cars is shown in Figs. 12 and 13,
in which n is a vertical steel shank 6 in. wide and about $\frac{1}{2}$ in. thick.
This shank is attached at one end to the hollow screw spindle P, working in a standard fixed to the floor of the car, whilst the other end
terminates with a sliding piece at right angles, carrying two small
inclined pulleys m m^1.   This slide is free to work in the horizontal
dovetailed guide M, which carries two corresponding inclined pulleys m^2
m^3 ; q is a handwheel fixed upon the screw spindle r, working through
the hollow spindle P, and in connection with a sliding piece N, which
works in a guide formed in the plate or shank n.   The sliding piece N
terminates with a wedge-shaped block, which is capable of being moved
vertically between the gripper shank slide n^1 and the back of the guide
piece M, and in this manner imparts a horizontal motion to the gripping
jaws o and pulleys m, m^1, m^2, and m^3.   When a car is to be run upon
the line, it is placed or pushed by hand over an opening in the road near
the depôt, and the gripping apparatus is then lowered into the cable
tube by the wheel q^1, when its proper relation to the pulleys and moving
cable is adjusted.   The wheel q is then rotated so as to open the jaws of
the gripping apparatus, which is effected by lowering the slide N and its
wedge-shaped termination.   The endless cable B is then lifted between
the inclined gripping pulleys, which are subsequently brought closer
together so as to clip the cable.   This action is effected by raising the
wedge piece with the handwheel.   If the gripping pulleys are brought
sufficiently close together to support the moving cable, they will only
revolve, and no forward movement of the car will take place.   But as
soon as the gripping pulleys are brought closer together by means of the

wheels before described, so as to allow the fixed jaws *o* to clip the travelling cable, the gripper and car will be propelled.

The small inclined supporting pulleys have sufficient play to allow them being forced back upon rubber cushions, and when the cable is thus gripped the pulleys are inoperative. The jaws which clip the cable are provided with soft iron packing pieces, which can be easily removed and replaced when worn out. It should be mentioned that the bottom of the gripper is fixed about an inch above the supporting pulleys C, and consequently the cable is raised clear of their grooves as it passes, as shown by the dotted circles *a b*, Fig. 7. When a car with its gripper arrives at a sudden change of grade on the line, and where the depression pulleys D are used, it will be seen from the **L**-shaped form of the foot of the gripping apparatus that the cable is forced down in order to permit it to pass under the pulleys. The principle involved in this construction (for clearing the pulleys) was described by Beauregard in 1869.

Note 8

The connection between the " dummies " and cars was at first effected by means of spiral springs, in order to prevent jarring when starting, but this precaution was subsequently found to be quite unnecessary, and it was soon proved that if the grippers were carefully manipulated there was no noticeable objection on this ground. The endless cables used on the line were constructed of steel wires, and were about 3 in. in circumference, and 6800 ft. in length. The strands were composed of 114 wires of No. 16 gauge, and weighing in their entirety about $4\frac{1}{4}$ tons. A cable to be employed was then passed through the up-and-down slotted street tubes of the line, thence over a grip pulley situated in the engine-house, where it was carefully spliced. The original engine employed for operating the grip pulley and driving the cable at a speed of about four miles per hour, was about 30 horse-power, having cylinders 12 in. in diameter and 24 in. stroke, fitted with Meyer's variable automatic valve gear.

The terminal pulleys and tensional apparatus were placed below the street surface in pits or vaults provided at the termini of the line, and having their retaining walls constructed of woodwork. The road has a gauge of 3 ft. 6 in., composed of an ordinary 30lb. rail laid flush with the street by packing with planks. All the timber used in the street construction is of what is termed " redwood," and which is stated to be capable of remaining in the ground in a sound condition for fully ten years.

Although the Clay-street cable railroad was opened for public traffic in August, 1873, about a month elapsed before the line was really completed.

At the lower or Kearny-street terminus a double turntable was provided. The available space at this point was very limited, and in view of this some ingenuity had to be exercised.   When a dummy car reached the foot of the incline, it was uncoupled from the common car and run on to the turntable, the slot in the latter allowing the shank of the grip to pass freely down.   The table was then turned round one quarter of a revolution.   The car was then run on the other table, which was turned back, and was so run on the up track.   The ordinary car was next brought on to the turntable, and transferred in the same manner and coupled to the traction car, ready for the ascent.   This course was necessary, as there were double lines ; and the travelling wire rope ran down beneath one pair and up under the other.   As the gripping attachments passed down under the street surface through the slot, it was necessary to have a similar slot in both turntables to allow of the grip car being turned.

The method adopted at the upper end of the road was more simple. A turnout was made for the cars, which ran down to a common single turntable.   A circular table thus connected both tracks with a slotted path described around a centre.   A small iron triangular frame connected the dummy at two points.   By pushing on the dummy, the centre of this triangle being held in position by appropriate means, the car was turned round in a very small area, and was ready for the return trip when attached to the other car, which had already been turned on the table.

The time occupied by the cars in travelling the entire length of the line was about eleven minutes, including stoppages.   The consumption of fuel involved in operating this line was about 4000 lbs. per working day.   The piston speed of the driving engine averaged about 400 ft. per minute, and the working pressure of steam varied from about 80 lbs. to 100 lbs. per square inch.

As before mentioned, the estimated cost of construction and equipment of the line was about 100,000 dols., and about 1000 ft. of cable tube were constructed in excess of that provided for, without the estimate being exceeded.

The following is a detailed account of the actual expenditure incurred in building and equipping this line:

	dols.
About 6600 ft. of track and cable tube	38,200
Tension apparatus and turntables	2,625
Engine, boiler, and gearing, &c.	5,000
Steel wire cable of about 6800 ft. length	4,050
9 dummy cars	8,500
7 cars with brakes and fittings	6,475
Site and buildings for engine-house, car depôt, and offices ...	9,000
Charges made for interferences with gas and water services in street	1,300
Superintending and incidental expenses and expenditure *re* franchise, &c....	10,000
	85,150

About 5230 ft. of horse track, 5 turnouts and points, 20 horses dols.
   and 3 cars   15,000

                  Total   100,150

From the above figures it will be seen that the estimated cost, equal to about 20,000*l.*, was only exceeded by about 30*l.*, and further, the cost per mile of single cable track was about 6000*l.* Also from the above it may be gathered that this inaugural cable tramway was constructed and equipped, with all incidental expenses included, at a cost of about 14,000*l.* per mile. It should, however, be remembered that the cost of labour and materials is much higher in the United States than in England.

It will now be interesting to take a brief glance at some of the early traffic returns of the line, and corresponding consumptions of fuel for the work then performed.

During the month of February, 1874, 76,500 passengers were conveyed over the line for a consumption of 39,755 lbs. of coal, and in May following 91,566 persons travelled by the line for a consumption of 37,848 lbs. of fuel. The coal then used cost the company about 12 dols. 50 cents per ton, delivered at the engine-house ; but later suitable coal was obtained for about 7 dols. to 8 dols. per ton. The traffic returns of the line kept on continually increasing, and during 1875 and 1876 the company carried an average of about 150,000 passengers per month.

The first cable used upon this line lasted in working order for about two years and three months, thus giving a daily working cost of 4 dols. 93 cents, or about 1*l.* per day. The second cable was put in the road during December, 1875, and ran twelve hours per day until October, 1877, or for 686 days, at a working cost of 7 dols., or about 28s. per day.

In 1877 the line had proved so successful that it was extended to Van, Ness Avenue. This involved the addition of about 2000 ft. more cable track, which was of a modified construction as compared with the first portion built. The general configuration of the tube and track frames

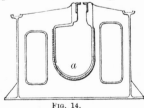

FIG. 14.

used is represented at Fig. 14, and was of such size and form as to be capable of carrying the rails as well as forming the tube in which the cable runs. The continuity of the tube between these frames was obtained by the light iron casing *a*, against which earth was filled and rammed. These combined tube frames and rail chairs weighed about 380 lbs. each, and therefore cannot be commended upon grounds of economy when ordinary iron castings in the United States were costing about 15*l.* per ton.

We will now direct our attention to the Clay-street line as it exists at the present time.   The endless hauling cable is now over 11,000 ft. in length, and is constructed of crucible steel wires formed into six strands of nineteen wires each.   The rope has an approximate aggregate tensile strength of about 70 tons per square inch of sectional area.   The terminal and engine-house pulleys for changing the direction of the cable are 8 ft. in diameter.   The third cable, which was put in the road in October, 1877, lasted until September, 1878, or about 340 days, but had to be repaired twice before the end of 1877.   The first instance of stranding was occasioned by the cable leaving one of the large engine-house pulleys, and the second was owing to a grip shank breaking and sticking fast in the tube ; but it is particularly worthy of notice that in neither case were the ends of the parted cable found more than 12 ft. apart in the tube, whilst the cars on the line did not travel more than such distance before being effectually arrested by the wheel and track brakes.   These accidents were of a most exceptional character, and may be assumed to have been due to the infancy of the enterprise, as they have not been known to recur.

The fourth cable ran until November, 1879, or 415 days, with satisfactory results ; whereas the fifth cable only lasted until April, 1881, or 110 days, and during this short life had to be slightly repaired on several occasions. The sixth cable ran about 396 days, or until April, 1882, whilst the life of the next cable exceeded 450 days.   The tensile strains upon the cables thus employed are by no means severe, and the principal injury done to them, apparently results from transverse strains from the numerous bends over the various pulleys.   The amount of wear and tear inflicted upon the cables by the nipping action of the car

Note 9

grippers is sometimes considerable.   Too much attention cannot be paid to the materials and manufacture of the cables, which should possess a high degree of toughness and flexibility.   As wire cables thus employed usually give ample signs of wear or approaching weakness, they can generally be repaired during the night without any inter-ference with daily traffic ; indeed an old or injured cable may be en-tirely removed and replaced by a new one in a few hours; without in any way interfering with the daily work.   Again, the machinery in the engine-room is so arranged that the cable must pass for some distance in open view of the engineer or attendant in charge, whose duty it is to make a frequent examination of it whilst running.

The cable is now operated by a horizontal engine, having a cylinder 14 in. in diameter, with 28 in. stroke, fitted with Ryder's variable automatic valve gear, and is driven at a velocity of about six miles per hour, for seventeen working hours per day—the piston speed being about 530 ft. per minute.   The engine is supplied with steam from a tubular boiler of about 6 ft. long by 4 ft. 6 in. in diameter, consuming about 1 ton 10 cwt. of fuel per day.   A duplicate engine and boiler is kept in reserve. The boiler furnaces are fitted with smoke-consuming appliances which communicate with a chimney shaft about 80 ft. high.

A five minutes' service is commonly run upon the line, with the exception of afternoons, when the cars depart every three minutes. The traffic is conducted with great precision and punctuality, and upon examining the timekeeper's returns throughout all seasons, it is a very rare occurrence to see note taken of any car being a half-minute late on the line. The travelling by these cable tramcars is generally admitted to be extremely pleasant, there being no appreciable noise, vibrations, or fluctuations in speed, such as is experienced in horse cars. The traffic returns show that about three times as many passengers travel up the hill as down.

It may be regretted that no diagrams of the engine's perform-ances are given, to demonstrate the amount of power expended in setting the cable and other machinery in motion, and in propelling the cars. It should, however, be understood that the conditions of traffic upon such a line are so variable, and subject to such continual and rapid fluctuations, that such determinations by indicator cards are practically of little value. In other systems of locomotion the frictional resistance in pounds per car ton, as also the propelling power exerted, can be more accurately determined than is the case with the system at issue ; the most reliable tests by which the performances can be judged are by the cost of operation, maintenance, and consumption of fuel.

Upon reference to Figs. 15 and 16, which represent respectively a sectional plan and transverse section of the Clay-street engine-room (15 ft. below the road level), the arrangement and operation of the cable driving, compensating and controlling machinery will be readily under-stood. S represents the driving engines in duplicate, which receive their steam supply from the boilers S^1, and actuate the cable hauling drum T through the intervention of the countershaft and spur gearing t. The direction of motion of the various parts of the cable B is re-presented by arrows. The cable on its inward passage to the engine-room is deflected at right angles by the large pulleys U U^1 (mounted in a pit or vault beneath the road), and thence passes to the driving clip pulley T, then over a sliding sheave or tackle arrangement V for taking up any undue slack, back to the said driving pulley, and finally out to the road tube again by the pulleys u u^1.

The arrangement provided for taking up any undue slack of the cable resulting from permanent stretching, simply consists of the mounted pulley V, which is capable of being moved along the guides v away from the driving pulley T. By moving the pulley V back or away from the driving gear, about 100 ft. of the cable can be taken up, or pulled into the engine-room, which amounts to about 1 per cent. of its entire length.

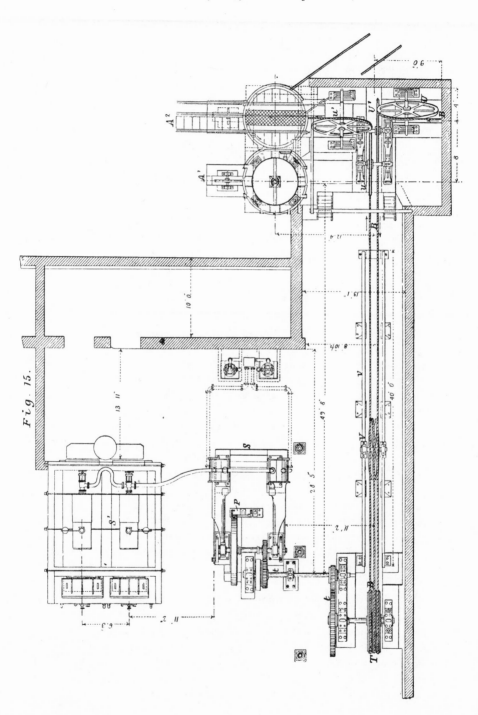

Fig. 15.

It will now be understood how the circuit of the endless cable B is effected and operated, or how it is caused to pass from the engine-room

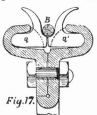

Fig. 17.

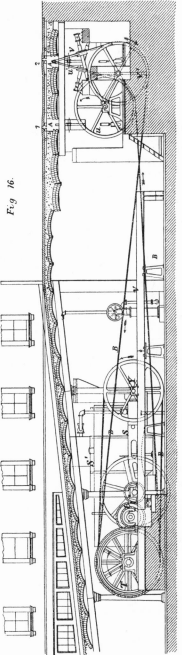

Fig 16.

by the pulleys $u\,u^1$ to the pulleys in the street tube, between the one set of lines to the one terminus pulley or set of pulleys, and similarly back in a parallel plane by the other track tube A^1 to the other terminus pulley or pulleys, returning in another portion of the tube A^2 over the pulleys $U\;U^1$, leading to the driving pulley T and slack-compensating gear V. In order to obtain the necessary adhesion or frictional resistance for driving the cable— without numerous turns over the driving pulley—the latter is provided with peripheral nipping jaws $q\,q^1$ as shown in Fig. 17, which represents a detached portion of the same to an enlarged scale.

At the Kearny-street terminus of the line the cable passes round a sheave or pulley mounted upon a tension carriage (similar to that shown in Fig. 4), having a counterweight of about 3300 lbs. arranged on a double purchase method, which automatically maintains the cable at a uniform tension requisite for the working of the line. This apparatus automatically compensates for any small fluctuations in the length of the cable, resulting from stretching or from variations in temperature, &c.

Wherever the small cable supporting pulleys C occur within the tubes A, small pits are provided for their reception, and to these access may be obtained through manholes. These small pulley pits may all be directly connected with the street sewer for the purpose of draining the cable tubes; or, say, every fifth one may be thus connected, whilst the intermediate pits drain into each other successively. In practice, no difficulty arises from these draining operations, and very little water or dirt is found to accumulate within the cable tubes or pits, which may be kept quite clean by dragging a properly shaped scraper through them about once every four to six months, according to the district and climate, &c. It has been practically proved that any wet or dirt getting into the cable tubes in no way interferes with the efficient operation of the system, and further that the slot or aperture in the road surface, through which the grip shanks pass, has never been known in practice to get clogged, or in any way materially obstructed.

Fig. 18 represents a pictorial view of the Clay-street Hill cable tramway, looking east from the company's premises at the corner of Leavenworth-street. From this view it will be seen that the line consists of a double track, practically quite straight in a longitudinal direction. The manner in which grades of the Clay-street line are cut by level crossings of streets, at right angles thereto, is also apparent in this view.

Having somewhat exhaustively described the construction and operation of the Clay-street Hill cable tramway, we will now pass on, to more briefly consider the more recent lines in the city of San Francisco.

Although all such endless cable tramways are founded upon the same general principle, yet no two lines appear to be constructed actually alike, and the modifications adopted in many cases do not seem to be the result of experience. This lack of similarity may be in many cases attributed to the patent mania which has beset the development of the system, and to the different interests fostered by the various engineers and others who were patentees.

The development or extension of street cable tramways in the far west of America was at first by no means rapid. The system was established step by step and under long and careful tests as to efficiency, economy, safety, effect upon other street traffic, and upon the adjoining property ; and it was not until the authorities and inhabitants became satisfied upon the above points that the system made much headway. Thus, we find that nearly $3\frac{1}{2}$ years elapsed between the successful inauguration of the first cable tramway up Clay-street Hill in August, 1873, and the opening of the next cable line, viz., the Sutter-street line, a portion of which was converted to the system in January, 1877. The unquestionable success of this section of line gave apparently a great impetus to the enterprise, and in April of the following year the California-street cable line was opened for public traffic, whilst other

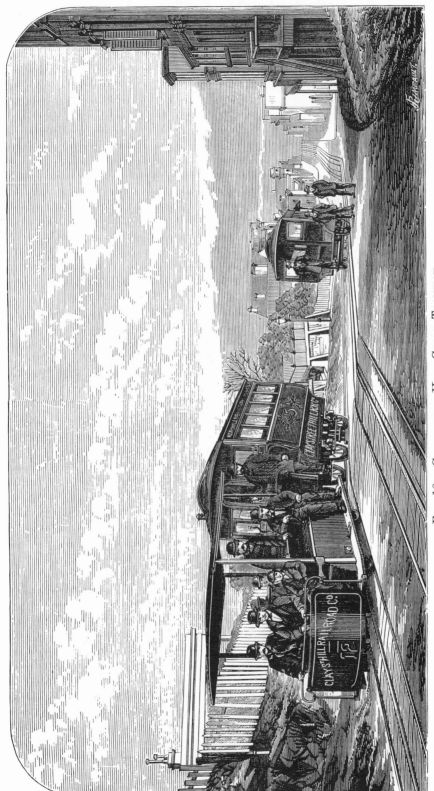

Fig. 18. Clay-street Hill Cable Tramway.

similar undertakings followed each other at about the same intervals of time. Thus, in March, 1880, the fourth cable line was opened on Geary-street towards Golden Gate Park ; in January, 1882, the Union, Presidio, and Ferrie's cable road commenced running ; and in October, 1883, the sixth cable tramway was successfully opened on Market-street, all within the city of San Francisco. Thus, about ten years elapsed between the first and the sixth line being opened, and during the whole of that time there had been a diligent collection of data establishing the successful performance of cable roads both mechanically and financially.

It is now proposed to direct brief attention to some of the general features of the Sutter-street cable line, and also to the chief differences in construction and operation which it exhibits as compared with the Clay-street Hill line.

The Sutter-street Railroad Company, whose lines had for many years been unsatisfactorily and unprofitably worked by horses, converted nearly the entire length of their lines to the cable system before the close of the year 1879. This company has now over $3\frac{1}{2}$ miles of line operated according to the system in question. The gauge of the line is 5 ft., and its maximum elevation above its initial point is about 170 ft., as will be seen upon reference to the longitudinal section of the road, as represented at Fig. 19 of the accompanying illustrations. The grades of this line, however, are comparatively light, and therefore it was not necessary to adopt a mechanical system of haulage.

The conversion of this horse tramway to the cable system was performed without interrupting the daily business of the line, and the reconstruction was executed in a substantial manner. The Sutter-street line extends further east than the majority of the cable lines in the city, thus intersecting the most important thoroughfares, Kearny-street and Montgomery-street, as shown in the section. The excellent control of the cable cars is therefore admirably demonstrated upon this line. After the conversion of the lines the traffic increased by 962,375 passengers the first year, whilst the shares of the company, which had been offered at 24 dols. under horse traction, were selling at 60 dols. This line now transports about 4,500,000 passengers per annum, which obviously forms the basis of a lucrative business.

Note 10

The original cable tube laid upon this road was practically similar to that of the Clay-street Hill line, with the exception that the tube was slightly different in configuration and that the intermediate tube frames had wrought-iron struts and ties secured to the castings. The type of cable tube now adopted by the Sutter-street Company is shown in transverse section at Fig. 20, and is composed of intermediate wrought-iron yokes or frames (old 60 lb. rails bent), with diagonal angle-iron struts C^1 carrying the slot beams C^4. These are tied back by bars C² connected with the rail sleepers C⁵, in order to insure that the proper parallel space shall be left between them for the cable grippers to pass through.   The continuity of the tube is obtained by ramming

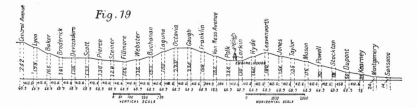

Fig. 19

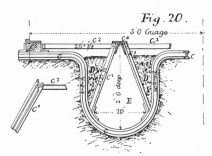

Fig. 20.

in concrete D at the back of suitable templates.   The actual available space or working clearance in the tube or channel E, is of triangular configuration, as shown in the section, and consequently has much greater internal dimensions than the type of tube used in Clay-street.

Prior to the close of 1883, the Sutter-street cable line was operated from more than one engine-house, an arrangement which was neither convenient nor economical.   The company have since erected and equipped a new and well-appointed engine-house, which should ultimately prove a great advantage, by concentrating their working power and machinery.   Originally there were two engine-houses, the one containing two engines and the other four, giving an approximate aggregate of 150 nominal horse- power.   The engine cylinders were 12 in. in diameter by 24 in. stroke, and worked at a piston speed of about 340 ft. per minute.   The working pressure of steam was 100 lbs. per square inch, supplied by six multi-tubular boilers, although it was ascertained that about 40 lbs. of steam was sufficient to set the machinery and cables in motion when the cars were not on the road.   The consumption of coal per working day of nineteen hours was about 24,650 lbs.

The cars and dummies of this company, seat alike eighteen persons, and weigh respectively 3000 lbs. and 2000 lbs. each.   The average intervals at which the cars depart is about every four minutes throughout the day, during which time they perform about 250 round trips.   Two hauling cables are employed to work the system, the main, or Sutter-street cable, being about 13,290 ft. long, and the branch, or Larkin-street cable, about 3712 ft. long.   These cables are each composed of six strands of nineteen crucible steel wires, giving a circumference of 3 in.   The speeds at which the cables are driven vary from about

500 ft. to 750 ft. per minute, while the average lives of the ropes appear to be only about ten to twelve months.

So far we have described cable traction as applied to the working of tramway traffic upon straight double tracks, and these are the conditions which exist upon the main line of the Sutter-street company. But near the termination of the Larkin and Market-streets branch, a sharp curve is to be seen in operation. The cable hauls the cars round this curve very effectually, but the cost of the underground apparatus was considerable. Between Larkin and Post-streets other curves are found. These curves are of small radii, varying from 40 ft. to 90 ft. ; they are on approximately level ground, and are traversed by the cars strictly by cable haulage, and not by momentum or gravitation. The construction and operation of the line at these points will be understood upon reference to Figs. 21, 22, and 23, which will now be explained.

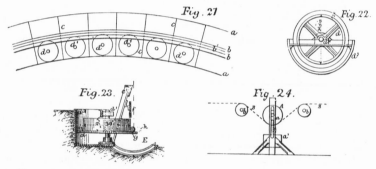

The diagrammatic plan in Fig. 21 is intended to represent a curved portion of the permanent way of a cable tramway ; in it *a a* are the rails and *b b* the slot beams, which are bent to the required arc, and supported by the tube frames *c* placed radially to suit the curvature of the road. On the inner side of the curve and between the frames *c* are placed a series of pulleys *d*, their distances between them varying according to the radius of the curve, but in the example here given the vertical axes of the pulleys are about 3 ft. 6 in. apart from centre to centre. In practice, the requisite intervals between the pulleys on curved portions of the line are determined by the maximum deflection that may be imparted to the cable, without injuring the shanks of the grippers, and this usually varies from 1 in. to 2 in.

Wherever pulleys exist proper access must be provided for oiling, inspection, and replacement; this may be obtained either by manholes communicating with the street surface, or by arranging the pulleys within pits or vaults having but one covered opening, by which a man may enter. In the example before us a number of manholes with suitable covering plates are provided, but in this country the interference with the street surface might reasonably be objected to. The construction and method óf mounting these curved pulleys is shown separately and to an enlarged scale in Figs. 22 and 23, the former representing a plan and the latter a transverse sectional elevation with part of the tube framing attached.

From these views it will be seen that ordinary pulleys d, fixed upon vertical axes d^1, are mounted in suitable guides and footstep bearings, capable of adjustment, the whole apparatus being self-contained within a casing d^2. E represents part of the cable tube with one diagonal strut c^1, to which a guiding bar or piece f is attached, and against which slides or rollers carried by the gripper shanks are caused to bear and travel, so as to relieve them of lateral and torsional strains.

This guiding bar should be arranged to come down close to the top of the pulleys, in order to prevent the cable passing between them or becoming jammed ; g represents the normal position that the travelling cable occupies, and h indicates the deflection the cable undergoes when a car with its gripper attachment is being hauled round such a curved portion of the line. When the car has passed clear of the various pulleys, the cable at once returns to its normal position. This arrangement of apparatus for conducting the cable and the cars round curved portions of the line has answered satisfactorily, but the cost of construction was excessive.

Later on we shall have occasion to consider, more simple and economical means of working the curved portions of cable tramways.

Fig. 24 shows a modified cable tension apparatus, as used in one place at the extreme west end of this line. At a glance, it will be seen that its functions are exactly similar to those of the usual horizontal tension apparatus, but that it is arranged to work in a vertical plane in order to economise space. B represents the cable, which is designed to pass over two small guide pulleys b b, and under a larger pulley A placed between the latter. The centrally situated pulley has attached to it a counterpoise or weight-box a^1, and the whole is arranged to work in vertical guides a.

It will be evident that when any undue strain is brought upon the cable, the counter-weighted pulley will be caused to rise in its frame, and conversely will return to its normal position immediately such strain is withdrawn.

Reverting to the engine-house appliances, the cable-driving apparatus differs somewhat from the arrangement described in connection with the Clay-street line, as will be seen upon reference to Figs. 25 and 26 of the drawings, which represent a side elevation and plan of the contrivance in question. A is a large fluted or grooved drum, fixed upon a counter-shaft a, and receiving motion from the prime mover, through the intervention of the spur gearing d D. Opposite this grooved drum and in about the same plane is provided a similar drum B, mounted in bearings and capable of horizontal adjustment by means of the sliding base C.   The endless hauling cable E is passed alternately backwards and forwards over these drums a sufficient number of times to obtain

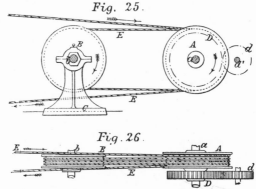

Fig. 25.

Fig. 26.

the necessary driving adhesion.   Positive motion is imparted to the drum A which hauls in the cable, as indicated by the direction of the arrows, the second pulley B simply acting as an "idler," and revolving by frictional contact with the running cable E.   When, however, the cable permanently lengthens by stretching, the drum D may be moved further back, so as to take up the resulting slack.

We will now pass on to examine the cable-gripping apparatus used upon this line.   The gripper (Fig. 27) consists of two vertically moving jaws a and b, which are caused to grasp or release the cable c, as desired, through the intervention of the lever d and link motion e. Upon the lower jaw of the gripper there are mounted two small pulleys $f f^1$, upon which the cable is supposed to travel when the apparatus is open.   Small conical pulleys $g g^1$ are arranged in connection with the upper jaw so that an extended opening movement of the lever d will also raise these pulleys so as to cast the running cable out of the gripper jaws.   This gripper, like the Clay-street apparatus before described, is of the so-called L-shaped type, but the former has to receive or discharge the cable in a horizontal direction, whereas the latter, it will be remembered, is capable of performing the same functions in a vertical plane.   It is obvious that in using the Clay-street type of grip, immediately the gripping jaws are sufficiently opened, the cable will drop out automatically, whereas in the Sutter-street class of apparatus the cable must either be mechanically ejected from the jaws, or be so deflected as to be conducted out of them when opened.   Both classes of grips have their respective defects as will be shown later on.

The Sutter-street gripping appliances are attached to the dummies by pins entering into the hollow terminations h of the carrying plate h^1. The projecting piece i on the side of the upper grip jaw a is the bearing slide or "skate," which relieves the grip shank j of shearing and torsional strains when the cars are being hauled round curved portions of the line. The way in which this is effected has already been described with reference to Figs. 22 and 23, that is, the grip shank is supported whilst going round curves by the slide i on the grip, bearing against the guiding bar f fixed on the inner side of the tube framing.

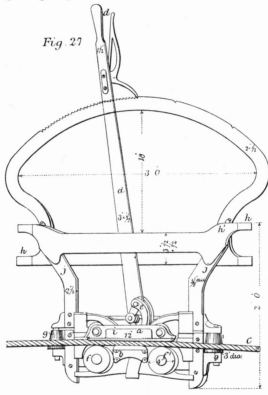

Fig. 27

From the relative positions of the vertical centre lines of the grip shank, and of the cable-nipping jaws, it will be evident that the cable does not travel directly below the continuous slot in the track. It is necessary that the pulleys should be carefully and accurately erected, as imperfect mounting may cause the cable to vibrate so considerably that a passing car may leave it off one or more of its pulleys. The succeeding car will probably replace it, but it is very desirable that the cable should be saved from such injurious treatment. The above described "grip," used on the Sutter-street line, is the joint invention of Messrs. A. Hovey and T. Day, and who were practically the first to employ this class of apparatus.

The next cable tramway that claims our attention is that of California-street, which was successfully completed in April, 1878. This

Note

11

line now consists of about 12,500 ft. of straight double track of 3½ ft. gauge, the highest part or elevation being about 265 ft. above its datum line at Kearny-street. The line, as originally constructed and opened for public traffic, was only about 8800 ft. long, but like the Clay and Sutter-street roads, its successful inauguration led to an early extension of the system.

The engine-house from which this line is worked is located in a valley, similar to that of the Sutter-street road, as will be seen upon reference to the longitudinal section given in Fig. 28, and from this it will be

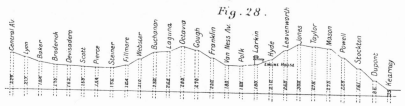

Fig. 28.

readily understood that the grades of the line are in some places exceedingly steep. In one place there is a rise of about 75 ft. in 413 ft., viz., between Stockton and Dupont-streets, equivalent to a grade of about 1 in 5¼. This is about the steepest incline yet worked by a cable tramway of the type in question, with the exception of a portion of the Union and Presidio line, which has a rise of about 3 ft. more in a similar distance.

The engines employed to operate the lines previously described are of the horizontal type, but upon this line vertical engines (marine type), capable of exerting about 200 horse-power, are used. The cylinders are 22 in. in diameter by 36 in. stroke, and are worked to a piston speed of about 570 ft. per minute. The boilers are of the horizontal multitubular type, 4 ft. 9 in. in diameter, with eighty 12 ft. tubes, 3 in. in diameter. The average working pressure of the steam used is 70 lbs. to the square inch. A pressure of 15 lbs. is stated to be sufficient to put the machinery and cables in operation when the cars are not on the latter. The approximate daily average consumption of fuel for nineteen working hours is 15,700 lbs. About fourteen cars and dummies are employed upon this company's system, and these depart about every five minutes, performing about 225 round trips per day. The cars and dummies used are heavier than those described in connection with the previous lines, and weigh respectively 4000 lbs. and 3000 lbs. each. The hauling cables used by the company are also heavier, being manufactured of Bessemer steel wires, formed of six strands of nineteen wires each, and presenting a circumferential measurement of about 4 in.

Although this system extends in one straight line from east to west, two endless cables are employed to haul the cars, the one extending from the Kearny-street terminus to the engine-house, and the other from the latter to the western terminus. Duplicate driving drums and conducting pulleys are employed, and are simultaneously actuated from the same engine and gearing. The engine-house is situated in a hollow about 4220 ft. west of the Kearny-street terminus, and therefore the cable used to work this section is about 8840 ft. long, whilst the section west of the engine-house is similarly operated by a cable of about 17,000 ft. long. These cables are driven at a speed of about 535 ft. per minute, or rather over six miles per hour, their working lives averaging about one year, although one cable used upon this line lasted for one year and ten months.

It will be evident, that as separate cables are employed to work the two sections on either side of the engine-house and depôt, all the cars, whether travelling east or west, must release and drop their respective cables at this point, and pick up the other when they have passed by gravitation or momentum the place where the cables make their communication with the operating machinery. This break in the continuity of the cables is, however, only for a few feet, and therefore causes little or no inconvenience. It should here be mentioned, that the type of gripper used upon this line is similar to that described upon the Sutter-street line, that is, it consists of a fixed and a movable clamping jaw operated by a lever and link motion, which receives or releases the cable laterally. In this manner it will be understood, that at places where it is necessary to drop the cable, the jaws of the grippers are opened wide, and the cable deflected out of them by a suitable arrangement of pulleys. Conversely, the other part of the same endless cable, or a separate and independent one, may be retaken on the other side of such break, by leaving the grip-jaws fully open and similarly deflecting the cable at a reverse horizontal angle, so that the former runs in to the latter, the apparatus being thereupon closed and the operation of haulage continued as before. Another way of obtaining substantially the same end, is to deflect a part of the car track in a similar manner, to or from the cable in a horizontal direction, so that upon opening the grip sufficiently at the requisite places, the cars and their gripping attachments are caused to run off from the cable, and similarly return to, and retake it when the break in the continuity of the cable has been passed. In some cases it is advantageous to make a slight depression or fall in the track, where it is intended to retake a cable, so that the grippers—caused to travel towards the latter as above described—partake of a compound motion in a vertical and horizontal direction, and in this manner are caused to close upon the running cable.

The cable tube employed upon this line is strongly constructed with frames of old 60-lb. rails, bent, and surrounded by concrete in a somewhat similar manner to the formation described upon Sutter-street, its internal depth being about 22 in.

Reverting to the engine-house, it may be remarked, that the vertical type of engines used, is scarcely suitable for the class of work, and the pulsations are sometimes to be distinctly felt when travelling upon the line. It will be readily appreciated, that any intermittent jerking of the cables is far from conducive to the comfort of passengers or economy in maintenance.

On other cable tramways in the States, the engines and operating machinery are situated at some distance from, and at about right angles to the track ; but on this line, the driving machinery is erected in a large vault immediately below the roadway, so that the cables are driven in the same plane, direct from the drums to the pulleys in the street tubes.

The cables are in this manner saved from some amount of bending, usually occasioned by deflecting the cables at right angles ; but, on the other hand, the benefit thus derived is apparently more than neutralised by the expense and inconvenience of such an arrangement. The method of driving the cables is also somewhat different to that practised upon other lines — that is, in lieu of taking two or more turns with the cable round a clip pulley or grooved drum, as previously described upon the Clay and Sutter-street lines, it is here preferred, to take only one turn round two driving drums in the form of the figure 8, as will be understood upon reference to Fig. 29. This method of driving appears generally undesirable, if experiences from mining, haulage, &c., are to be observed, *e.g.*, in colliery winding, the under and over rope is found to wear more rapidly than the top rope.

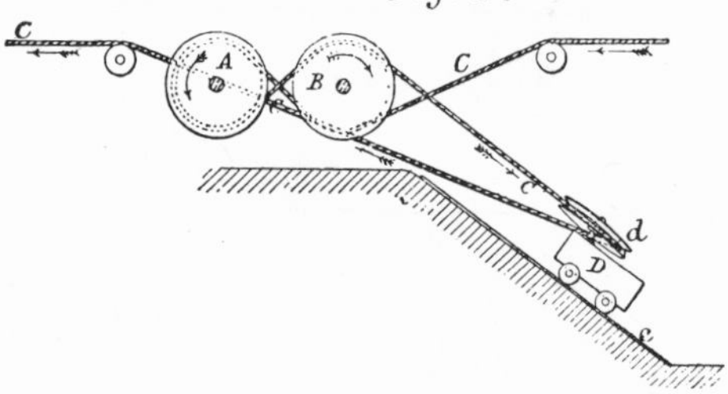

Fig. 29

Note 12

A and B represent two grooved driving drums or pulleys, mounted in the same plane, and both receiving positive motion from the same source of power, through spur gearing. The grooves of these drums are "lagged" or faced with wood packing, in order to avoid injuring the cables.

The cables C are passed round their respective drums, as represented by the direction of the arrows in the engraving. In reality, there are two such sets of driving pulleys in the vault, situated side by side, the one set operating the Kearny-street cable, and the other that of the Western cable. The tensional apparatus D used in combination with the above machinery is primitive, if not undesirable, and consists simply of a truck carrying a pulley *d*, and mounted upon an angularly arranged rail bed *e*. The outgoing portion of the cable, after leaving the drums, passes round the pulley *d* before returning to the street tube. The truck or wagon D carrying this tension pulley is loaded with scrap iron or other weights, and in this manner maintains the cable taut. This apparatus, it will be seen, is somewhat rough, and should the cables strand at any time, it would probably be found smashed at the bottom of the incline. It should be clearly understood that the haulage cables, if maintained efficiently taut, behave more like rigid rods, and are practically free from sagging or vibration, which is an essential desideratum upon a cable line. When there is any appreciable "sag" it will be generally exhibited upon the outgoing portion of the cable, which is being paid out at the back of the cars hauled upon the line.

Referring to the question of the utility of facing the drums and pulleys, &c., with wood or similar soft packing, no doubt, theoretically, it is a correct measure to adopt, but practice, on the other hand, indicates that it cannot be economically or conveniently carried out, neither do the results obtained show any appreciable advantage over those given by other lines not following this practice. All the cables used on these mechanical tramways are kept well coated with a mixture of vegetable tar and linseed oil, which is usually allowed to drip on the cables as they leave the engine-rooms on their outward passage to the street tubes.

Fig. 30 represents a plan of a portion of a cable tramway track, with

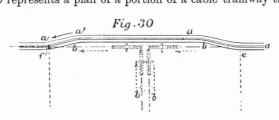

Fig. 30

a lateral deflection or offset, for dropping and regaining the cable at an engine-house pit, where the continuity of the cable is interrupted. Let it be assumed that a car is travelling (in the direction of the full arrow) upon the track *a*, and that upon arriving in the proximity of the machinery pit *e*, the operator on the dummy or car platform throws open his gripping apparatus, releasing the running cable *b*, which continues travelling in the same line. Thereupon the car would diverge and travel by momentum *viâ* the curvature *a¹*, and when on the opposite side of the pit *e* would return into the running line of the cable at *f*, where it would receive the outgoing portion of same, as indicated by the dotted arrows.

This operation of slipping and catching the cables, may be necessary at more than one place on a cable tramway, and will depend upon the nature, extent, and ramifications of the system. In any case, wherever any unavoidable obstructions occur in a line, such measures are necessary, as, for instance, where a cable runs from the track to the engine-house or operating machinery ; at terminations of a line; at shunting points; on curves worked by gravitation ; where cables cross from another line ; where it is desired to drop one cable and pick up another, &c. It will therefore be understood that, where these operations have to be effected, great care and some experience is most necessary on the part of the drivers, for if they do not open their grips at the proper time and places, they will certainly break or injure the cables or grips, or derange some of the machinery. The drivers employed upon the lines in the States are, however, so competent and dexterous that such troubles seldom arise.

Releasing the cables at these critical places is obviously of more serious consequence than retaking them, for in the latter case, should any driver overrun the proper points arranged for catching a cable, the car will either have to be pushed or drawn back again, or the cable lifted into the gripper by means of a hand-hook provided for the purpose.

These devices should be arranged as far as possible upon level portions of the lines, as if constructed upon heavy grades, a failure in regaining the cables may cause an accident by the cars running away by gravitation. In all cases, however, the cars are equipped with efficient and powerful continuous wheel and slipper brakes. Much care must be exercised in the construction and operation of such portions of a cable tramway, and the passing of such places must be effected either by momentum, gravitation, or by some auxiliary assistance of pushing or pulling.

Fig. 31 represents a diagrammatic plan of the arrangement of the tracks and turn-outs opposite the car depôt.

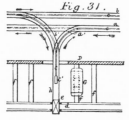

D represents a portion of the front wall of the depôt, the flooring of which is provided with car siding tracks f and a traversing bed d, upon which a carriage or traverser e is mounted. G is a car on one of these sidings, which when required to be put in service upon the line, is transferred upon the traverser e. In this manner the traverser and car would be subsequently brought back in line with the outgoing track h, and upon which the latter would be transferred. C^1 represents the hatchway through which the gripping appliance is lowered from the car into an extension of the cable tube. The car is then pushed or drawn out of the depôt on to the main line, where it picks up the cable and proceeds ; a and b represent the " up and down "

main line tracks ; *c* the slots through which the grippers work, and $a^1 b^1$ the respective in and out curves from and to the car depôt, the direction of their traffic being indicated by the arrows.

Fig. 32 is a diagrammatic plan of a common type of terminal arrangement employed upon cable tramways.

B represents a portion of an endless cable travelling round the terminal pulley A, nearly centrally below the tracks *a* and *b* of a cable line. The terminal pulley is mounted upon a counter-weighted carriage, as already described, and the whole is arranged to work within a suitable vault or pit *a* below the roadway.

The up-going or departing cars (*viâ* track *a*) can take the cable within some distance close up to the terminus pit, but the down-coming or arriving cars (*viâ* the line *b*) must release the cable at D, or where the track converges into the crossover road b^1, and where the shunting operations are effected in the following manner :

Upon a train arriving at or about D, the dummy is uncoupled and the cable let go, so that the dummy travels by momentum *viâ* the crossing b^1 to the up line *a*, when the brakes are applied so as to bring it to rest in front of the second crossing b^2. The ordinary car is then allowed to travel on in the same manner by the last-mentioned crossing b^2, so as to get behind the dummy now waiting upon the up line *a*. The cars are then re-attached, and the cable regained, when the up journey is commenced. These shunting operations, which are similar to "fly shunting" upon railways, are necessitated by the employment of the dummies or independent cars for carrying the gripping appliances. Later on we shall have occasion to refer to the use of ordinary cars provided with the necessary cable-gripping apparatus, and by this arrangement the above complications may be materially reduced, or avoided.

Fig. 33 represents a side (sectional) elevation of the lower terminal

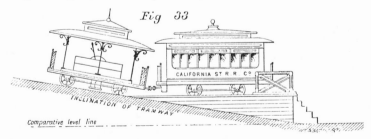

Fig 33

CALIFORNIA ST R R Cº

Comparative level line

platform erected upon the California-street line. It will be readily understood, and has been before mentioned, that it is desirable to arrange the termini of cable tramways upon approximately level ground, and therefore in instances where this cannot conveniently be done, a terminal platform is sometimes erected as shown in the figure in question. It will be seen that the ordinary passenger cars are arranged to stand upon the level, whereas the dummies stand upon the natural inclination of the road in a suitable manner to readily pick up the hauling cable.

We will now pass on to examine the construction and working of the cable-gripping apparatus carried by the dummies upon this line and as shown in side elevation at Fig. 34. It will be seen at a glance that there is a very close analogy in this apparatus to that employed upon the Sutter-street line. Practically it is the same type of grip, but upon close examination, the general arrangement of the working parts will be found to be more conveniently carried out than in the former example, in which it can be seen that the essential operating parts are designed to travel in the cable tube beneath the street surface.

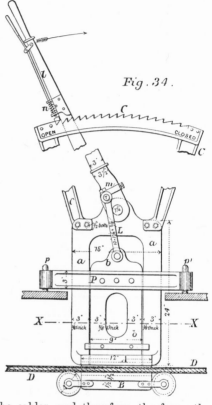

Fig. 34.

In practice, more or less dirt, grit, and wet must penetrate the cable tubes, independently of the tar and oily matter that is brought in by the cables, and therefore, the fewer the moving parts of the gripping appliances that run within the tubes the better, and the more reliable their action should be.

In the example before us, it will be seen that the link L, for communicating the motion from the lever l to the gripping jaws A and B, and also the necessary gear m for adjusting their play, is arranged to be accessible from the car platforms, and is clear of the cable tubes. These gripping appliances are connected with the dummies by means of pin attachments p p^1 carried by an auxiliary framing mounted upon the axles of these vehicles, or arranged with slides and springs in order to permit of lateral vibrations, without injuriously straining the grip shanks. From this method of mounting, it will be seen that the bottom jaw B of the grip with its plate b is rigidly attached to the frame P, which is connected with the dummy framing, whilst the top jaw A is capable of receiving a vertical reciprocating motion upon moving the operating lever *l*. In other words, the lower jaw remains stationary, whilst the upper one, with its connecting plates *a* and quadrant frame *c*, is forced down upon the former by moving the lever *l* over, and thus the continuously running cable D may be either grasped or released as required. When the gripping jaws are closed, obviously the motion of the cable is imparted to the dummy or car, whilst conversely, when the upper jaw is raised, the cable is left running inoperatively upon the lower jaw, and the vehicle can be brought to rest by applying the brakes.

Another difference in the construction and working of this gripper, as compared with that used by the Sutter-street Company, is the absence of the conical pulleys for ejecting the cable from the jaws. In the present example, offsets are provided in the track, where it is necessary to drop the cable, so that upon opening the grippers they are caused to travel off the cable as already described when referring to Fig. 30. The dotted line X X, Fig. 34, is intended to indicate the approximate street level, so that it will be understood that all the parts below this line travel within the cable tube, whilst those above it are clear of the street surface. The shanks and jaws of the grips are constructed of cast steel; the carrying frames, quadrants, and operating levers of wrought iron. The jaws are provided with soft iron packing pieces secured in Babbit metal. Wood, brass, and white metal liners have also been tried in the grips used by this company, but soft cast iron has been found to answer sufficiently well, and proves far more economical. The aggregate weight of these gripping appliances is about 250 lbs. each. The operating levers are provided with ordinary spring catch-rod devices *n*.

It may here be mentioned, that jaws similar to A and B can be cast on the other side of the shanks *a* and *b*, so that they may be capable of engaging with a cable on either side. Some such arrangement, or the employment of two separate grippers to each dummy or car, would be necessary if the cables did not occupy the same position in relation to the centre lines of the up and down tracks. In practice, however, it is generally found convenient to arrange the cables similarly, as regards the slots in the tracks of both roads, then only one set of grip jaws is required upon the apparatus, and the turning of the dummies or cars rendered unnecessary. The foregoing remarks refer to the L type of gripping apparatus already explained.

Later on will be described, a central cable-gripping appliance, which bears a common relation to the cable, whether upon the up or down lines.

All these gripping devices are fixed in the centres of the dummies or cars, so as to effect a uniform draught, and in cases of those operated direct by means of levers, a sufficient clearance for working them has to be provided upon the dummies or cars.

In the employment of all lateral or side operating grips, and of the type described upon the Sutter and California-street cable lines, care should be taken that the cables do not fly out of the jaws of the apparatus if there be any curved portions of line upon which it may be desired to open the grips to allow a car to stop. In practice, however, if the curves be short, a rule may be made that no passengers shall leave or enter the cars until such portions of the line are passed. On the other hand, should the exercise of such a rule prove inconvenient, or if the curves upon a line be long and frequent, auxiliary guard plates may be attached to the jaws of the grippers, so as to prevent the cable leaving them upon opening the apparatus to allow a car to stop.

The fourth cable tramway in San Francisco was constructed about two years after the California-street line, the route selected being Geary-street, a central and densely populated thoroughfare connecting some of the principal business centres and attractive resorts of this beautiful western city. The gradients upon this line are, however, comparatively unimportant, as will be seen upon reference to the longitudinal section represented in Fig. 35.

The Geary-street cable tramway was completed in March, 1880. The length of this line is about 13,200 ft., the gauge 5 ft. The Market-street terminus is 35 ft. above datum level, and the maximum elevation attained is about 350 ft. above this base.

The construction of the permanent way and cable tube used upon this line is shown in the transverse and longitudinal sections, Figs. 36 and 37 respectively. The central slotted tube A is practically of similar construction to other examples already described, and with the exception of drawing attention to its very compact or small section (viz., about 7 in. by 1 3in. in the clear), a very cursory explanation will suffice to make its construction understood.

B represents one of the intermediate trough-shaped castings which form the principal elements of the tube. These carry the slot

Fig. 35.

beams or rails *b* (in this case ordinary inverted rails), so arranged as to leave a parallel opening or clearance *c* between them, through

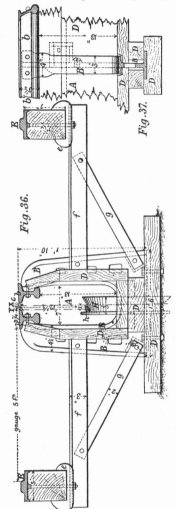

Fig.37.

Fig.36.

gauge 5 ft.

which the cable grippers operate and travel. The sides, bottom, and foundations of this tube are chiefly composed of woodwork D, as represented in the drawing, the side planks, however, being so arranged as to be capable of being readily withdrawn and replaced by concrete, if desired. The rails E are laid upon longitudinal wooden sleepers carried in chairs *e* connected with the tube frames by transverse and diagonal bracings *f* and *g*.

The cable-supporting pulleys H, situated at suitable intermediate distances along the tube A, are of special design, as will now be explained. The type of cable-gripping apparatus used upon this line differs from those employed and described upon earlier lines, inasmuch that the jaws are arranged to engage and hold the cable in the same vertical plane as the slot in the tube, as just referred to, in contradistinction to the **L**-shaped type of apparatus.

In consideration of the action of this type of gripper, and of the accepted desirability of allowing the cable to travel out of the plane of the slot, in order to prevent some amount of wet and dirt falling upon it, a special form of supporting pulley was designed so as to meet both requirements. These pulleys are about 3 in. broad, and are formed with inclined or conical peripheral surfaces terminating with vertical flanges, as shown in Fig. 36. X indicates the centre line common to the tube slot, grip shanks, nipping jaws, and cable when the latter is engaged in the jaws, and Y shows the position of the hauling cable when running free upon its carrying pulleys H.

It will now be understood, that although the passing cars drag the cable into the same plane as the tube slot, it is caused to so return to its supporting pulleys and slide down their inclined surfaces, as to run, when free, under cover of one of the slot rails *b,* as shown at *h,* Fig. 36.

Figs. 38 and 39 represent a side elevation and a part end view

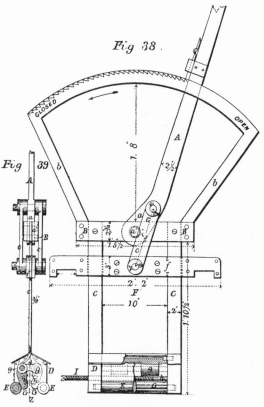

Fig 38.

Fig 39.

respectively, of the Geary-street Company's gripping apparatus above referred to. A is the operating lever, terminating with the bent enlargement *a* working upon the fulcrum a^1 carried by the plate B to which the quadrant frame *b* is attached. To this lever there is pivotted a double link *c,* the opposite extremity of which is connected to the carrying plate or bar *f,* which is suitably attached to the central grip framing of the dummy car. C are the vertical shanks or actuating plates, fixed at their top ends to the quadrant plate B, whilst their lower extremities terminate with the framing D provided with horizontal rollers E. The lower framing bar *f,* connected to the car, carries the central shank plate F terminating with the jaws G, mounted upon hinged joints *g,* so as to be capable of moving radially to or from each other as the rollers E are raised or lowered in a vertical plane. These swinging jaws are fitted with suitable metallic packing pieces *h,* which may be readily replaced when worn out from pressure or friction upon the cable I. In this apparatus it may be observed, that no small friction or carrying pulleys are provided for the cable to run upon, when the jaws are released, and as in some of the other gripping appliances already described.

In the above illustrations the gripping apparatus in question is shown in its open position, and the cable is therefore assumed to be running inoperatively through it. When it is required to close the apparatus in order to impart the movement of the cable to the dummy or car, then all that is necessary is to pull over the lever A, whereupon the same, with its quadrant frame and shank attachments C, will be raised up bodily about the lower pin or fixed fulcrum of the link *c*, and thus the pair of rollers E, carried at the lower extremities of C, will be caused to force the swinging nipping jaws G closer together so as to tightly grasp the cable between the concave dies or packing pieces *h*.

Upon examining these engravings, it will be seen that the nipping jaws and the cable carried within them, lie in the same vertical plane as the shank connections C and F (as indicated by the dotted line Z, Fig. 39), and therefore, at places where the cars are upon the line, the cable for some distance is held immediately beneath the slot in the tube. The degree of importance to be attached to maintaining the cables always under the cover of the solid portion of the tubes, as effected by the employment of the **L** type of gripper, we will not pause to discuss, as indeed there appears little or no practical evidence either for or against such arrangement.

The Geary-street gripping apparatus resembles that previously described upon the Clay-street line, inasmuch as their construction necessitates receiving and discharging the cables in a vertical direction, whereas the Sutter-street and California-street appliances perform the same functions laterally, or in a horizontal direction. It will be readily apparent, that in the employment of the former type of apparatus, care must be exercised that the cables are not repeatedly dropped out of their jaws, when it is really intended to only let them run through them inoperatively. But when such slips have occurred, the cables have been rapidly regained by the use of handhooks, owing to the very convenient and accessible position that the cables always bear to the jaws of the gripping appliances. It is evident that in the case of the **L**-shaped type of apparatus, that it is more difficult to drop a cable unintentionally (except when stopping on curves as before alluded to) than in the last example, but on the other hand it should not be lost sight of, that at places where it is necessary to relinquish a cable and again retake it, the vertically acting type of grip has the advantage.

Let it be assumed that a dummy upon the Geary-street line has arrived at the engine-house machinery pit, situated beneath the roadway, and it is therefore necessary to release the ingoing cable promptly ;

then all that is required, is to simply throw open the grip to its full extent, whereupon the cable at once falls out of the jaws by gravitation clear of the apparatus. When the car has travelled over the pit by momentum, the outgoing cable is so raised by a suitably located pulley, as to conduct it into the jaws of the open grip, which are then closed and the system of haulage continued.

Reverting to the engine-house, car depôt, and offices of the Geary-street Railroad Company, which are situated about 8000 ft. west of Kearny-street, they may be mentioned as amongst the best-arranged and appointed premises of the kind. The building, which is constructed chiefly of wood, is located in a valley at the corner of Buchanan-street, the car depôt and offices being chiefly arranged upon the street level, whilst the engines and machinery are situated in the basement, and an elegant gallery is erected round such spacious room, to which there is direct access from the street.

The engines employed to operate this line are two in number, one of which is kept in reserve. They are of the horizontal type, with cylinders 18 in. in diameter by 48 in. stroke, provided with automatic (variable) valve gear, and work to an average piston speed of about 370 ft. per minute. Steam is supplied to these engines by three steel boilers about 16 ft. long and 4 ft. 4 in. in diameter, having sixty-three steel tubes 3 in. in diameter. The average working pressure of steam used is about 70 lbs. to the square inch, although it is stated that 10 lbs. pressure of steam is quite sufficient to set the engines, machinery, cables, and pulleys in motion when no cars are being hauled upon the line. The approximate daily average consumption of fuel for nineteen working hours is about 5 tons.

The dummies and cars used by this company weigh respectively 4800 lbs. and 4000 lbs. each. The extra weight of the dummies over that of the ordinary cars (which is an exception), may be remarked, but this is to be chiefly attributed to the heavy angle irons used in their construction and to some metallic embellishments, which, although presumably ornamental, are by no means essential. From eighteen to twenty of these dummies and cars are used daily throughout the system, their intervals of departure varying from 3 min. to 6 min. according to the period of the day and the traffic.

Two cables are employed to operate this line, the one east and the other west, of the engine-house, and measure about 16,600 ft. and 11,000 ft. respectively, or 27,600 ft. together, for about 26,400 ft. of single track. These cables are composed of six strands of nineteen crucible steel wires, the average linear velocity at which they are driven being about 600 ft. per minute.

These cables are driven by plain grooved drums and followers mounted on countershafts, practically similar to the arrangement already described on the Sutter-street line, but the motion from the prime or engine shaft is in this case communicated to the former through rope belting, in lieu of spur gearing, and by this arrangement the noise of the working parts is much reduced. In cases where engine houses for operating such mechanical systems of haulage are unavoidably located in densely populated districts, the question of silently-acting machinery should not be disregarded.

The average life of the cables run upon this line is about eleven months, which is below the average of those on most other lines. Individual cases may, however, be cited in which the lives of the cables have met every expectation ; for instance, one lasted for eighteen months after running at the rate of about six miles per hour for $19\frac{1}{2}$ working hours per day. However, it appears to be now generally admitted that the average lives of the cables used upon the Geary-street line are somewhat below most of the other company's returns. This is attributed by some persons to the additional wear inflicted upon the cables by the employment of top boxwood bearing pieces at the changes of grade on the line, in lieu of proper depression pulleys, and also to the cables being unduly exposed to wet and dirt from the road, owing to their being so much under the tube slot. The importance to be attached to such explanations appears, however, small, and far more evidence supports the contention that these results more likely arise from slipping or sliding with the grippers towards the Kearny-street end of the line, and to the complex bending of the cable at the lower terminal pit where a turntable is located.

Some small degree of slipping upon the cables must at times necessarily occur, but the practice of reducing the speed of the cars by allowing them to slip upon the cable must prove detrimental to the lives of the ropes. In practice, no appreciable slip is necessary in order to start a car smoothly. The closing motion, whether communicated by a handwheel or lever, should be steady and uniform until the cable is tightly held. When once a car commences moving upon such gradual application of the power, there is no occasion to give the lever or wheel of the apparatus a final pull, and thus unnecessarily jam the cable, a practice, however, by no means uncommon amongst cable car drivers. The maximum pressure and adhesion is obviously required for starting the cars and not for maintaining them in motion.

On the whole, the Geary-street cable tramway certainly affords a good example of the system in question, both as regards economical construction and mechanical efficiency. The construction and equipment of this line cost about 10,000*l*. per mile, and it has earned as much as 17 per cent. upon its capital. About $37\frac{1}{2}$ dols. have been called up per share, and the stock has attained the value of 98 dols. and upwards.

Before quitting the Geary-street Company's cable system we would direct brief attention to the complex nature of the traffic throughout the street upon which this line is laid, as it affords valuable evidence regarding the highly efficient and reliable manner in which the traffic upon a properly constructed cable line can be conducted. The line, it will be remembered, is about 13,200 ft. long, consisting of separate up and down tracks throughout, laid without appreciable curves. Independent of the ordinary street traffic of a heavy character, which has to be contended with, the route of the line in question is either intersected or interrupted upon no less than six separate occasions by other tramway systems, and as will be understood upon reference to the diagrammatic plan given at Fig. 40. From this figure it will be seen, that the Geary-street cable line commences from the turntable A, located at the eastern or Market-street terminus, and extends in a westerly direction towards the Pacific shores ; *a* and *b* represent the up and down tracks respectively of the line, from which it may be noticed that tramway traffic in the United States is conducted in an opposite manner to the practice observed in this country, that is, the " up " traffic is conducted upon the right-hand line or side of the street.   Passing from this lower terminus, a few feet westerly, to Kearny-street (see also section, Fig. 35), the line in question is at first completely intersected by the horse tramway of the North Beach and Mission-streets Company, marked B on the plan, whilst a branch of the same (C) joins the Geary-street cable lines immediately west of Kearny-street. Besides this special interference at the very commencement of the cable traffic, it should be mentioned that the ordinary vehicular and foot traffic along and across

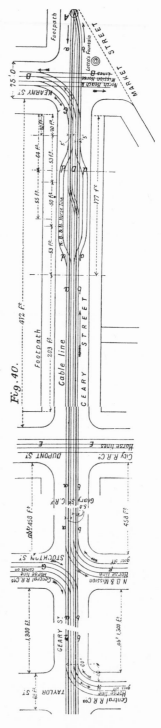

Fig. 40.

Kearny-street to Market-street is exceptionally heavy, these being the two principal streets in the city.

Progressing west, we next find the cable and North Beach and Mission-streets horse cars travelling over the same lines until arriving at D, when the former continue their straight course, whilst the latter deviate to either side to the passing-places *d*, and subsequently rejoin the cable line a short distance further on, where the cable and horse traffic is again jointly conducted over the same way. Continuing a westerly course for about 412 ft., the line in question crosses Dupont-street, from which it is cut by the horse lines E of the City Railroad Company. About 458 ft. further west, the horse traffic of the North Beach and Mission-streets Company is diverted from this cable line at F, Stockton-street, but whilst this extra traffic is got rid of here, another company's horse lines immediately obtain partial running powers over the line in question, viz., those of the Central Railroad Company, as represented at G on the plan. Continuing for about 1300 ft. in the same direction, the Geary-street cable line crosses Taylor-street, where the horse traffic of the Central Railroad Company leaves the former as indicated at H. The line then extends for a distance of some 1650 ft. further without similar interruption, or until it arrives at Larkin-street, where a branch of the Sutter-street cable line crosses Geary-street. At this point the drivers of the Geary-street cars have to release the cable and travel over the interruption by momentum, retaking it on the other side, for the Sutter-street Company having the previous right of way, have carried their cable above that of the other company.

Towards the western terminus of the line, Fillmore-street is cut about 825 ft. west of the engine-house (on the corner of Buchanan-street) along which a branch horse line of the Central Railroad Company runs, which thus again intersects the Geary-street cable line.

From the above facts it will be understood that the operation and control of the cars upon this cable line must be highly efficient, or collisions would be continually occurring, and therefore it admirably serves to exemplify with what precision and safety, cable tramways may be operated.

The pictorial illustration given at Fig. 41 (see Frontispiece) represents a portion of the Geary-street cable line with a dummy and coupled open car thereon, and is an accurate reproduction from a photograph, thus conveying a very good idea of the general appearance of the cars and permanent way of this and other cable lines.

In describing the Clay-street cable line, attention was directed to the fact that the drainage of the slotted underground cable tubes was effected by connecting them at suitable intervals with the drains or sewers in the street. Some such provisions are common to all street cable tramways, the intervals of connection varying from about 40 ft. to 200 ft. according to circumstances or requirements.   In some cases it may be convenient and admissible to connect, say, half a dozen pulley pits together before communicating with the street sewer, whilst in others it may be desirable or compulsory to connect each pit separately.   In Europe it may be considered necessary to trap all such connections, but practice proves that such measures are usually quite unnecessary.   Touching upon this part of our subject the following extract from the "Annual Hygienic Report" for 1880 by the medical officer for the city of San Francisco, may be read with interest :

"The engineer, under whose supervision this road was constructed, found it necessary for purposes of drainage to connect the tube through which the cable runs with the sewer in the street, by pipes 4 in. in diameter.   These pipes are placed at intervals of 40 ft., and so thorough does the ventilation seem to be, that no complaint has been made of any offensive odours from this sewer since the construction of this line. Speaking from a sanitary standpoint, I believe Geary-street to be the most desirable thoroughfare to live on.   The offensive and mephitic vapours, which under certain degrees of pressure penetrate the dwellings of other streets in the city, here escape into the open air in a form so diluted as to be both inodorous and innoxious."

Note 13

The Union, Presidio, and Ferries Cable Tramway is the next cable traction scheme in San Francisco to claim our attention.

This line consists of about 10,500 ft. of double track, constructed to a gauge of 5 ft., and the nature of the route along which this line is laid is represented in longitudinal section at Fig. 42.   Upon reference to

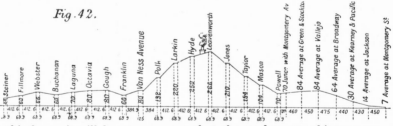

Fig. 42.

this figure, it will be at once seen that the grades upon this tramway are extremely severe, and, as previously mentioned, the line affords a capital illustration of the capabilities of the system in question, this being about the steepest tramway (proper) ever successfully constructed and operated.

The steepest gradients upon this line, and which occur about Polk and Larkin-streets, vary from about 1 in 4½ to 1 in 5.   The engine-house, car depôt, and offices are situated at the summit of a hill between Leavenworth and Hyde-streets, or about midway between the termini, as shown in the section above referred to.

The permanent way and tube are substantially constructed, the latter being formed with cast-iron frames, connected with rolled channel iron, whilst the continuity is obtained by the employment of a sheet-iron tubular casing. The construction and equipment of this line bears generally a close resemblance to those already described.

About 2600 ft. from the eastern terminus, there exists a curved portion of way (at the intersection of two streets), where the cable is suitably deflected by two horizontal pulleys 8 ft. in diameter. Here the operators upon the approaching cars have to release the cable, and travel round the curved portion of line by momentum and gravitation ; the site of the deflection being situated in a depression, it is conveniently located for such auxiliary method of locomotion. After passing this curve the operators upon the cars retake the cable on the opposite sides. There is, however, nothing particularly advantageous or instructive in this method of working or running over curved portions of line, and such practice would hardly be allowed in this country.

The gripping apparatus used, is exactly similar to that already described upon the Clay-street line, although somewhat more heavily constructed to suit the rolling stock. The dummies and cars weigh alike 4000 lbs. They run at about five-minute intervals, thus making about 220 trips per day of nineteen working hours, the service being performed by twelve cars of each kind.

Two crucible steel wire cables are used to work this system, the one 10,500 ft. and the other 11,000 ft. long, both being alike 3 in. in circumference ; the speed at which they are driven averages about 600 ft. per minute. The hauling engines are of the ordinary horizontal type, with suitable valve gear, such as previously described in connection with other lines, their cylinders being about 18 in. in diameter by 36 in. stroke, and working to a piston speed of about 350 ft. per minute. Steam is supplied to these engines by three multitubular boilers, 16 ft. long by 4 ft. 6 in. in diameter. The average working pressure is about 80 lbs. to the square inch, and it has been found that about fifty per cent. of such pressure is necessary to set the machinery and cables in motion, without the cars. This is in excess of the previous examples mentioned, and is mainly due to the extremely heavy gradients upon the line. The driving motion is transmitted from the crankshaft of either engine to the drums or pulleys through the intervention of leather belting, in practically a similar manner to the rope-belting used in the Geary-street engine-room, but with less advantage as regards silence in working. The driving drums used for hauling the cables are provided with gripping peripheries, as employed upon the Clay-street line. These drums are fixed upon a countershaft, which also has keyed upon it a large driving pulley, 25 ft. in diameter, and around which a colossal leather belt passes from the driving pulley, fixed

Note 14

upon the prime motion shaft as before mentioned. From the nature of the heavy gradients upon the various cable lines in San Francisco, some sceptisim naturally arises as to the safety of stopping cars upon such declivities, when the cables are released? It should, therefore, be made clear that the cars are never released from the cable, nor stopped upon such gradients as those alluded to above. The stoppages always take place at level crossings, which occur at about every 412 ft. along the line, as represented in the diagram at Fig. 43.

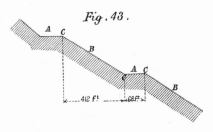

Fig. 43.

In this figure, A indicates the manner in which the transverse streets intersect the cable lines with level crossings, and upon which the cars are stopped to pick up and set down passengers; B represents the angular relation that the route of these lines bears to such intersecting thoroughfares. It is at these angular changes upon such lines that the cable depression pulleys are placed, and as indicated by C in the diagram.

The introduction of the dummy car for surmounting such irregularities, has been already sufficiently described with reference to the Clay-street line. All the cars are, however, equipped with sufficiently powerful brakes to bring them to rest upon almost any gradients if necessary, although it is not requisite or advisable to resort to such a practice.

The Union, Presidio, and Ferries Cable Tramway was opened for public traffic at the close of December, 1881.

We will now pause to examine the principal features of interest exhibited in the construction, equipment, and operation of the cable lines belonging to the Market-street Cable Railway Company, and which makes the sixth cable tramway enterprise in San Francisco.

This system was opened for public traffic at the close of August, 1883. The Market-street Cable Railway is one of the most important undertakings in the category of cable tramways, and possesses so many points of peculiar interest that a rather detailed description may be acceptable. Hitherto we have considered the question of cable traction as applied to the working of tramway traffic upon more or less severe gradients, under which circumstances the superiority of the system over all others known should be readily admitted. We shall now, however, have occasion to investigate an extensive system of cable haulage chiefly upon level ground, and over the greater portion of which animal traction had been previously effectually utilised for a long time.

For some years the southern parts of the city made comparatively slow progress, as contrasted with the northern portions, whilst the unusual length of Market-street—although the principal thoroughfare of the city—was by no means conducive to the improvement of such conditions. However, for some years past, a well-laid and well-equipped horse tramway has run along this street, but the necessary slowness with which the traffic was conducted under animal traction rendered the extreme trip at best decidedly tedious. Since the conversion of the chief horse lines to the "cable system," the traffic has been conducted at a speed of eight miles per hour, so that the entire trip from the Ferries to the Valencia terminus of the line can now be effected in about thirty-five minutes, whilst the cars depart from the former terminus at intervals of from two to three minutes throughout the day of twenty running hours. From the above facts the extensive and important character of the traffic to be accommodated will be readily apparent.

Fig. 44 represents a diagrammatic plan of this company's tramway

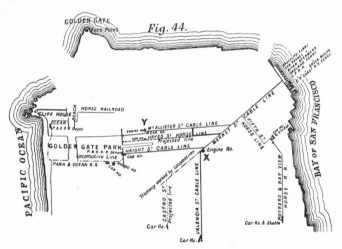

Fig. 44.

system, including the Market-street, Valencia-street, McAllister-street, and Haight-street cable lines ; the Park and Ocean and the Castro-streets locomotive sections, and also the Ocean Beach, Hayes-street, Fifth-street, and Potrero horse lines, all of which are shown and correspondingly designated. Beyond these lines in operation, which exceed eighteen miles of track, certain projected extensions are indicated upon the plan by the dotted lines. The ramifications of this company's system will be seen to extend east and west from the Bay of San Francisco to the Pacific Ocean. It may be seen that the greatest portion of the lines are now operated by the cable system, *i.e.*, those running through Market-street in a south-westerly direction, then extending southerly along Valencia-street, with branch lines projecting due west, *viâ* McAllister and Haight-streets. The approximate aggregate length of the cables employed to operate these lines is 100,000 ft., equivalent to over seventeen miles of single track.

It is also intended to extend the cable system a mile further— along Market-street, towards the west—a route which is at present worked by steam locomotives, and as indicated upon the plan. The cables of the Market-street (or main line), Valencia-street, and Haight-street lines are operated from the engine-house marked X, whilst that of the McAllister-street branch line is operated from an independent engine-house marked Y on the plan.

Market-street, as before mentioned, is the principal thoroughfare in the city of San Francisco, which has at present a population of over 230,000. Into this main street all others of importance (from the north-west and the south) open, *e.g.*, Montgomery, Kearny, Dupont, Stockton, Geary, Sutter-streets, &c.; and consequently the congested state of the traffic upon the street in question may be easily imagined. There is only one fare charged by this company, viz., 5 cents ($2\frac{1}{2}$d.), and transfers are given to any of the company's branch lines without any extra charges. The McAllister branch cable line has a good traffic to " Golden Gate Park," and the branch line at Haight-street makes a second route to the same locality, but the latter is considered the more important of the two.

At the junction of Haight-street, every alternate car is switched off from the Market-street or main line to go the western route. The steepest gradient upon Haight-street (which traverses a hilly district), is a rise of about 1 ft. in 10 ft.; Market-street is practically level, although at some parts it has an inclination of about 3 ft. in 100 ft. A longitudinal section of Haight-street is given at Fig. 45, and will convey

Fig. 45.

an idea of the character of the route taken by this branch cable line. The practical inauguration of this company's extensive system was looked for with some anxiety, owing to the very crowded state of the thoroughfares along which it was to operate. Besides ordinary vehicular traffic, the cars of about half a dozen other horse lines traverse the route in question.

At first it was considered by some, that this extended application of the cable system was inadvisable, even if it did not verge on the impracticable, whilst others thought the traffic would have to be conducted at such a slow pace that the system would be rendered unpopular, and present no particular advantage over the old horse cars. These conjectures have, however, proved to be erroneous, and experience has since demonstrated that the traffic upon this company's system can be conducted at the rate of nearly eight miles per hour, with safety and satisfaction. The average number of stops made by these cable cars throughout an entire trip is about thirty ; and, taking these into consideration, the average speed maintained throughout the journey is at the rate of about $7\frac{1}{2}$ miles per hour, which is more rapid travelling than attained on any of the other cable lines, leaving, of course, horse traction quite out of the question. We will now turn our attention to the permanent way and cable tube employed by the Market-street Railroad Company, and for which purpose we will refer to the transverse section represented at Fig. 46, and the perspective sectional elevation shown at

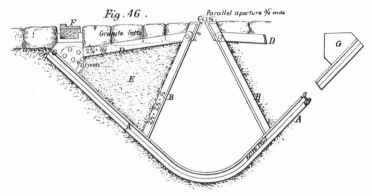

Fig. 46.

Fig. 47. It was determined to build this line in a rigid and substantial form, and with such view the component elements of the tube and way were arranged as one rigid, or self-contained structure, as represented in the engravings. Referring to Fig. 46, the cable tube and way, will be seen to consist of **V**-shaped frames A, composed of old bent rails, and having attached to them the diagonal angle-iron struts B, and tie-bars D. This may be recognised as substantially similar to the type of frame used upon the Sutter-street line previously described. The continuity of the tube is obtained by ramming in the concrete E, at the back of suitable templates, which are subsequently withdrawn. The rails F are laid upon longitudinal sleepers carried in the wrought-iron chairs G, attached to the frames A. These composite wrought frames or yokes for carrying the central angle-iron slot-beams C, and track-rails F, are placed about every 3 ft. throughout the lines, and the whole tube is supported upon small vertical concrete foundation piers placed at intervals of 9 ft., as shown in Fig. 47. At the eastern terminus of the line, piles were driven, in addition to the above-named precaution, as auxiliary supports to these foundation piers. A main street sewer, with house drains in connection (and into which the pulley pits drain at suitable intervals), are also represented in this figure. Altogether, there

FIG. 47. MARKET-STREET COMPANY'S PERMANENT WAY AND CAR.

are about 9000 of these supporting piers used throughout the system, their bases being about 10 ft. below the street surface, likewise about 25,000 of the frames are employed. The rails used were manufactured at the Pacific Rolling Mills, from imported " Bessemer steel " blooms, and weigh 38 lbs. per yard run.

The small cable-supporting pulleys, fixed in the slotted street tube (see Fig. 47), are placed 30 ft. apart, and possess the peculiarity that they are cast in one piece with their axles. Their over-all diameter, is 15 in. ; and their axles are mounted in lignum-vitæ bearings. Each of these pulleys is placed in a small pit, to which access can be obtained from the street through small manholes, suitably protected and closed by wrought-iron plate covers. At places where there is any sudden change of grade upon the lines, " depression " pulleys are used to keep the cable down in its place, as previously described upon the Clay-street line. The device for achieving the same end is, however, somewhat different on this company's system. In the present case, the depression pulleys are carried by counter-weighted levers, mounted in horizontal attitudes beneath the tube slot. This contrivance permits of a limited vertical depression when the gripping appliances are passing, but secures the immediate return of a pulley to the normal position when the cars have cleared the same.

We will now examine the method adopted for operating curved portions of line, and which always present special mechanical difficulties. A curved portion of way upon this system is encountered at the junction of Market and Valencia-streets, opposite the main engine-house X (Fig. 44), and where their intersection forms an obtuse angle of about 55 deg., with a curve of 80 ft. radius. The novel feature in the arrangement consists in the employment of an independent auxiliary cable to work this curved portion of line, and arranged to run at half the speed of the main cables. The advantage and reason of such a device will be apparent when we reflect, that it would be a most hazardous practice to run round the curved portions of any tramway at a speed of eight miles an hour, as collisions with ordinary street vehicles would be the probable result.

Note 15

The Market-street and Valencia-street cables pass round their respective guiding pulleys into the engine-house, and between these the said short auxiliary endless cable is arranged to operate, receiving its motion from a driving drum fixed upon the crankshaft of the engine. This cable is conducted to and from the curved portion of the line to be operated, by suitable leading or guide pulleys, and whilst rounding the curve it travels over vertically arranged pulleys. The arrangement will be better understood upon reference to the diagram shown at Fig. 48, upon which the names of the streets and respective functions of the cables are indicated. The " auxiliary cable " runs round the horizontal pulleys *a*, *b*, vertical pulleys A, and around those of *c* and *d*, back to the driving drum.

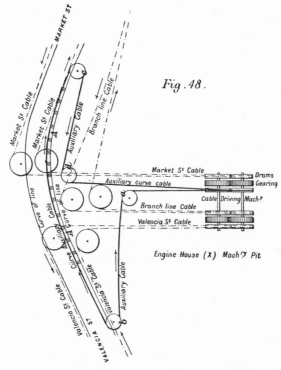

Fig. 48.

It may be noticed that this auxiliary cable, only travels under the one line running towards Market-street, because there exists a slight falling gradient from Market-street towards Valencia-street, so that the cars run round the curve in question towards the latter street, by gravitation to the point where they pick up the other cable. In travelling in the opposite direction, the cars have to travel up hill, and, therefore, they are connected to the auxiliary cable and are hauled round the curve towards the eastern terminus, until they can take hold of the main or Market-street cable. The auxiliary cable is driven at the rate of four miles per hour, and obviously the strains upon it are small as compared with those on the main line cables; consequently, the grips of the cars are relieved from any great lateral strains whilst passing the curve.

From the arrangement above described, it will be evident that the operators upon the various cars upon arriving at the engine-house have to release the main cable, pick up the auxiliary cable, drop it again, and re-take the other main cable, in the manner already described in a previous account of this subject. The cars have only about 8 ft. to travel by momentum in order to change cables; whilst the entire distance travelled upon the auxiliary cable is about 120 ft.

At such parts of the line, where it is necessary for the drivers to release or take a cable in the manner above mentioned, large iron notice-plates are provided by the roadside, having inscribed upon them the necessary instructions to be observed, as, for example, the words, "Let go here;" "Take on here;" and "Stop here," &c. At night these plates are well illuminated, so that the words may be clearly visible.

Immediately before approaching the curve above described, some rather novel shunting devices are encountered for switching off the Haight-street branch cars from the Market-street or main line. To carry out this subsidiary traffic, the main line cable has to be released and the branch one picked up. Movable switch points or tongues are not only required upon the track for diverting the traffic, but similar appliances have to be provided for the grip slot in the cable tube. If this were not done, the car-wheels might be shunted whilst the grip shanks might continue their course. In such event the result would be to break the grippers, or damage, if not sever, the cable. Switchmen are therefore employed to shunt the traffic by operating the rail and slot tongues, which simultaneously actuate safety appliances situated some 30 ft. away. The whole of the road-bed is formed by inter-paving with granite sets, as represented at Figs. 46 and 47 of the illustrations.

At the Ferries or Market-street terminus of the system a large turntable is provided (30 ft. in diameter), upon which the cars are turned, so that their open or fore portions, in which the gripping and braking appliances are provided, are always kept in the front. Upon releasing the cable at this end of the line the cars are carried on to the turntable by momentum, whilst the return of the cars to the place for retaking the cable is effected by gravitation through a slight fall in the tracks.

At this eastern terminus are laid four sets of lines, one for receiving the incoming traffic, and the other three for distributing the departure traffic, *i.e.*, the Valencia-street, Haight-street, and McAllister-street cars are all transferred, and depart from their special separate sidings. A short distance from the turntable mentioned, these three outgoing tracks converge into the main line. By this means the despatch of the cars can be carried out in rapid succession. The turntable is provided with two sets of lines, so relatively disposed, that it is always maintained in a proper position for receiving and transferring the cars. It is intermittently revolved in one direction by the continuous movement of the hauling cable, through the intervention of suitable gearing. The latter consists mainly of a friction drum, which is rotated by the cable, and is mounted so as to be capable of being moved into contact with the periphery of the turntable. In this manner the cable can be rotated by frictional contact at about one-fifth the speed of the cable.

The cables used by this company were manufactured by Messrs. Roebling and Sons, of New Jersey, and are constructed of six strands of nineteen crucible steel wires each laid round a manilla core. These cables are about $1\frac{1}{4}$ in. in diameter, and weigh $2\frac{1}{2}$ lb. per foot run. Five of such cables are used to operate this company's system, viz., the main line or Market-street cable, which is 24,125 ft. long ; that of Valencia-street, 20,194 ft. long ; that of Haight-street, 20,000 ft. long ; McAllister-street, 20,490 ft. long, and that of McAllister and Fulton-streets branch, 6000 ft. long. The last two cables are similar to those first described, but were manufactured at the California Wire Works in San Francisco. The McAllister cables are driven from the small and independent engine-house marked Y on the plan, Fig. 44. The speed at which the main cables are driven is about eight miles per hour. The strands of these cables are at first filled up externally by applications of vegetable tar, but the subsequent lubrication is effected by castor oil. The application of any mineral or animal oils or fats to the cables is avoided.

The next important department to investigate, is that concerning the construction and arrangement of the machinery for driving the cables. The engine-houses are located at the junction of Market and Valencia-streets and towards the west end of McAllister-street. Our chief attention should, however, be directed to the former and more important of the two. The Haight-street branch line, which is also operated from the principal engine-house, springs from the Market-street line in a north-westerly direction, and forms with it an angle of about 35 deg.

In the rear of the engine-house X, are provided fuel bunkers, presenting accommodation for over 2000 tons of coal ; and in the yard behind, an artesian well is sunk, for supplying the boilers, &c. The principal part of the basement of the premises is covered with brick flooring, and with the foundations for the boilers, engines, feed-heaters, pumps, tension machinery, and guiding pulleys, &c. One of the marked external features of the building is the chimney shaft, the base of which is carried 9 ft. below the boiler-room floor, or about 24 ft. below the street level. The foundation of this shaft is 30 ft. square, and its section throughout is in the form of an eight-cornered star, its total height being 175 ft. The effective sectional area of the shaft is about 44 square feet.

The operating power is supplied by two pairs of compound condensing engines, having high and low-pressure cylinders 24 in. and 34 in. in diameter respectively, with 48 in. stroke. The low-pressure cylinder has about double the capacity of the high-pressure cylinder, and the two are directly connected. Only one pair of these engines is required to operate the system, the other pair being kept in reserve. These compound engines were constructed by local manufacturers, and appear to give satisfaction. Each set of engines ordinarily furnishes 400 indicated horse-power, but is capable of working up to fully 700 indicated horse-power. These are the only compound condensing engines used for operating a cable tramway in this city ("the home of the cable system"), and therefore the anticipated comparative economical results will be watched with interest. The spur-pinions fixed on the crankshafts for transmitting power to the hauling drums are 4 ft. in diameter with 20 in. faces, and gear into spur-wheels 12 ft. 6 in. in diameter, fixed upon the driving countershafts. This spur gearing is constructed with diagonal or helical teeth. The boilers are of the Babcock and Wilcox type (special horizontal multitubular), composed of four sections of 250 horse-power each.

The cables are driven by drums in a similar manner to that adopted upon the California-street line already described, *i.e.,* the cables are wrapped round them in the form of the figure 8 ; and known as the " American system of driving." The driving drums or pulleys are 12 ft. in diameter, with grooved peripheries lined with wood, which arrangement, in combination with the tension apparatus, secures sufficient adhesion to haul 24,000 ft. of cable heavily loaded. To the automatic tension apparatus this result is chiefly due, and by it, the cables are kept close upon the peripheries of the " drivers." In contradistinction to the above-mentioned system of driving, the method of taking one or more complete turns with a cable round drums, is termed in the States the " English system of driving." The first-mentioned system is supposed to injure the cables less, but in practice there appears no evidence in support of the alleged superiority, and colliery engineers consider such method of hauling or winding is attended with inferior results. Any system of driving or hauling that tends to minimise the bending of the cables and inflict such limited compressive strains, all in one direction, appears a movement in the right path.

Reverting to the latter method, in which one or more complete turns are taken with the cables around the driving drums, or in which similar open turns are taken round a pair of such pulleys as previously described upon the Sutter-street line, it must be admitted that it also exhibits some defects. For example, at the places where the cables first come upon the drums or pulleys, the peripheries wear more rapidly than at the points at which they leave them. This differential wearing of the circumferences of these " drivers," produced by this method of driving, has on some occasions caused expense and annoyance. The defects of the methods in question may have been long recognised, but the difficulty has been to devise something better, and at the same time to provide the necessary driving adhesion. In the Market-street Company's system the requisite motion for actuating these driving drums is communicated by

spur gearing fixed upon the main and countershafts. In this manner
the driving shafts are caused to make one-third the number of revolutions of the engine. Four pairs of driving drums are provided for
operating the four separate cables (see Fig. 48), but only one pair of
engines and one set of gearing are commonly used to actuate them.

The method of maintaining a uniform tension throughout the cables
has been previously discussed ; but in the case at issue, there are some
novel details connected with the arrangement which may be instructive.
The cables are, on a hot day, several feet longer than upon a cool one, and
these continual changes have to be automatically compensated for.
Further, there is the permanent stretching of the cables to be allowed
for, and which, in the course of their lives, may vary from 1 to 2 per
cent. of their entire lengths. Thus, in the case in point, this might
mean an ultimate increase in the length of the longest cable of about
250 ft. It should be understood that each cable is provided with a
separate or independent tension apparatus.

Fig. 49 represents the type of tension apparatus employed in this
company's engine-house,
and in which A is a
large and heavy carriage
mounted upon the track
bed B, upon which a
smaller supplementary
carriage E is placed. The
former carriage A can be
freed so as to be moved
along the track B (which

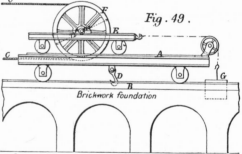

Fig. 49.

is about 165 ft. long), to take up the slack arising from the stretching
of the cable C, and by which arrangement 330 ft. of each cable may be
taken up. The smaller counter-weighted carriage E, carrying the large
vertical pulley F around which the cable C passes, is also free to travel
upon the lower one, and serves to automatically compensate for any
fluctuations of tension arising from changes of temperature, and the
effect of the cars upon the lines. When the tail-weights G, attached to
the upper carriages, show signs of permanent settling, it is an indication that the cables are permanently stretching. The lower carriages
should then be moved back upon the rail-beds (by means of tackles)
until the slack is taken up and the upper carriages stand well forward,
whereupon they may be fixed in such positions by hooks D, arranged to
engage in suitable rack-bars.

The cable-gripping apparatus, carried by the fore part of the composite cars, is represented in side elevation at Fig. 50, and will be seen
at a glance to very closely resemble the type of apparatus used upon the
California-street line already described. A is the lever for opening

and closing the nipping jaws pivotted at B upon the quadrant plate, and provided with an intermediate adjustment C and link D, connected at its lower end with the frame E, which carries the shank-plates F, terminating with the lower grip jaws *f*, and provided with the small cable-supporting pulleys *h*.

The central grip shank-plate G carries the quadrant frame of the operating lever upon the top extremity and the upper grip jaw *g* at its lower end. Both of these jaws are provided with an independent screw adjustment. This gripping apparatus is attached to the cars by the frame E, so that it will be understood that the outer shanks F and bottom jaw *f* remain practically stationary whilst the upper jaw *g* with its connection is raised or lowered to or from the former, so as to grasp or release the running cable as required.

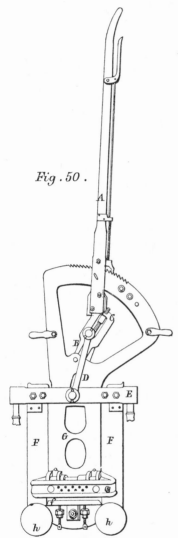

Fig. 50.

This apparatus, like that on the California-street line, is of simple construction, with as much mechanism as possible above ground, and is readily accessible from the cars. The gripping apparatus is constructed of cast steel, and the jaws are packed or lined with soft iron dies capable of being easily replaced. It should be understood that these gripping appliances are not rigidly attached to the main framing of the cars themselves, but are mounted upon and carried by bogie trucks. By this arrangement the vibrating motion of the carriage springs is not imparted to the grips and the cable.

From the side elevation given at Fig. 47, showing the type of this company's composite cars, it will be seen that they practically consist of a combination of an ordinary passenger car and an open dummy car built in one framing. This arrangement necessitates a very long rigid framing, viz., of 34 ft., and therefore the necessity of mounting the cars upon the bogie system is very apparent. The leading bogie truck of each carriage or car carries the gripping apparatus and brake levers,

whilst the rear or trailing truck is provided with suitable track brakes.
This arrangement will be understood upon reference to Figs. 51 and 52,

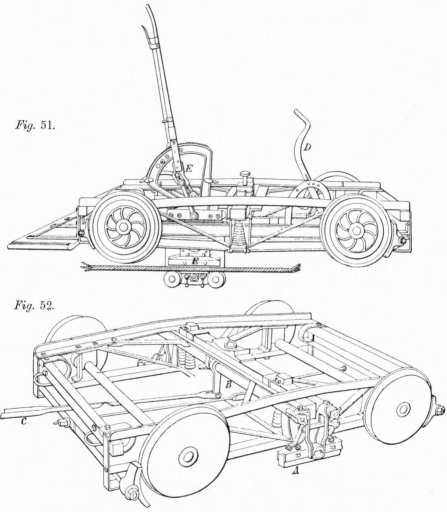

Fig. 51.

Fig. 52.

which represent side perspective views of a leading and trailing bogie
truck respectively.   All the bogie wheels are provided with the ordinary
brakes, as shown in the illustrations, in addition to the special track
brakes A, worked from the rocking shaft B, which receive their motion
from the leading truck through the intervention of rod connections C.
The trucks themselves will be seen to be of the ordinary bogie type,
having their connections with the framing or bodies of the cars through
a single bolt attachment.   These composite cars weigh about $4\frac{1}{4}$ tons
each, but the braking appliances are stated to be so efficient that they

can be arrested within a few feet, when running at a speed of eight miles per hour. The brakes are worked by the levers D and their connections, situated upon the leading trucks, as represented in Fig. 51. The gripping appliances E are mounted upon and carried in the fore part of the leading trucks or immediately behind the front axles, and the drivers upon the open car platforms stand directly over them.

This construction of car was adopted to meet the requirements of the traffic, and at the same time to allow of the old horse cars being converted for the cable system at a reasonable cost. The forward portions of these cars are open, as shown in the illustration, so that the drivers may have a clear view of the road. The cars are provided with large alarm gongs to warn foot-passengers and drivers of other vehicles of their approach, and at night they are further equipped with powerful headlights. Guards or fenders are also applied to the cars to prevent persons from getting run over.

At the Valencia-street terminus a spacious car depôt is constructed 420 ft. long by 100 ft. wide and two stories high, the cars being elevated from the ground floor by mechanical lifting apparatus. The Haight-street cars are housed in a separate depôt, provided for their accommodation.

The Market-street cable tramway, concludes the list of lines to be noticed within the city of San Francisco, and it is alike both satisfactory and interesting to be able to remark that here the method of traction in question has proved as great a financial as a mechanical success. No cable line in this city has, it appears, yet proved a losing undertaking, but, on the contrary, the various cable tramway stocks now stand from 15 to 50 per cent. above their original value. The original ordinary shares of the Market-street cable lines were eagerly taken up at 1 per cent. premium.

There is now about an aggregate of forty miles of cable tramways in operation in this city. We have previously called attention to the fact that from 25 to 28 per cent. of the population of San Francisco travelled daily by the various tramway companies, at the commencement of cable tramway enterprise. About nine million passengers are stated to have travelled over the Market-street cable system of tramways alone in one year, or about 10 per cent. of the population daily. Further, it is stated that over *twenty* millions of persons are conveyed by the combined cable lines of this city in the course of a year, or about 23 per cent. of the population daily, disregarding the performances of the horse and locomotive tramways in the city.

At the opening of the Industrial Exhibition of San Francisco in August, 1881, the Honourable W. Morrow, in an address, appropriately remarked: "In this city, under our own eyes, we have seen a revolution in street railroads. . . . . The simple principles involved and their ingenious adaptation mark the value of the invention and success of the undertaking.   What a revolution has been made in the mode of trans-porting passengers in this city !   The hills have fallen down before it, and are now more accessible, and certainly more desirable for residence, than the level portions of the city.   Where the goats used to frolic on California-street Hill, mighty railroad kings have built their palaces," &c. Whilst the Elevated Railway of New York and the Underground Railway system of London bear their respective interests, San Fran-cisco, similarly, evinces worthy pride concerning her cable tramway achievements.

Note 18

Before passing on, it may be mentioned that in August, 1884, another cable tramway was opened in Los Angles, California, being a system of about 1½ miles long.   It consists of single track with suitable intermediate passing places.   The cable tube employed is similar to the Clay-street line construction.   The gauge of the track is 3 ft. 6 in. The type of grippers employed are similar to those used on the Sutter-street line, whilst the system is operated by a pair of Corliss engines having cylinders 14 in. in diameter with 30 in. stroke.

CHAPTER III.

CHICAGO, PHILADELPHIA, AND NEW YORK, &C., CABLE LINES.

WE will now leave the city of San Francisco and California in order to follow the introduction and development of the system in the eastern cities of the United States, and will first pause at the enterprising city of Chicago, Ill., which has a population of over 500,000 souls. Having previously given several examples of the cable system, with somewhat exhaustive particulars regarding its applications, constructions, and operations, it will be now unnecessary to devote much space to the subsequent cable lines which may claim our attention, as in principle and construction they are very similar to those already described. San Francisco is unquestionably entitled to the credit of inaugurating the cable system, but the Chicago people were not slow in appreciating the achievements of the smaller city at the Golden Gate, and availing themselves of their experience. It was about the beginning of 1881, that Chicago began to take a real interest in the cable system and its capabilities, and about that time a Mr. Holmes (now president of this city's lines) went to San Francisco with the view of studying the system and introducing it into Chicago. We learn that this gentleman was not only perfectly satisfied with the result of his western visit, but also returned deeply impressed with the advantages offered by the use of cable traction. Mr. Holmes was evidently pleased with the paramount merits of the system, and when he experienced this pleasant method of transit, without horses, locomotives, or other visible means of propulsion, he apparently concurred with the enthusiastic utterances of some of the Chinese inhabitants of that city, who exclaimed on beholding the first cable car in motion, " No pushee, no pullee, no horsee, no steamee : Melican man heap smart."

Shortly after Mr. Holmes's return from the west, he submitted his views to a number of practical engineers, who prepared the plans, &c., for the construction of a cable line in their city. Subsequently Mr. Holmes laid these plans before the Mayor of Chicago, who expressed an opinion that if the enterprise could be carried out it would prove a success. With such an assurance and support, an application for powers to construct a cable line was laid before the Municipal Council, and was passed without opposition.

Afterwards, some party cries were raised about the ill consequences of obstructing the streets during construction ; and, again, there were rumours that the horse-car drivers in the city would all rise in arms. But such prognostications proved unfounded, and the works were rapidly proceeded with.   No difficulties were experienced in raising the funds, although it was intended to spend about 2,000,000 dols. (about 400,000*l.*) on that considered virtually an experiment, for reasons hereafter stated.   The actual commencement of the works was started about August 12, 1881.   The Chicago cable lines are laid upon practically level ground, similar to the Market-street Company's system in San Francisco, previously described ; but it is to be observed that the former were in operation by January, 1882, whereas the latter was not constructed until August, 1883, and therefore Chicago was the first to demonstrate the advantages of the system for operating tramways upon flat ground.

This enterprise in Chicago was decidedly a most bold undertaking, because the success achieved by the system in the Far West was no true criterion for its satisfactory introduction into the eastern States, where the climate was very different.   In California the weather is uniformly warm, and is decidedly favourable for the efficient operation of such a mechanical system of traction.   On the other hand, the climate of Chicago is variable and extreme.   In the summer the temperature may exceed 100 degs. Fahr., whilst, conversely, in the winter the thermometer sometimes indicates 10 degs. to even 15 degs. below zero.

**Note
19**

Further, rain, hail, and snow fall periodically in great abundance, and might be expected (from the consequent variable expansion and contraction) to cause endless difficulties with the cables, pulleys, tube, its slotted opening, or its draining connections, &c.

The cable lines of the Chicago City Railroad Company have, however, now been in successful operation for about five years, working twenty hours per day and involving the operation of over 20 miles of metallic cable, weighing about 120 tons.   The application of the system to the working of tramway traffic in this city has proved highly satisfactory, and in winters when heavy falls of snow have stopped or retarded railway and horse traffic in this city and locality, the cable trams have been maintained in operation without a hitch.

The introduction of the cable system into New York and Europe, appears mainly due to the crucial tests it has undergone in Chicago, and towards the close of 1883 we may find the town clerk of Edinburgh, on behalf of the Lord Provost's Committee, communicating with the town clerk of Chicago regarding the operation of the cable system in that city.   Amongst his tabulated questions, we find one : " In general has the working of the cable tramway system been proved to be a success ?"—the reply from the States being : " Complete success in all

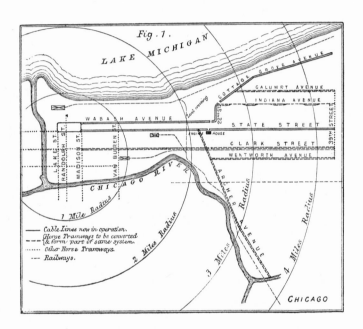

Fig. 1.

CHICAGO CABLE TRAMWAYS.

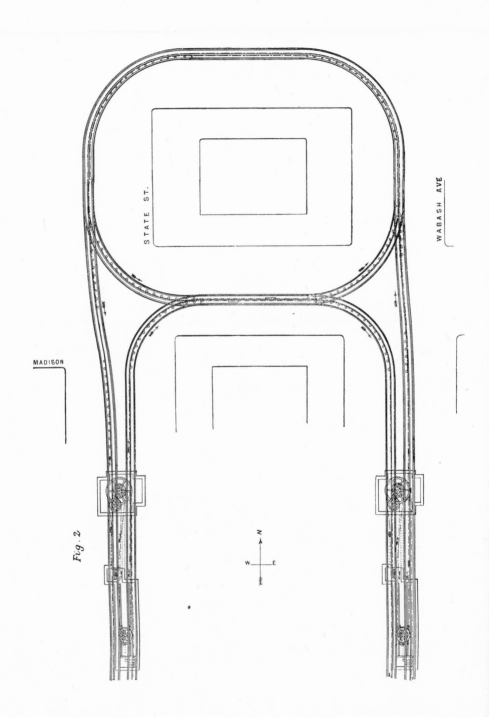

Fig. 2

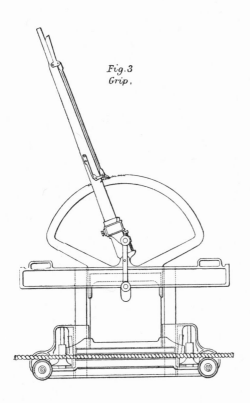

Fig. 3
Grip.

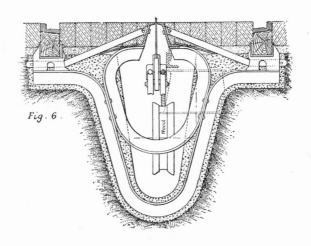

Fig. 6.

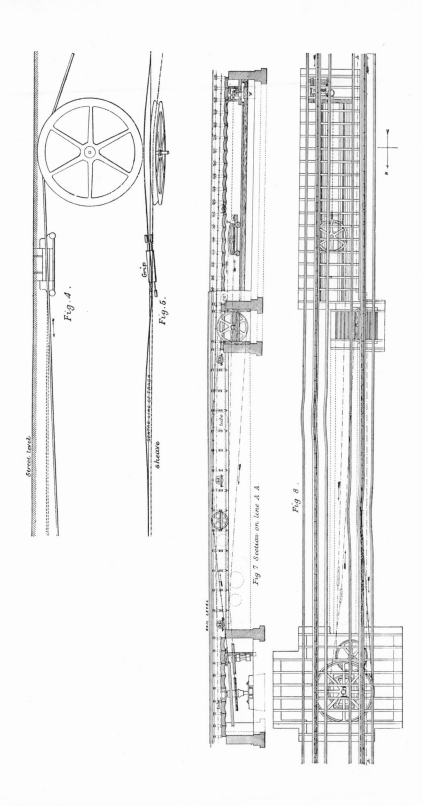

Fig. 4.

Street level.

Fig. 5.

sheave

CENTRAL LINE OF FLANGE

Grip

RAIL LEVEL

tube

Fig 7 Section on line A A

Fig 8.

N

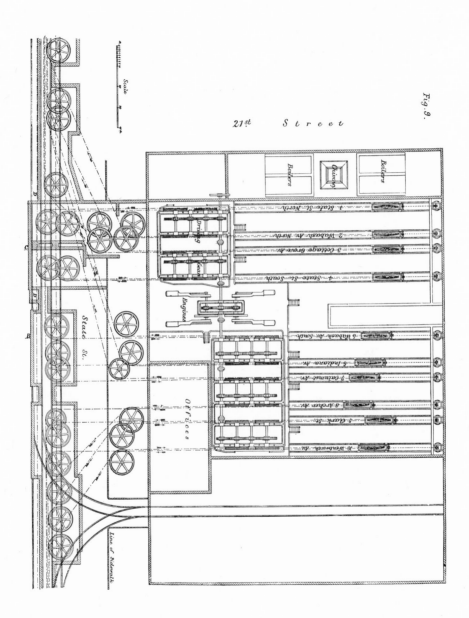

Fig. 9.

21st Street

Boilers Chimney Boilers

1 State St. North
2 Wabash Av. North
3 Cottage Grove Av.
4 State St. South

Driving Gear

Engines

5 Wabash Av. South
6 Indiana Av.
7 Calumet Av.
8 Archer Av.
9 Clark St.
10 Wentworth Av.

Offices

State St.

Scale

Line of Sidewalk

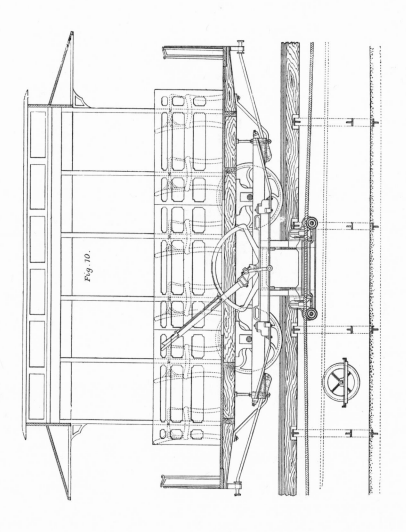

Fig. 10.

respects. This winter just closed was by far the most severe for many years, and the cable system operated without the loss of a single trip." These tabulated queries and replies, issued and received by the city of Edinburgh, will be again referred to later on.

The tramways of Chicago are divided into three separate districts, and worked by independent companies, viz., the southern, northern, and western; the first-named, however, only concerns us. The above combined system incorporates about 155 miles of track.

The conversion of any portion of the Chicago City Railroad Company's lines to the cable system was by no means necessary, as the company was working its lines very successfully with horses, and their financial condition was satisfactory. Since conversion the original 100 dols. stock is quoted at about 300 dols. From 70,000 to 100,000 passengers are carried daily by this company's cable system, on about 19 miles of single track, with an expenditure of about 400 mechanical horse-power. By the alteration, the daily toil of over 1000 horses and 200 stablemen, &c., have been dispensed with, besides the continual expenses of shoeing, harnessing, sickness, food, &c., consequent upon the employment of horses. The traffic is very heavy indeed, and efficiently supports a two to three-minute service, commonly consisting of a train comprising a dummy and three or four ordinary cars. A small diagrammatic map relating to the southern system of Chicago tramways is given at Fig. 1 on the Plate A.

This City Railroad Company's tramways extending upon the south side of the city, are laid upon practically level ground. The portion first converted to the cable system was upon State-street, the main and principal thoroughfare of the city, but engines and apparatus were provided at the same time for extending the scheme to include several endless cables and a few auxiliary ones for working curved portions of line. The city end of the system, has its cables driven at a speed of about seven miles per hour, with the exception of the curved or auxiliary portions of way, where they are driven at four miles per hour, whilst the outer or suburban cables can be driven up to ten miles an hour. The terminal arrangements worked by belts or auxiliary cables, driven at lower speeds, are represented at Fig. 2 on the special sheet of illustrations.

The principal streets operated by the system are those of State-street and Wabash Avenue, the traffic of which is worked by two main cables to each, distinguished as North and South State-street and Wabash Avenue and Cottage Grove cables; and it is the South State-street and Cottage Grove cables that are driven at the highest speed above mentioned. Possibly, two instead of four main cables might operate the system, had it not been deemed advisable to work some portions at a greater speed.

The following Table gives the various sections of this company's system, with particulars respecting the locations, functions, and lengths of the cables employed upon it:

Sections.	Situations.	Cable. — Feet.	Lengths. — Miles.
Wabash Avenue Line	From engine-house *via* 22nd-street to Madison-street and return, including extras for pits, splicing, &c. ...	23,608	
Cottage Grove Avenue Line	Engine-house to pit, south of 39th-street and back, including extras ...	27,770	
22nd-street Line ...	Amount involved in street and pits, &c., including extras...	2,684	
Auxiliary Line ...	In and from pit in Wabash Avenue and Madison-street, around belt, with extras	4,339	
		58,401	11.061
North State - street Line	From engine-house to Madison-street pit and return, with extras... ...	20,290	
South State - street Line	Engine-house to pit south of 39th-street and back, including extras ...	23,792	
Belt Line	From pit on State-street at Madison-street end to Wabash Avenue, with extras	4,361	
	Total	106,844	20.236

Note 20

The length of the Cottage Grove cable, which measures over five miles, is worthy of notice, as being amongst the longest in use.

The company's engine-house, from which the whole system is operated, is situated about midway on the State-street section, and the manner that the various cables are disconnected from the cars and others picked up at this point, has already been described in the previous chapter.

In order to avoid the inconvenience that would arise from shunting the cars at the northern terminus of the system, they are conducted by an auxiliary or belt line cable from the main line on State-street to that on Wabash Avenue, before mentioned. The underground slotted tube through which the endless cable travels, is about 3 ft. deep, and a section of same is given at Fig. 6. The cables used by this company are about 4 in. in circumference, weighing about $2\frac{1}{2}$ lbs. per linear foot. The gripping apparatus is practically very similar to those employed upon the Sutter-street, California-street, and Market-street lines already described, and as shown at Fig. 3.

Two engines, of about 250 horse-power each, are employed to operate the system, although in practice the power actually required seldom exceeds 400 horse-power. A duplicate pair of engines are kept in reserve, a provision which also applies to the boilers, which are constructed by Messrs. Babcock and Wilcox. The engines are of the horizontal condensing type (by Wheelock), equipped with automatic variable valve gear ; the cylinders being 24 in. in diameter with 4 ft. stroke, whilst the ordinary working pressure of steam is about 60 lbs. per square inch.   The speed of the engines is about sixty-five revolutions per minute.

The dummies and cars used by this company are similar to those already described, but weigh about 5000 lbs. and 5800 lbs. respectively. About 150 of these vehicles are employed in ordinary daily service. A section of a dummy car is given at Fig. 10.

The special arrangement, employed for raising the cables at terminal and other parts, for bringing the same within reach of the grips, is shown at Figs. 4 and 5 in side elevation and plan respectively.

Figs. 7 and 8 show the construction of underground street vaults with arrangements of machinery provided therein, for operating and controlling the haulage cables.   In the first figure, T represents the tension apparatus with its counterweight W, the functions of which have been previously described.

Fig. 9 represents a sectional plan of the engine-house and shows the relative arrangement of the engines, boilers, driving machinery, and tension appliances at the rear of same.   In the front will be seen the arrangement of pulleys beneath the street for directing and controlling the operation of the cables.

Regarding the practical results of the adaptation of cable traction generally to this company's system, it is satisfactory to be able to state that the enterprise has been crowned with both mechanical and financial success.   In the verbatim account, of the last annual meeting of the American Street Railways Association, held in New York in October last, may be found a special and favourable report by a select committee upon the cable system.   Remarks were made about patents and alleged inventions, and it is interesting to read with what care any direct replies to such queries are avoided ; in fact, we, read the chairman of the Committee of Investigation (also president of the Chicago cable system) evasively replying, " I make no mention whatever of patents . . . . There are a number of patents merged into the cable system, but as to the merits of same I offer no remarks whatever . . . I wish to say nothing about patents whatever," &c.

A Mr. Wharton then asked : " What percentage of power is required to move the cables upon the Chicago system ?"   **Note 21**

The chairman replied about 480 horse-power, of which about 350 horse-power is absorbed in setting the machinery and cables in motion.

A Mr. Richardson said : " I should like to ask whether the company (Chicago) is engaged in further developing the system ?" To which the chairman answered : " Thirteen miles more will probably be constructed next season and plans are in preparation."   **Note 22**

Inquiries were then raised as to how frequently the Chicago system (especially) had temporarily stopped operations through any breakdown of the cables or machinery, &c.? The chairman replied: "I will say directly to that point that the main cables were operated nine months without a single moment's delay on any account: a few weeks ago a little interruption occurred by the breaking of one of our cog-wheels."

Questions were next asked regarding the average lives of the cables. To which the chairman replied: "Dependence may be placed on the ropes running without any flaw for a term of twelve months."

Comparisons between the cost of working tramways by the horse and cable systems were afterwards raised. To this query the chairman replied: "The cable can be operated for one-half; *i.e.*, the expense of operating the cable cars is one-half that of the horse cars, for the same amount of service."

Note
23

Later, we find the chairman advocating the Chicago type of grip, with fixed horizontal jaws, in preference to those provided with gripping wheels or rollers; and he goes on to state that in Chicago they have hauled ten connected cars, containing 1000 persons, with one cable gripper, whereas on the Brooklyn Bridge line, in New York, they are unable to haul more than one car, owing to the employment of their type of wheel gripper. It is estimated that the present system now worked by cable traction would take about 2700 horses to maintain the same service as at present afforded the public. Before conversion only sixty cars were run upon these lines, but within two years after the substitution, from 150 to 180 cars were running daily and conveying about 27,000,000 passengers per annum.

Every midnight a careful general inspection is made of all appliances and machinery, &c., so that everything is kept in complete order for regular business.

In the beginning of 1883, the Union Passenger Railroad Company, of Philadelphia, constructed a short experimental cable tramway between Columbia Avenue and Renz Park, a distance of about $1\frac{1}{4}$ miles of double track, the site being about three miles from the centre of the city. This route is chiefly level, excepting for one part, where the gradients vary from about 1 in 10 to 1 in 12. The engine-house was situated at the Avenue terminus, and contained a duplicate service of horizontal engines, of about 100 indicated horse-power each, making nearly 200 revolutions per minute. A steel wire cable was employed of $1\frac{1}{4}$ in. diameter, driven at a speed of about seven miles per hour. Perhaps the most peculiar feature of this line was the employment of an entirely cast-iron slotted cable tube, which was buried beneath the street surface, and which, with other details of indifferent engineering, mainly contributed to the collapse of this scheme. This cast-iron cable tube had the appearance of a slotted "gas or water main," and turned out to be as expensive and cumbersome as inefficient.

The type of gripping apparatus used was also rather novel, and consisted of radially moving transverse nipping jaws, operated by a vertically-moving cam-plate, actuated by a rack and pinion motion worked from the cars. In the types of grippers previously described, the hauling cable is either picked up from below or at about right angles to the nipping jaws, but in the grippers at present referred to, the cable was taken in from the top of the apparatus; the reason of this is, however, not clear, as it appears that it would entail greater difficulties in ejecting the cable.

Note 24

This introductory line was not, however, maintained in operation for many months; it worked all right mechanically, but the wear and tear was considerable and the traffic small. The ill-success of the undertaking, however, was not attributable to the system, but the result of little experience and indifferent engineering, combined with the "Patent plague," which at this time continually diverted people from lines of approved practice to vague and untested modifications.

However, the Philadelphians were in no way discouraged by this comparative failure, as they were convinced of the advantages of the system. Accordingly they started a more important and extensive scheme, involving about twelve miles of their most important streets, comprising Market-street and Columbia Avenue. This line has only been recently opened, so that at present little is known as to results beyond that at first the new and untried form of tube which was adopted has given them trouble and anxiety. The

Note 25

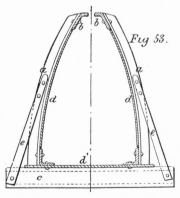

Fig 53.

construction of this cable tubeway is shown at Fig. 53, and will be seen to consist of a number of wrought-iron members; *a* being bent angle irons, carrying the slot beams *b*, secured to the piece *c*, and tied by the bars at *e*; the continuity of the tube is formed by the side and bottom plates *d d'*. This design has the appearance of an elaborate and costly construction, and it is not surprising that trouble and expense have been involved.

Engine stations are employed for operating this system on Market-street and Columbia Avenue. The introduction of the cable system into the Pennsylvania capital—the centre of America's mechanical engineering intelligence—was not altogether that which would have been expected.

The clear breadths of the streets in Philadelphia, traversed by the cable tramways, vary from 60 ft. to 25 ft. The heaviest gradients are about 5 per cent. ; the sharpest curves about 35 ft. radius. Dummy cars are not used. The speed of the cables is about eight to nine miles per hour. The internal clearance of the cable tube is 12 in. by 33 in. About seventeen miles of track are now built, and it is proposed to extend the system to twenty-one miles. The streets traversed were previously worked by horse cars. The cost is given as at 11,000*l.* per mile of track, without its equipments. The present system is said to pay 8 per cent. per annum on the par value of the stock.

We will now pass on to New York City, a capital which ranks on terms of equality with any others in the world, whether for combined magnificence of situation and structures, or for general intelligence and commercial enterprise. Any one who has visited this city since 1883 cannot have failed to have noticed that great engineering achievement, the Brooklyn and New York suspension bridge, to which structure we now have occasion to direct our attention, as being daily traversed by cars operated by the cable system. This great work took upwards of thirteen years to complete and involved an expenditure of over 3,000,000*l.* As the cable line of railway extends right across this bridge from the Brooklyn to the New York terminus or side, it will not be superfluous to make ourselves acquainted with the principal dimensions of this colossal undertaking.

The length of the main river span is 1595 ft. (at an elevation of 135 ft. from high water line), the length of each land span is 930 ft., whilst the length of the approaches is 2533 ft., thus giving an aggregate distance of rather over $1\frac{1}{8}$ miles, which is practically the length of the cable railway. The breadth of the bridge is 86 ft., so that the lines of railway can extend up one side and down the other with a footpath between.

The question of the most suitable system of traction to be employed upon this structure, was one which engrossed the most careful and lengthy consideration of the engineers and executive direction. Loco-motives were considered out of place, as being objectionable to foot-passengers on account of smoke, steam, and noise, &c., whilst horse traction was deemed expensive and dirty, besides being unsuitable for dealing with a fluctuating and heavy traffic. Therefore it followed that as little or nothing was known respecting the practical application of compressed air engines or electric motors to such purposes, the solution of the problem almost necessarily fell to the cable system, and this was accordingly selected.

As no foot or vehicular traffic is allowed, nor necessary, upon the route of this line, the haulage cable is not arranged to operate within a slotted tube beneath the road surface. The endless steel wire cable is

1½ in. in diameter, 11,450 ft. long, and weighs 3½ lbs. per foot run. The cable-driving drums are 12 ft. in diameter, and very similar to the Chicago apparatus. The motive power for operating the cable consists of two horizontal steam engines, having cylinders 26 in. in diameter, and 48 in. stroke, and making fifty-seven revolutions per minute. Steam is supplied to these engines by four Babcock and Wilcox multibular boilers of about 100 horse-power each. The cable is driven at a speed of ten miles per hour, and the estimated engine power requisite to run it with its dependent machinery, but without any rolling stock, is stated to be 35 horse-power. The average consumption of fuel per working day of twenty hours, is given as 6 tons.

Note 26

The rolling stock comprises twelve passenger cars 48 ft. long, and six cars 49 ft. long, their weights unloaded and loaded being respectively 10 and 20 tons. Two such cars coupled together are usually run, but the maximum number of cars on the road at the same time seldom exceeds twenty. As many as 7200 car trips have been performed in a day, whilst the maximum number of passengers transported in such time has exceeded 40,000. The total number of passengers transported or conveyed by this tramway from September 24, 1883, to January 1, 1885, exceeded 70,000,000, which at practically 5 cents per head, means a very considerable sum of money. The line was opened for public traffic in May, 1883, and has given general satisfaction. The system, however, of employing terminal locomotive for shunting purposes appears as unscientific as uneconomical. The engine and machinery room or site, is provided under one of the arches forming part of the Brooklyn approach. The gripping appliances attached to the cars are of the " roller or wheel type," somewhat similar to that described upon the Clay-street line, but as they are not required to travel within a slotted tube the various parts are larger, but the general efficiency of this type of gripper appears doubtful.

Before quitting the city of New York, there is yet another cable railway of even more recent date and importance that claims our brief attention, viz., the Tenth Avenue line, from 125th-street, to a distance north of about 3¼ miles, and which was successfully inaugurated in the fall of last year, and has been satisfactorily maintained in operation since such period.

This system differs chiefly from others already described, in the novel feature, that duplicate cables and independent engines, with actuating gear, are provided, so as to insure the continuous operation of the road under all probable conditions arising from accidents or temporary " breakdowns " of any kind—a good idea if not too costly. The system was devised by Mr. Miller, the engineer to the line. One of these cables is kept in constant operation for propelling the cars on the road, whilst the other is maintained by its side in readiness should the first

Note 27

one break down. The machinery is so arranged that in the event of any interruption of work, the loads or cars can be readily transferred from the one cable to the other, and for this purpose the gripping appliances (which are of the Chicago or **L** type) are constructed with double gripping jaws, so as to be capable of catching hold of either cable as occasion may require. In this manner, if necessary, the cables may be run alternately for, say, twenty hours each, thereby giving ample time for inspection or repairs, &c.

The engine-room contains two of " Wright's automatic cut-off engines " of 300 horse-power each, the cylinders being 28 in. in diameter with 40 in. stroke ; the flywheels are 18 ft. in diameter and weigh about 16 tons each. The spurwheels are 6 ft. and 13 ft. in diameter, and the shafts 12 in. in diameter, by 100 ft. long, coupled at their centres, so as to be readily detached or uncoupled. These shafts are mounted in ten bearings.

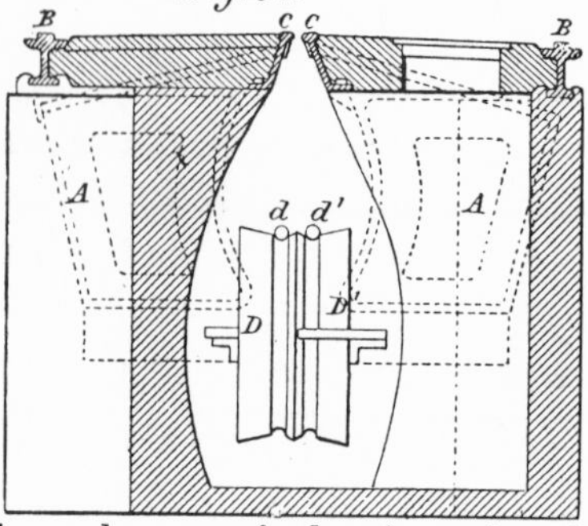

A transverse section of the tube and pulley pit is represented at Fig. 54, in which A A are the tube frames, B the rails, C the slot beams, and D D¹ the duplex supporting pulleys upon which the duplicate cables *d d¹* are carried.

Fig. 54.

Each spur pinion on the engine shafts drives a train of gearing carrying a pair of grooved driving drums which are of exactly similar

Note 28

design, so that they may be interchanged   required. Around each pair of these drums a cable is wound, similar to the Chicago operating mechanism ; in fact, in many features, this arrangement bears a close resemblance to that system ; for example, the vertical tension apparatus, &c., working, however, in combination with a differential weighted lever device, which is apparently an improvement. The two cables capable of being operated in the same tube or section (by throwing one part of the driving mechanism out of gear and another part into gear by means of an ordinary clutch) are arranged to run in parallel planes about 3 in. apart. Each cable is about $6\frac{1}{4}$ miles in length, and the longest yet in use for such purpose. A pair of small auxiliary vertical engines are provided to each section of machinery for the purpose of slowly hauling round the cables after working hours, with the object of careful and systematic inspection, without the employment of the main engines. Steam is supplied to these engines

Note 29

by four return tubular boilers of 150 horse-power each.

It may be here mentioned, that Mr. Miller has also supplied similar designs for the Kansas City Cable Tramway, a line of about $2\frac{1}{2}$ miles in length. This line is now in successful operation. St. Louis, also, boasts of a cable line, whilst Omaha and other cities have apparently decided to adopt the system.

Note 30

We will now turn to Cincinnati, an important city in the States which lies on practically level ground, whilst its suburbs are situated upon pleasing hilly country. Owing to its physical surroundings, primitive systems of cable haulage or elevators have been employed in this district for some twelve years past, *e.g.*, the Price's Hill, Elms' Hill, Mount Auburn, and Mount Adams, &c., cable railways. Cincinnati now, however, has a street cable tramway of the modern type, viz., a line from Court and Broadway to McMillan and Gilbert Avenue, a distance of about $1\frac{1}{2}$ miles of double track. There are seven curved portions of line in this distance, and an elevation of about 300 ft. is surmounted. Hitherto the horse cars took about thirty minutes to climb the Gilbert Avenue hill, a journey now performed by cable traction in about ten minutes. A novel feature in this enterprise is the use of the cable line, or a part of it, as a common section of horse tramway. Upon the horse cars arriving at the hilly portion of the line, gripping appliances are attached to their axles, and the traction continued by the agency of cable haulage. Another feature claimed in connection with this line, is the reasonable cost of the construction, a point where plenty of room for improvement exists, providing always the economy is not achieved by the introduction of an imperfect or unreliable system.

Note 31

After this section of cable line has been efficiently tested, it is to be extended to Fountain-square and Walnut Hill, making $3\frac{1}{2}$ miles of double track.

Practically, the construction and appliances employed are similar to others already described. The cable tube is 27 in. deep, and attention has been given to the arrangement of the pulleys, in the matter of their adjustment, accessibility, and replacement, &c. The cost of this roadway is stated to be at the rate of about 15,000*l.* per mile of double line.

It will now be appreciated that, notwithstanding the strong opposition against the system, resulting from prejudice and vested interests, its introduction and development in the eastern States has made steady progress. Quite recently an elevated cable railway has been constructed from the Hoboken Heights to the Landing, New York.

Note 32

CHAPTER IV.

NEW ZEALAND CABLE TRAMWAYS.

THUS far our attention has been entirely engaged upon the organisa-
tion, introduction, and development of the cable railways system
within the United States of America, where the system has made steady
progress year by year. We shall now quit the experiences of our
Transatlantic cousins, and turn our attention to the reception the
system in question has met with in other parts of the world. With
this object we will first advert to the British colony of New Zealand, in
order to pursue our subject with something like chronological sequence.

About six years ago Messrs. Reid and Duncan, having devoted some
special attention to the system of cable traction for street purposes,
brought before their fellow citizens a scheme for connecting the city of
Dunedin with the contiguous localities of Roslyn and Maori by means
of a cable tramway. Speedily the requisite financial assistance was
obtained, and the construction of the line at once commenced, and after
a few months the works were brought to a satisfactory completion.
This cable line has now been in successful daily operation for about five
years, and consists of 3500 ft. of single track, with passing places; it
surmounts an elevation of about 500 ft. in its course. There are two
reversed curved parts in the line of about 200 ft. radius, but no difficulties have been apparently experienced in working such portions of
contra-flexure in the track. The engine-house is located upon the
summit of the high-lying land.

After the mechanical and financial success of the Roslyn Cable
Tramway had been demonstrated, we find the inhabitants of Mornington
fostering a similar scheme for providing a method of locomotion from
the high ground of this suburb to the centre of the city of Dunedin.
Towards the close of 1882 the works of this tramway were commenced,
and in March, 1883, the line (which is about one mile long) was successfully opened for public traffic. It is worthy of note that most of the
work was carried out by local labour and manufacturers. The Mornington Cable Tramway is of 3 ft. 6 in. gauge, with a double line throughout.
The greater part of the route is practically level, whilst other portions
have gradients up to 1 in $6\frac{1}{4}$; there is one curve on the road of 250 ft.

radius.   The slotted cable tube is about 24 in. deep, and is composed of bent rails (40 lbs.—forming the rail and slot-beam supports), substantially imbedded in concrete.   As, however, this construction is practically similar to the Australian cable tubes, to be hereinafter illustrated and described, it is not necessary to give further particulars of this part of the New Zealand practice.

The cables employed upon this line are about 3 in. in circumference and are composed of crucible-steel wires.   The tube pulleys are 11 in. in diameter and are placed every 30 ft. apart, whilst the terminal sheaves are 10 ft. in diameter.   The engines used for working this system, are of horizontal high-pressure type, with cylinders 13 in. in diameter and 27 in. stroke, fitted with automatic expansion gear and capable of indicating 78 horse-power each.   The steam is supplied by a duplicate service of multitubular cylindrical boilers 10 ft. long by 4 ft. 6 in. in diameter.   Dummy and passenger cars of the ordinary American type are used.

The grips and brakes are all operated by direct-acting levers, similar to those described upon the Sutter or California-street lines, U.S.A. The cable is driven by a clip drum similar to the arrangement described on the Clay-street line, U.S.A., whilst the tensional apparatus is of similar known type.   The capital of this tramway was originally subscribed and held by only thirty-two shareholders.   This line has now been in operation for about four years, and has given satisfaction.

Messrs. Cradock and Co., of Wakefield, have supplied several wire ropes for these tramways, with successful results, one having recently run for about twenty-three months in continual daily service.   The five separate ropes supplied by this firm were—with one exception— $2\frac{3}{4}$ in. in circumference, the longest one, 3800 yards, was of 3 in. circumference.

CHAPTER V.

CABLE TRACTION IN EUROPE AND AUSTRALIA.

WE will now take a glance at the limited progress that has been made in Europe with the cable system of traction.

It may be remembered that nearly a whole year elapsed, from the date of Parliamentary powers, authorising the construction of the Highgate Hill Cable Tramway, London, N., before any practical signs of life in the scheme were exhibited. The construction of this tramway was, however, commenced at the close of October, 1883, and the line was opened by the Lord Mayor for public traffic on the 29th of May, 1884. This line is nearly one mile in length, commencing at the Archway

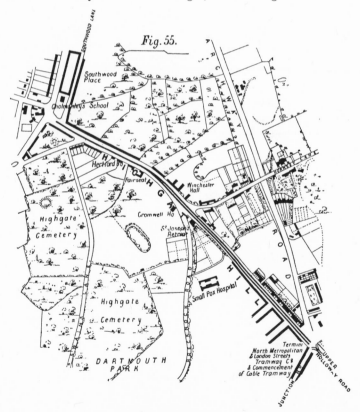

Fig. 55.

Tavern, Upper Holloway, and extending in a north-westerly direction up Highgate Hill to one end of Southwood-lane, Hornsey, as indicated on the map, Fig. 55.

The greater portion of the line is double throughout, and is of 3 ft. 6 in. gauge ; but, upon approaching and traversing the High-street Highgate, there are about 1000 ft. of single track with passing-places, which is not a favourable condition for cable traction. Further, there are many curves at various parts of the road, varying from 3000 ft. to 250 ft. radius, except at the points and the engine-house turn-out, where the radii are 75 ft. and 40 ft. respectively. The gradients along the road vary from 1 in 11 to 1 in 75, the steepest portion being near Hornsey-lane, and the most level, through the High-street at the summit of the hill.

From the above particulars it will be understood that this cable line is subjected to severe physical conditions, and well demonstrates the mechanical capabilities of the system. The character of the road necessitates frequent deflections of the cable in both vertical and horizontal planes, occasioned by the grades and curves, and it should be noticed that at certain portions of the permanent way (where the double tracks converge into single lines, as before referred to) the two parts of the endless cable, which run in opposite directions, are conducted through the same underground tube ; these are trying requirements, and necessitated special arrangements. The line passes through, or touches, three parishes, viz., St. Mary's Islington, St. Pancras, and Hornsey, so that some of the parochial difficulties and enactments that were met with may be imagined. The tracks with points, switches, &c., are of ordinary construction, and are similar to the systems used in Manchester and Huddersfield, &c. Although this type of permanent way was adopted it should be understood that nearly any other system would do as well, and many better, for it certainly was not cheap, nor easy to lay.

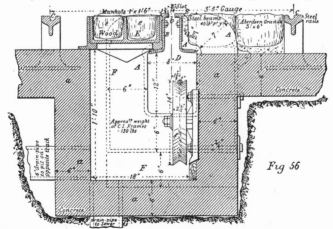

Fig 56

Centrally between the up and down rails and below the street surface is laid a continuous rectangular tube or trench (1 ft. deep by 8 in. wide), see Fig. 56, in which the endless cable travels ; the top of this tube has

a central opening or slot *b*, about $\frac{5}{8}$ in. wide, through which the mechanical gripping appliances carried on the cars operates in order to pick up
or release the movement of the cable.   The tube D is composed of cast-
iron frames A, which carry the steel girders B, forming the narrow
parallel opening *b* in the roadway, and is built in with intermediate
fillings *a* of Portland concrete ; C represents the ordinary tramrails or
track.   Along the axis of the tube are provided a series of vertical
supporting pulleys *f* placed 40 ft. apart ; these carry the cable and
maintain it in its proper working plane.   The cross section, Fig. 56, is
taken through a pit F, provided with one of such pulleys, and with a
manhole E to give access to it.   On curved portions of the road
the pulleys are formed with larger flanges and their axes of rota-
tion are fixed at an inclination of 45 deg., as shown in Fig. 57.

Wherever these pulleys
occur small pits F are
provided, to which access
is obtained by manholes E
opening into the streets.
The covers of these pits
are accurately made in
order to prevent rocking,
whilst their surfaces are
formed to receive wooden
blocks *e*, to maintain the
continuity of the paving.
All these pits are formed

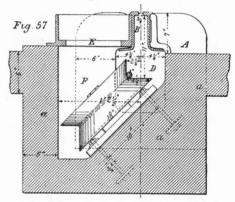

Fig. 57

with walls of concrete rammed behind suitable templates.

At the termini of the line the endless cable passes round two sheaves
or pulleys, 8 ft. in diameter, the northern one being mounted to rotate
on a horizontal axis, whilst the southern terminal pulley is similarly
mounted in a horizontal plane upon a vertical axis, arranged upon a
movable carriage, suitably counterweighted so as to maintain a uniform
tension of the cable, during variations of temperature and fluctuations
in the traffic.   These pulleys and terminal gear are arranged in brick
pits or vaults formed beneath the road.

The underground cable tubes above described, drain into the adjacent pulley pits, which are at convenient intervals connected with
the main sewer by trapped earthenware pipes.   The construction of
this cable-tube did not necessitate extensive excavations, the maximum
for the reception of the cast frames A, before referred to, being only
about 24 in. deep, whilst between these frames, the bottom of the
cable-tube is 18 in. below the street surface.   The whole of the road
surface between the tracks and in the margins prescribed by the
Board of Trade, is filled in with 3 in. by 6 in. Aberdeen granite setts
grouted with Portland cement.

The permanent way does not in all cases occupy the centre of the road ; this variation was made in order to ease the curves, which are all more or less objectionable to the cable system.

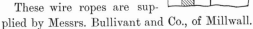

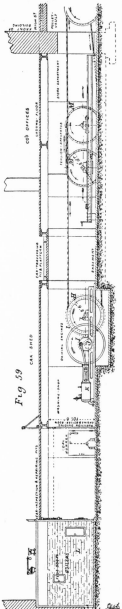

Fig. 59

The cable employed on the line is constructed of the best crucible - steel wires twisted into strands and closed round a hemp core. It is about 3 in. in circumference (or about $\frac{15}{16}$ in. in diameter), and weighs about 5 tons complete.

Fig. 58

These wire ropes are supplied by Messrs. Bullivant and Co., of Millwall.

The cable is rendered endless by means of a long splice (about 45 ft. in length) of a very uniform character, so as to work smoothly from the driving drum over the respective pulleys. It is driven by a Grant and Ritchie " grip pulley " or drum H, the periphery of which is shown in section at Fig. 58. This pulley is fixed on a countershaft h in the engine-house and is operated through the intervention of a train of spur gearing I i, driven from the prime or engine shaft J, as shown in Fig. 59.

The hauling cable, after being conducted by pulleys clear of the engine-house, goes down the hill over the small vertical supporting pulleys mounted in the tube on the east track, thence round the large horizontal southern terminal sheave (mounted on the compensating carriage), whence it goes up the hill in a similar tube and manner in the west track. At the northern terminus of the line the cable passes over the large vertical sheaves, and returns in a similar way to the driving pulley in the engine-house ; thus completing its circuit, as may be understood upon reference to Fig. 59.

The cable is held in such a state of tension that the " sag " seldom exceeds 2 in., whilst the gripping apparatus attached to the cars have only to raise it about an inch in order to clear the pulleys. At curved portions of the road the angle pulleys are located so as to reduce the deflection of the cable to a minimum when the cars pass such places—an important considera-tion for reducing the lateral strains upon the grip-shank.

The engine-house, car depôt, and offices are situated at the top of the hill on the east side of the High-street, and have a substantial frontage, composed principally of red and white brickwork relieved by plinths, pillars, &c., of worked Portland stone. This structure was, however, unnecessarily expensive. The outside dimensions of these premises are about 130 ft. long by 30 ft. wide.

A longitudinal section of the basement of the building, is given at Fig. 59 already referred to. In this portion the whole of the operating machinery is located, whilst the ground floor on the street level is chiefly arranged for the car depôt, repairing pits, &c., the offices being situated above. The narrow and irregular character of the site would not permit of the premises being built at right angles to the road, and hence they are inconvenient for traffic purposes. Indeed, there can be no doubt that the site of the building is very unsuitable, for in the first place, its relative position to the roadway has necessitated some very heavy road-making, in order to attain a suitable gradient to the premises, and, secondly, its angular relation to the road renders the efficient exit and entrance of the cars very difficult. Further, the location of the engine-house at the top of a severe gradient, where the grips release one part of the cable to pick up the other, is most undesirable if not dangerous.

The engines for operating the machinery and cable are two indepen-dent motors of about 25 nominal horse-power each (by Messrs. Grafton and Co.), fitted with automatic variable expansion gear, so that the power of the engines will automatically vary to meet the fluctuat-ing working requirements of the system. The boilers L, situated in the rear of the engines, are by Messrs. Babcock and Wilcox. They afford a duplicate service of 50 horse-power. All the machinery is in duplicate. The engine in service drives, through the spur gearing I *i*, a countershaft *h*, on which the cable-driving drum H is fixed, so that the cable is driven at a uniform velocity of from five to six miles per hour, as required. As the cable leaves the drum or pulley H it passes on its way out to the road, over two com-pensating sheaves M M¹ capable of having their axes moved further apart by slides *m*, and screw spindle gearing *m*¹, and by which any permanent slack in the cable (resulting from stretching) may be taken up. Changes in the length of the cable arising from variations of temperature and working strains, are, as before mentioned, compen-sated by the counter-weighted pulley carriage in the lower terminal pit. The cars used upon the Highgate line are of three types, and demonstrate how any existing rolling stock can be adapted to the

system, and that the employment of "dummy cars" (*i.e.*, independent
hauling cars for carrying the grippers and other mechanical contrivances),
is unnecessary if not unsuitable for traffic in this country. Some
of the cars employed on this line are of the ordinary type, with the
gripping apparatus worked direct; others are mounted on bogie trucks,
similarly equipped and worked; and lastly, some "dummies or auxiliary
hauling cars," are employed. The last arrangement may be useful in
exceptional cases, but their common use on passenger lines, whether
level or of fairly uniform gradients, such as are usually found in this
country, appears unnecessary and a source of danger and inconvenience.

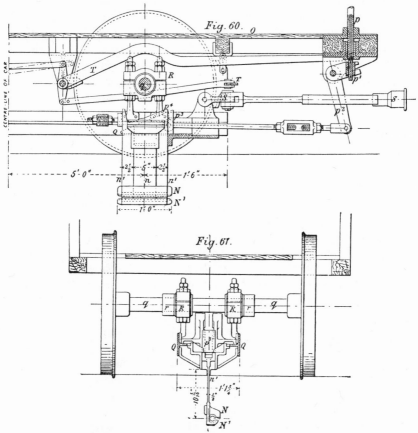

Fig. 60.

Fig. 61.

The gripping apparatus provided upon the cars (see Figs. 60 and 61),
is a device consisting of two movable jaws N N[1],which engage or release
the cable at the will of the operator, who, standing on the car platform
O, works a hand-wheel connected with the screw p and mechanism
p, p^1, p^2, p^3. The jaws of the gripping apparatus travel in the slotted
tube beneath the road surface, and are opened and closed by vertically
sliding plates or attachments n, n^1, passing through the slot in the

H 2

tube. It should be understood that immediately the cars are taken on to the road, the cable is pulled or guided into the "grips." When it is desired that a car should stop, the bite on the cable is released, so that it continues running inoperatively, until the grip is again closed. When the cars arrive at the termini or opposite the engine-house, the cable is conducted out of them in the same way as on the California-street and Chicago lines, &c., U.S.A.

The manner in which the gripping operations are performed will be readily understood from Figs. 60 and 61, the former being a part longitudinal section and the latter a transverse section of a car platform and under gearing, &c., as used on the Highgate line. The screw termination of the operating handwheel spindle is shown at p ; this works into a block-piece p^1, carried by the forked termination of the lever p^2, the other extremity of which is connected to a rod, terminating with a "wedge piece" p^3, which works into a tapering hood-piece p^4 attached to one of the gripper or stem-plates n. In this manner it will be seen that upon turning the handwheel in one direction or the other the lever p^2 will be caused to push or pull the wedge p^3 in or out of the hood-piece p^4, and thus open or close the gripping jaws N and N^1. The type of gripper is nothing more than the common L principle, used on the San Francisco and Chicago lines, &c. The arrangement of gearing for transmitting motion to the apparatus is supposed to be novel; it is, however, a somewhat weak arrangement and has not given great satisfaction, the motion being slow and uncertain, and the wear and tear considerable. These gripping appliances are carried on longitudinal framings Q hung upon the car axles q in adjustable bearings R, as shown in the engravings, lateral play being limited by the fixed collars r. S shows the arrangement and connection of the coupling drawbars, whilst T indicates the arrangement of the brake levers, &c. Continuous wheel-brakes are applied to all the cars, as well as slipper brakes, the latter consisting simply of wooden blocks which may be forced down upon the rails by common toggle lever arrangements. The cars with their gripping and brake appliances, &c., were supplied by the Falcon Car and Engine Company. At Fig. 62 is represented in plan a set of the terminal junction points and switches, as used at Highgate ; $c\,c^1$ indicate a pair of ordinary tramway points ; $b\,b^1$ represents the "grip slots," which form a junction at X, and at which point a spring tongue piece y^2 is introduced, in order to guide the gripper shanks, so that they shall take the correct slot ; E are the manhole covers to the "point pulleys." The chilled castings for these junctions and other work were made by Messrs. Miller and Co., of Edinburgh, a speciality to which they have devoted much attention with marked success.

This firm has recently manufactured the special points, crossings and junction work, &c., for the Melbourne Cable Tramways, and are well known to the tramway community in connection with such class of work

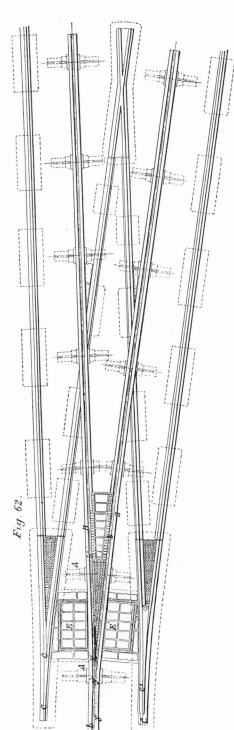

Fig. 62.

and especially for their chilled iron wheels, which wear about twice as long as crucible - steel wheels. These manufactures are carried out upon thoroughly scientific bases, and hence the Americans, who once had a practical monopoly of this trade, have recently encountered powerful competition by this British firm. Too much attention can scarcely be bestowed upon the question of really good and reliable chilled castings, a manufacture full of difficulties and about which very little was known in this country until recent years.

The entire works at Highgate are substantially and well executed, but some of the designs have turned out to be hardly satisfactory. Strictly, the character of the road is unsuitable to the system, and it was looked upon more as an introductory line, the site being recognised to lack many requirements, as also an immediate lucrative future. It was, however, a difficult matter to obtain powers to introduce a new system upon an appropriate elevation near the centre of London, and therefore it is only just to state that this line affords no true criterion of the financial capabilities of the

Note 33

system.   However, considering its performances under very unfavour-
able auspices, and from a standpoint of only comparative efficiency, the
line has furnished data of unquestionable importance and success, as will
be explained.

A matter of vast importance was the efficiency of " the brake apparatus" applied to the cars, and to this question the Board of Trade
devoted much careful attention.   Major-General Hutchinson, R.E., on
May 18, 1884, made some very crucial trials with these appliances, *e.g.*,
a descending car was released from the cable and allowed to run down
the hill by gravitation until the speed indicator showed it had attained
a velocity of about twenty-five miles per hour, when orders were given to
apply the brakes, and the car was then brought comfortably to rest
within twelve yards.   The result of this experiment was considered very
satisfactory, the " slipper or track brakes" giving valuable assistance.

The merits of direct-acting toggle lever track brakes was identically
described by Mr. Bodmer in 1845, in the early days of railways.

The true cost of constructing and equipping the Highgate Hill line
was about 18,000*l.*, *i.e.*, for the entire roadwork (proper), machinery, cars,
and " dummies," which with the cost of land and building was raised
to a total of about 25,000*l.* A large amount of money was unnecessarily
expended upon the engine-house, car depôt, and offices, &c.   In the
above amount no account is taken of Parliamentary expenses, promoters' and patentee's charges, parish work, &c., which were heavy items.

We will now pause to briefly inquire into the practical results of the
operation of this small cable system, which has now been running for
nearly three years.   With this object in view every reasonable allowance should be taken into fair consideration, *e.g.*:

1. It is the first line of the kind built in this country, and therefore
high expenditure, some indifferent details, and administration, &c., may
be in some measure allowed for.

2. The conditions of the line are unsuitable to the " system," *e.g.*,
numerous curves ; single lines, with passing places ; a short length of
line and consequently small car mileage returns ; a very small traffic of
a uniform character to support the line, &c.

So far as winter weather is concerned, we know that it has worked
successfully through severe seasons without interference with the daily
operations.   It may be remembered that during the severe snowstorm
which occurred at the close of December last, and when so much general
damage was effected—besides the traffic of our railways and tramways
being greatly obstructed or stopped—the cable line in question was
worked without trouble or delay. In some summer months the cars have
earned as much as 4s. per mile run, *e.g.*, bringing a total revenue of 1850*l.*
(during the months of June, July, and August), with a working expenditure of about 715*l.*, being equal to about 39 per cent. of the gross

receipts. Such returns, it is believed, are hitherto unprecedented in the tramway annals of Europe. The daily consumption of fuel (sixteen working hours) is about 1½ tons. Notwithstanding the heavy cost of construction and equipment of this line, its actual or legitimate expenditures did not exceed that of the average capital account of horse tramways in London, whilst its working expenses are far less. In certain financial details the line is heavily handicapped, from which it can scarcely be expected to prove a lucrative investment.

Assuming the line to be located on about level ground, locomotives could scarcely do the work under 7d. per car mile, or ideal compressed air motors under 9d. per car mile, to say nothing of their drawback or imperfections, whereas the cable system, if judiciously applied, can certainly be worked for 5d. per car mile, including depreciation. A common mistake lies in assuming that the system can be universally applied with similar success ; in some instances even animal traction may be more advantageously employed.

With reference to the two slight accidents which occurred upon the Highgate line on the 31st of July, 1884, and 8th of January, 1885, the Board of Trade issued reports concerning the cause of these mishaps, and from these it would appear that the system is entirely exonerated from blame.

From these documents it will be seen that the cause of the first-mentioned accident " was primarily due to the negligence of both the driver and conductor of dummy car No. 6 attached to the ordinary car No. 3, in not having the ' slipper brakes' coupled up before starting down the hill." It appears the driver's attention was previously called to the state of the " brake connections," and he simply replied, " Never mind that thing." The officer of the Board of Trade then continues : " The second cause of the collision was the failure of the driver to seize the cable before starting from the depôt," &c. With regard to the second accident referred to, the report similarly states : "The primary cause of this accident was the breach of regulation No. 7, which states the cars shall not be allowed to descend the tramway by gravity, but shall always be attached by the grippers to the cable." " Secondly, the want of sand in the sand-boxes provided on the cars contributed to the accident."

As it may be interesting and instructive to some, a reproduction of the Board of Trade rules, regulations, and bye-laws issued by them in respect of the employment of cable traction upon street tramways, is here annexed :

Regulations.

I. The carriages to be used on the tramways shall comply with the following requirements, that is to say :

(*a*) Each wheel shall be fitted with a brake block which can be applied by a screw or treadle, or by other means, and each carriage, except the dummy carriages, shall be fitted with a slipper brake capable of being applied by the driver or conductor of the car.

(b) A governor (which cannot be tampered with by the driver) shall be attached to each stationary engine, and shall be so arranged that at any time when the engine exceeds the number of revolutions sufficient to move the cable at a speed of six miles an hour, it shall cause the steam to be shut off.

(c) Each carriage shall be numbered, and the number shall be shown in a conspicuous part thereof.

(d) Each carriage shall be fitted with a suitable wheel-guard to push aside obstructions, and each dummy and bogie carriage shall be fitted with a special bell to be sounded as a warning when necessary.

(e) Arrangements shall be made enabling the driver to command the fullest possible view of the road before him.

II.   Every carriage used on the tramways shall be so constructed as to provide for the safety of passengers, and for their safe entrance to, exit from, and accommodation in such carriages, and for their protection from the machinery used for drawing or propelling such carriages.

III.   The Board of Trade and their officers may, from time to time, and shall, on the application of the local authority of any of the districts through which the said tramways pass, inspect the stationary engines, cables, or carriages used on the tramways, and the machinery therein, and may, whenever they think fit, prohibit the use on, or in connection with the tramways of any of them which, in their opinion, are not safe for use.

IV.   The speed at which such carriages shall be driven or propelled along the tramways shall not exceed the rate of six miles an hour.

V.   The ordinary carriages shall be connected with the dummy carriages by double couplings.

VI.   The dummy carriages shall be provided with gates which shall always be kept closed so as to prevent passengers leaving such carriages at the " off side."

VII.   The carriages shall not be allowed to descend the tramways by gravity alone, but shall always be attached by the gripper to the cable, except when stopping or when passing the spot near the engine-house where the cables cross.

VIII.   The conductor of an ordinary carriage shall not leave the rear platform of the carriage during the ascending journey.

Penalty.

Note.—The company, or any person, using such mechanical power on the tramways contrary to any of the above regulations, is, for every such offence, subject to a penalty not exceeding 10*l.*, and also in the case of a continuing offence, to a further penalty not exceeding 5*l.* for every day, after the first, during which such offence continues.

Bye-Laws.

I.   The special bell shall be sounded by the driver of the carriage, from time to time, when it is necessary as a warning.

II.   Whenever it is necessary to avoid impending danger the carriages shall be brought to a standstill.

III.   The entrance to and exit from the carriages shall be by the hindermost or conductor's platform, except in the case of the dummy carriages.

IV.   The carriage, or carriages, shall be brought to a standstill immediately before taking any facing point both on the upward and downward journeys.

V. The company shall place, and keep placed in a conspicuous position inside of each carriage in use on the tramways, a printed copy of these regulations and bye-laws.

Penalty.

Note.—Any person offending against or committing a breach of any of these bye-laws is liable to a penalty not exceeding 40s.

The provisions of the Tramways Act, 1870, with respect to the recovery of penalties, is applicable to the penalties for the breach of these regulations or bye-laws.

Signed by order of the Board of Trade this 26th day of June, 1884.

HENRY G. CALCRAFT,
An Assistant Secretary to the Board of Trade.

(Later) Regulations.

IX. Every dummy carriage shall be fitted with a slipper brake.

X. No carriage shall leave the depôt on any downward journey unless the cable is properly gripped and the slipper brake connections are in proper order.

XI. The conductor of an ordinary carriage shall not leave the carriage on the downward journey.

Penalty.

Note.—The company or any person using mechanical power on the tramways contrary to any of the above regulations, is, for every such offence, subject to a penalty not exceeding 10*l.*, and also in the case of a continuing offence, to a further penalty not exceeding 5*l.* for every day after the first during which such offence continues.

Signed by order of the Board of Trade this 16th day of October, 1884.

HENRY G. CALCRAFT,
An Assistant Secretary to the Board of Trade.

Adverting to more recent movements with the system in Great Britain, in 1884 powers were obtained to construct about five miles of cable tramways in Edinburgh, with the view of opening up the northern districts of this beautiful capital. This cable system is designed and located to serve the northern districts of Stockbridge, Trinity, and New-haven, *viâ* Royal Circus and Frederick-street and Cannon Mills, Pitt and Hanover-streets to Princess-street respectively. The steepest gradient will be about 1 in 13 to 1 in 14. The Cannon Mills section is now in an advanced stage of construction. **Note 34** **Note 35**

The Corporation of Birmingham, acting under reports and opinions of their Public Works Committee (supported by Sir Frederick Bram-well as their consulting engineer), have unanimously agreed upon the construction of a cable tramway system within their borough. The necessary financial arrangements have been satisfactorily arranged, and the works are progressing. The present system will consist of about four miles of double track ; the average steepest gradients being about 1 in 20 to 1 in 13, and the sharpest curve about 45 ft. radius.

It is proposed to construct and work the system in two sections, the first being from Colmore-row *via* Snow-hill and Holyhead-road to Handsworth, a length of 2 m. 7 fur. ; the second section extend- **Note 36** ing from Colmore-row to Selly-road *viâ* the Bristol-road, thus making an aggregate distance of about four miles. The gradients above referred to are upon the first-named section, those in the latter being very light. The gauge of the track will be 3 ft. 6 in. The report of the Public Works Committee contains a tabulated series of replies from the authorities of San Francisco, Chicago, Philadelphia, New Zealand, &c., in answer to inquiries made by the mayor of Birmingham respecting the efficiency of the cable system, and to an extent influenced by these replies, the Committee arrived at the following conclusions :

" 1. That the cable system is practical and suitable for the routes proposed.

"2. That under proper regulations it appears to be as safe, if not safer, than steam, and as safe as horse traction.

" 3. That with a frequent service of cars, it appears to be cheaper to work than horse traction, and as cheap as steam traction, *even with the extra capital outlay.*

" 4. That it possesses advantages over steam traction in being more free from noise, entirely free from smoke, steam, or fumes, and less unsightly.

" 5. That it avoids cruelty to horses.

" 6. *That it possesses advantages over both steam and horse traction,* in uniformity of speed, in admitting of more frequent service, in power of expansion to meet sudden emergencies at little increased cost, in being able to ascend steep grades with ease, and generally it appears to possess fewer inconveniences and annoyances to the householders on the line of route, interferes less with vehicular traffic, and affords greater advantages to the users of such cars than other systems in practical work."

The last conclusion is an able epitome of the true merits of the system, and which appears strong evidence in favour of its extended application.

Due consideration was given to locomotives, compressed air, and electrical motors, but the two latter were discarded at an early stage as impracticable or uneconomical.

It may be worth noticing that the authorities "in order to form an idea as to whether the central slot rails would be likely to be a source of trouble in the crowded streets of Birmingham," laid a short length on Snow-hill, just above the station gates, but "it has not given rise to any complaints." It may also be mentioned that at the close of 1883 a somewhat similar trial section was laid at Kirkdale, Liverpool.

Perhaps about the most important reply given by the mayor of San Francisco (Cal., U.S.A.), to the queries of the Birmingham authorities, in reference to the cable lines of that city, was that "all these roads pay dividends from 8 to 24 per cent. per annum."

Another important conclusion arrived at by this Inquiry Committee was that the cost of working the cable system appeared about 3d. per mile less than that of working by locomotives and 6d. less than horse traction, under average favourable conditions.

We will now turn to a recent accepted project for the application of the "endless cable system of traction" *to the working of underground railways.*

The project referred to, is Mr. J. H. Greathead's underground railway system, to extend from King William-street, City, to the Elephant and Castle, which works are rapidly advancing, and are expected to be completed and open for traffic within twelve months.

Note 37

As regards the novelty of the application, little can be said, as the system, *per se,* has been known and used for years in mines, and only proves how "history repeats itself;" further, in 1864, Mr. P. Barlow advocated a somewhat similar system of cable haulage for working traffic in tunnels or subways.

During a discussion upon the Paper by Messrs. B. Baker and W. Barry upon the Metropolitan (Underground) Railway, read before the Institution of Civil Engineers last session, Mr. Greathead, M.I.C.E., directed attention to the present uneconomical and obnoxious working of locomotives upon this system, *vide* vol. lxxxi. of the Proceedings of the Institution.

Independent of the evolution of highly objectionable and deleterious gases and products of combustion, combined with difficulties of ventilation, Mr. Greathead further called special attention to the large proportion of locomotive power that is practically wasted upon the Metropolitan system, and as a result of careful investigations, he stated that "the proportion of power actually or effectively utilised for carrying the live load (*i.e.,* passengers) was only something like 2 per cent. of the total average power exerted." In conclusion, Mr. Greathead mentioned that he believed "the 'cable system' of traction could frequently be utilised for the above stated purposes with more satisfactory results," as it avoided vitiated atmosphere, and gave greater facilities for quick services at as high speeds and at considerably less cost.

Reverting to Mr. Greathead's project before alluded to, and for which Parliamentary powers were granted in the session of 1884, it may be mentioned that a company has been formed to carry out and work the enterprise, under the title of "The City of London and Southwark Subway Co., Limited"—and an excellent undertaking they appear to have in hand.

This cable railway will commence at King William-street (adjoining the Monument Station of the Metropolitan Railway), whence it will proceed under the River Thames, and Borough High-street, Blackman-street, and Newington Causeway, a distance of about 1½ miles. There will be four stations on the line, viz : at King William-street, London Bridge (Surrey side), Dover-street (Borough), and Elephant and Castle. Two separate metallic tunnels are being constructed (of about 10 ft. internal diameters), the one for the " up " and the other for the "down" traffic.   On a portion of the line there is a gradient of about 1 in 30.

The haulage cable will be driven at a uniform speed of about fifteen miles per hour, and it is intended to despatch cars or trains at about every two minutes' interval.

With respect to the system and designs for the construction of the tunnels, by Mr. Greathead (the company's engineer), much originality and ability have been displayed, the entire scheme being fully endorsed by Sir John Fowler (the company's consulting engineer), and Mr. Benjamin Baker, M.I.C.E.

The cost of the entire works, including land, buildings, hydraulic and mechanical machinery and equipments, &c., is estimated at about 300,000*l.*, or less than one-half of the capital expended per mile upon the underground portion of the Metropolitan Railway.   The works are rapidly and successfully advancing, and now one tunnel is carried through to the south side of the Thames.   The portion completed presents an admirable appearance, combining efficiency with simplicity. The process of construction is carried on in a very simple, efficacious, and silent manner ; the metallic walls are quite watertight, a matter of vast importance when we remember the usual permanent expense incurred from leakage or percolation.   As such examples, the Mersey and Severn Railway tunnels may be cited, where many millions of gallons of water are being daily pumped out, owing to the unavoidable porous nature of brickwork constructions.   Mr. Greathead's method of constructing his metallic subway, varies according to circumstances.   At present the tunnelling is being effected by means of a cutting annular shield, which is forced forward by hydraulic rams, the dislodged and contained soil being dug out and removed by trollies and hoisting apparatus in the usual manner.   The operations may, however, when necessary, be carried on by the action of impinging currents of water, forced against the resisting materials encountered in front of a "tunnelling shield." The materials thus dislodged in front of the shield would be forced backwards through pipes into receptacles situated in the excavated or completed part of the tunnel.   Tools and boring appliances may be used in front of the shield if required.   As the earth or materials can be thus dislodged and scoured away, the shield, with its cutting edge and front protecting plate, would be forced forwards by presses or rams.   Before, however, the shield is propelled, a cast-iron tube (built up of segments bolted together) is formed within the same, so that as it advances, it leaves behind it a complete metallic and water-tight tunnel.

Various methods and apparatus, devised by Mr. Greathead, for preventing any settling of the structure ; counteracting the pressure of external air, water, or semi-liquid matter ; removing deposited débris ; scouring and flushing the circulating pipes, &c.; facilities for entrapping and removing detached boulders ; devices for the employment of tunnelling tools through the shield, &c., are very ingenious and deserve special notice, which the limits and title of this treatise unfortunately preclude.

The thickness of the metallic segments forming the tunnel lining is about 1 in. The gauge of the lines is to be 4 ft. $8\frac{1}{2}$ in. Commodious cars are to be provided, and hydraulic lifts arranged at the stations for conveying passengers to and from the street level, according to which arrangement no waiting below will be necessary.

It may also be mentioned that the company has this session made application to Parliament for powers to extend this cable subway to Clapham—thus making a distance of about three miles.

The financial prospects of the scheme certainly appear good, when we consider that the approximate number of persons who pass over London Bridge in the course of a year must amount to something like 55,000,000. Carrying capacity for about 100,000 persons per day can be provided, although an estimated revenue sufficient to pay 12 per cent. per annum upon the capital to be expended, is based on only carrying 33,000 passengers daily at one penny each ; the working expenses are assumed at about 27 per cent. of the gross receipts, a feasible estimate, when we consider the capabilities of cable traction and the heavy (metropolitan) traffic reasonably expected.*

Similar cable traction subway projects are engrossing careful attention, and several other cable tramways are under serious consideration, but sufficient examples have already been given of lines in actual practice. It is, however, a great hindrance to the system, that many of the most important tramway leases expire in a few years, so that existing companies will not seriously consider the advisability of adopting or converting some portion of their lines to the systems, until they are in a better position to judge whether their leases will be renewed, and if so, upon what terms and conditions.

On the Continent serious attention is also being given to the system, *e.g.*, in parts of Belgium, Germany, Switzerland, Italy, Spain, and Portugal, &c., but most of these countries move slowly in such matters, and require much time for preliminary formalities, &c.

In some of these countries much room exists for the advantageous application of cable traction, owing to hot climates and excessive gradients for the working of which animal power is totally unsuitable. It should not be lost sight of, however, that in some foreign countries, the import duties placed upon materials and machinery, &c., are so excessive,

---

* For a more detailed description of this work see Appendix.

that mechanical enterprises are seriously "handicapped," and consequently countries are sometimes debarred from the benefits of modern
applied sciences.

During the construction of the Highgate Hill cable tramway,
London, a similar project was promoted in the City of Melbourne,
Australia, and the requisite colonial Parliamentary powers for the same
were obtained in November, 1883.

Before such powers were actually granted, it was arranged that
Mr. F. B. Clapp and Mr. G. Duncan, the future managing director
and engineer respectively to the enterprise, should visit America and
Europe in order to collect all useful available information respecting
modern systems of tramway traction, so that the best or most approved
constructions and methods of locomotion might be adopted. The
Australian authorities wisely laid stress upon their desire that an
engineer of some special technical experiences should be retained, as
they considered it would probably prove an expensive and unsatisfactory matter to have " to educate an engineer to the cable business."
It was appreciated that such a system would have to be very carefully
designed from practical experience, otherwise " breakdowns " or
vexatious delays and losses would probably arise. Ultimately it was
decided that the various local authorities should build the tramways
themselves, and lease them for working to a company for thirty years.
This decision rendered necessary the formation of some legal " trust."
The requisite election of trustees was accordingly arranged, comprising
members of the city and municipal councils, Alderman O'Grady acting
as chairman.

The engineer, &c., having settled the requisite plans and specifications for the works, estimated to cost about 800,000*l.* (independently of
rolling stock, &c., which the working company has to provide), the next
and most important matter was to raise the money for such operations.

At the close of October, 1884, the Commercial Bank of Australia
and the Royal Bank of Scotland (representing the City of Melbourne
Bank, Limited), were instructed to negotiate a loan in London of
500,000*l.* for this business enterprise, under the following title and
terms : " Colony of Victoria. The Melbourne Tramways Trust Loan,
for 500,000*l.*, in 4½ per cent. debentures, guaranteed by the city of
Melbourne and the suburban municipalities jointly and severally.
Issued under Acts of the Victoria Legislature."

This loan was well received in London, so that but little delay was
occasioned in raising sufficient capital to commence this important
tramway undertaking.

Fig. 63 is a plan or map of the city of Melbourne, with its surrounding localities, and on it are marked—in full black lines—the various
routes of authorised " cable tramways" which are about thirty-four miles

in length. Further, there was to be 16 miles of horse lines, thus giving
an aggregate of 50 miles of tramways to be constructed. The total

**Note
38**

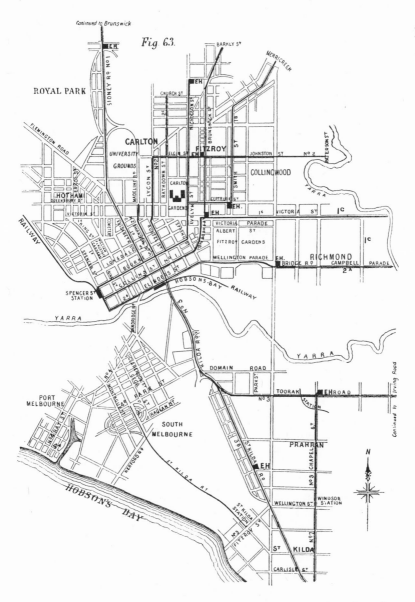

Fig. 63.

estimated cost of construction is about 950,000*l.*, exclusive of equipments of rolling stock, &c.

In the scheme, as at first projected, the approximate value of

materials, plant and machinery, &c., to be imported into the colony
was about as follows :

		£
Rails and appendages	... ...	88,000
Slot beams ...	... ...	44,000
Tube frames...	... ...	36,000
Wire ropes ...	... ...	13,000
Tie-rods, bolts, &c....	... ...	12,000
Engines and machinery	... ...	22,000
Portland Cement ...	... ...	91,000
Total value	... ...	£306,000

According to clause 14 in the fourth schedule of the principal Act of
Parliament, the whole of the lines above referred to must be constructed
by October, 1889 ; this will require vigorous action to be complied
with.

The Richmond and Brunswick sections have been already satisfactorily constructed, and are opened for public traffic. The system
will cost about an average of 20,000*l*. per mile ; the heavier horse
line costing about 14,000*l*. per mile, exclusive of equipments, land and
buildings.

Steel rails varying from about 67 lb. to 87 lb. per yard will be laid
throughout the system. The total approximate engine power, estimated
to be employed in working these cable lines, is 2000 indicated horse-
power, which will be distributed over the system from eight independent
engine-houses (E H), located as shown on the map, Fig. 63. The
engines are to be of the high-pressure horizontal type throughout, fitted
with automatic expansion gear, the average size of the cylinders being
24 in. in diameter by 48 in. stroke.

The boilers to be used will be of the Babcock and Wilcox type
The engines will be driven at about forty-five revolutions per minute,
imparting a velocity to the cables of about 575 ft. per minute through
the intervention of the usual gearing. The driving and tension appliances are to be similar to those employed upon the Market-street line
(U.S.A.), as previously described.

The cables will be composed of steel wires measuring about $3\frac{1}{2}$ in. in
circumference, and having a tensile resistance of about 90 tons per
square inch of sectional area. The longest cable to be used in one
length, will be about $4\frac{1}{2}$ miles or through $2\frac{1}{4}$ miles of double track.
The longest cable line, however, will be about $4\frac{1}{4}$ miles of double track.
Cables, manufactured by Messrs. Bullivant and Co., of Millwall, E.,
and Messrs. Craddock and Co., of Wakefield, have been sent out to
Melbourne for these lines. These ropes contain about 24 tons of wire
in one continuous length, *i.e.*, without "tucking or splicing" a strand
and involve special machinery for their manufacture.

The maximum gradient upon the system is about 1 in 14, but the majority are light.

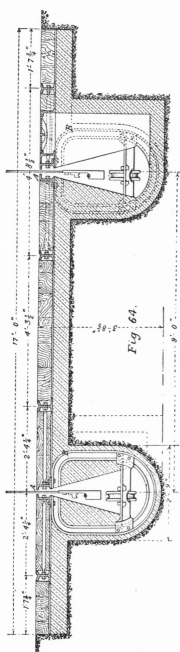

Fig. 64.

Dummy cars with one ordinary car attached will be used throughout the system; the former with their brakes and gripping appliances will be similar to those used upon the Sutter-street line (U.S.A.). These cars are to be capable of seating twenty-two passengers, but no outside accommodation is allowed to be provided.

A transverse section of the permanent way and cable tube used in Melbourne is represented at Fig. 64. The width of the grip-slots A in the street surface, is about $\frac{7}{8}$ in.

It will be seen that the tube frames are formed of bent rails B, imbedded in concrete, and as already described upon the New Zealand lines. The working company is to pay the interest upon the borrowed capital, and it further has to pay to the "Tramway Trust" $1\frac{1}{2}$ per cent. per annum during the first ten years of the lease, 2 per cent. during the second ten years, and 3 per cent. during the third period of ten years' lease. The last amounts will be set aside to form a "sinking fund" for redeeming the debentures at maturity, and will thus ultimately secure the entire system for the local authorities free of cost to them. The working company is allowed to charge 3d. fares during the first ten years of the lease, after which the result of working will be reviewed, and may be the terms revised.

On certain sections, a fixed number of workmen's cars are to be run at half-fares, but the introduction of the general 3d. fare is considered to place the company in a strong financial position. This tramway undertaking should prove remunerative, if the ultimate capital cost be not too heavy.

The operation of threading the cable from the engine-house at Brunswick-street to Spencer-street and back, a distance altogether of $3\frac{1}{2}$ miles, was watched with great interest by a large number of spectators. The rope weighed 28 tons, and was manufactured by Messrs. Cradock and Co. This was rolled on an immense drum, and had to be drawn from same through $1\frac{3}{4}$ miles of covered track and back again. The end of the cable was made fast to the gripper of a dummy car, which was drawn forward by a gang of men, carrying the rope with it. In a short time, however, the resistance became too great to be overcome in this way, and horses were employed. Eight animals were harnessed, but proved too few, and four more were added. These carried the car along for a time until the gripper suddenly snapped, and operations had then to be suspended until it was welded. A fresh start was made two hours after, and the terminus was ultimately reached without any serious mishaps. The cable was then led round the end pulley by means of a short auxiliary piece which had been previously placed in position, and then the return journey was made with twenty-four horses.

Six wire ropes have been supplied this company by the above well-known firm, making an aggregate length of 45,400 yards and weighing 134 tons. The longest rope was 8300 yards, and all were made of patent crucible-steel wires, to $3\frac{5}{8}$ in. in circumference.

It is now proposed that some of the horse tramways already planned and authorised shall be modified to permit of rope traction being used. The new lines are to be in Hotham, City of Melbourne (West Melbourne), South Melbourne, and Port Melbourne. The modification will necessitate the alteration of routes and largely increase the expenditure. " The South Melbourne line will be 1 mile 75 chains, and cost 38,750*l.* ; the Port Melbourne line 2 miles 30 chains, and cost 54,625*l.* ; buildings, 9000*l.* ; land, 6000*l.* ; engines and gearing, 15,000*l* ; gas and water pipes, 3000*l.* ; drainage, 19,000*l.* ; total, 145,375*l.*, or 90,000*l.* more than the projected horse lines. The Hotham and West Melbourne systems will cover 3 miles 35 chains, and cost, for construction, 68,750*l.* ; for land, 6000*l.* ; for buildings, 10,000*l.* ; for engines and gear, 12,000. ; for pipes and drainage, 5000*l.* ; total, 101,750*l.*, or 80,750*l.* more than the horse line. The cost of completing the present authorised schemes for the northern lines is, for cable tramways, 769,000*l.* ; for horse tramways, 19,800*l.* For the southern lines, for cable roads, 275,000*l.* ; for horse roads, 82,009*l.* The total cost of the present authorised tramways is 1,146,400*l.*"

Note 39

A cable tramway of about three miles has also been built in Sydney, and been satisfactorily working for the past year, the haulage rope having been supplied by Messrs. Bullivant and Co. The borough authorities of Balmain, Sydney, have recently invited tenders for the construction of a cable tramway in their district, and for which powers have been granted. Powers are also being applied for another cable line along King-street, College-street, Boomerang-street, and Park-street, to William-street, &c.

Cable traction for operating tram or railway cars, and in which the haulage cable is arranged to work within a slotted street tube, has been known and used for some time past in Portugal, and as may be seen in operation at Bragga and Lisbon. For example, a small **Note** cable tramway was built about five years ago in the latter city, up the **40** Calçada da Lavra, and which is operated by a small steam engine at the elevated terminus of the line ; a section of the slotted cable tube is given in Fig. 65. The gradients up these streets (Calçada) in Lisbon are very steep, *e.g.*, from 1 in 6 to 1 in 10. About eighteen months ago another somewhat similar cable tramway was constructed in

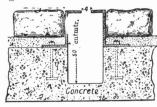

Fig. 65.

this city, viz., up the Calçada da Gloria. The slotted cable tube is similar to that shown in the last figure, but in this case the cars are worked hydrostatically, *i.e.*, tanks are provided under the cars, which are alternately filled with water at the elevated terminus and emptied at the lower one, and in this manner it will be understood that the descending or " down" cars pull up or raise the "up" cars; in fact, similar to the water car elevators in use at Scarborough. The cars are fixed permanently to the cable, whilst brake and pinion wheels are arranged on the axle of the cars, to travel in a " racked rail," so as to arrest the descent of the car or cars should the cable slip or strand.

It may be readily imagined that the presence of these rack rails in public thoroughfares does not improve the appearance or safety of the streets. Financially, such cable lines give satisfactory returns, but mechanically, the engineering details are indifferent, and in some cases the permanent ways give indications of "settling." Steam engines, however, have been found to work these lines more economically than water ballast, except in cases where water can be procured practically free of cost, and the conditions of a line are peculiarly suitable for such class of gravitation working.

A metropolitan underground cable railway has been successfully **Note** working for the past ten years in Constantinople, from Galata to Pera **41** The tunnel is built of brickwork. About 7000 persons are carried daily upon this line, the gross receipts for the last year having exceeded 12,000*l*. The total number of passengers carried last year was 2,348,247. The line is laid on a steep gradient and is only about ¼ mile in length; it is the property of an English company. The construction and equip-ment, &c., of this railway cost about 250,000*l*.

CHAPTER VI.

TECHNICAL CONSIDERATIONS AND COST OF CONSTRUCTING AND WORKING THE SYSTEM, &c.

It now remains to examine and consider an average cost of constructing and equipping a cable system of tramways under reasonable conditions.   At the present time a cable tramway (of say three miles) can be constructed and equipped in this country to meet average conditions at a cost of about 16,000*l.* per mile of double track, or for about 9*l.* per yard run of double line.   For example, the construction and equipment of the first mile of double track can be executed for, say about 18,000*l.*; the second mile, 15,000*l.*; and the third mile, 14,000*l.*; total, 47,000*l.*—or an approximate average cost of 16,000*l.* per mile of double track.   As some portions of the construction and equipment are common to a line independent of its length (*e.g.*, engine-houses and appliances, terminal pits and their machinery, &c.) the greater the distance the lower should be the average cost of any convenient linear measurement.

The expenditure incurred in the first mile of double line, as above referred to, would be composed of items about as follows:

	£
For permanent way and tube, &c., pulleys, man-holes, &c.	11,000
Buildings, *e.g.*, engine-house, car depôt, pits, &c., say	2,500
Engine and boilers, with setting	1,300
Pit, machinery, pulleys, &c.	250
Driving gear and sundries	200
Steel wire cable	300
Cars, grips, and fittings	1,200
	£16,750
Engineering and superintendence	850
	£17,600
Sundries	400
Total	£18,000

It is obvious, that the expenditure for buildings, is an elastic item, and might be more than the amount above allowed, and will vary according to the type to be erected, &c. The prices allowed for plant and machinery, &c., are based on recent tenders.

The above general and approximate estimate, however, does not include any extraneous expenses which may be necessary, for such as acquirement of land or interference with roads, drains, gas or water services, &c. These, however, are not necessarily big items.

The cost of providing the slotted cable tube (with its pulleys, manhole frames, and necessary equipments) over any ordinary tramway construction may be about 30s. per yard run of single track.

An average cost of about 16,000*l.* per mile of double line throughout a system of, say about three miles, may at first appear a considerable expenditure, but it should be remembered that the average capital disbursement of our horse tramways is about 14,500*l.* per mile of street, whilst in London the capital accounts of some tramways have exceeded 26,000*l.* per mile. The capital expenditure of a good locomotive tramway may be about 14,000*l.* per mile or more, according to conditions and requirements.

If an existing tramway, of the usual type, has to be converted to the cable system, *i.e.*, necessitating the raising and relaying of the paving ; excavating ; building and equipping the cable tube, &c., the above work would cost about 10,000*l.* for the first mile of double line.

It has been practically demonstrated that the cable system under average suitable conditions has a working advantage of about 50 per cent. over animal traction and 25 per cent. over locomotives, besides presenting an unquestionable saving in maintenance of way, and being able to work gradients hitherto impracticable.

From the foregoing, it may be deduced that the average first cost of constructing and equipping a cable tramway, under reasonably suitable conditions, may be from about 15 per cent. above that of our good horse lines.

Note 42

The extremely high cost of many cable tramways in the United States appears in many instances to have been unnecessary, but nevertheless they seem to pay handsomely. The cost of constructing and equipping some of the cable lines in San Francisco, has attained 30,000*l.* per mile of single track, an amount that is unjustifiable after making due allowance for the high cost of labour and materials. The Chicago cable system is stated to have cost a similar figure, and even with this enormous expenditure it has proved to be a financial success. At the last annual meeting of the American Street Railway Association the following particulars were given concerning some expenditures, &c. connected with the twenty miles of cable tramways in Chicago, *i.e.* :

		dols.
Street construction, cost per mile	105,000
Cost of engine-house	50,000
,, machinery, engines, and boilers, &c. ...	150,000
Cable grips and attachments	75,000
Number of cars operated 260	
Horse-power required 500	
,, in reserve 1500	
Life of cables ... ... 6000 miles	

On this occasion similar information was given concerning the Cin-
cinnati-street Railroad Company, now operating a cable system of
three miles, *i.e.* :

		dols.
Street construction, cost per mile	30,000
Cost of engine-house	19,500
,, machinery, engines, and boilers, &c. ...	18,000
,, gripping appliances, &c.	8,600
Cars operated 20	
Horse-power required 73	

The cost of the Geary-street permanent way was only about 2*l.* per
foot run.

Upon examination we may find that in some cable lines in the
United States, compound wrought-iron tube frames (placed 3 ft. 6 in.
apart), and costing about 30s. each, have been adopted, whereas the
Highgate Hill (London) tube frames cost only 5s. each. Again,
the cable-driving apparatus in the United States cost, in some cases,
about 1000*l.* as against rather less than 200*l.* at Highgate, and so on
throughout many entire constructions. If the cable system is to make
successful progress in this country, engineers should, after studying
the practice of the past, carefully devise and pursue some original
and more economical methods of carrying the system into effect and
not follow indiscriminately that which has gone before. Originally in
America, as in this country, the cable system was handicapped with
exorbitant charges and claims for alleged patent rights, and which
unquestionably largely contributed to the apparently high cost of
construction.

At the last annual meeting of the American Street Railway Asso-
Note 43 ciation before referred to, Mr. G. B. Kerper, chairman of the Committee
on the " Progress of the Cable System of Motive Power in the United
States of America," communicated the following information and
opinions :

" To street railroad companies operating lines in small cities . . . .
the present cost of construction has placed the adoption of the system
out of the question." " The minds of engineers throughout the country
have been directed to the solution of this objectionable feature."

" The question of the right to construct a tunnel or tube with a slot to suitably operate a cable therein, with a grip either by dummy or direct attachment to a street car, is one that may be disputed but cannot be sustained. Such is the opinion of our prominent attorneys with whom we have consulted, substantiated by evidence sufficient to warrant this statement." No valid claim can be reasonably upheld for the system broadly whether in America or in this country, where the practice in all essential details and particulars has been copiously published and illustrated prior to the dates of any patents now in force.

Mr. Kerper further stated : " I should say that all companies carrying any excess of 5000 passengers per day, and operating lines with heavy gradients, will find it to their interest to make the change. We have found (referring to the Cincinnati cable roads), as in Chicago, that the greater facilities and rapid transit gained by the change have increased our traffic about 70 per cent."

It appears admitted, that about 50 per cent. of the average driving power exerted by the engines is commonly absorbed in setting the cables, pulleys, and dependent machinery in motion, but as the motive power is usually concentrated at one source, the loss is not so large or important as in the employment of locomotives, with which considerable loss is experienced by the frequent stoppages. Tramway locomotives may at times develop from about 25 to 35 horse-power, an amount which appears disproportionate to the performances of even animal power. In the uses of endless cable traction, as applied to mining industries, more economical results have been attained ; in such cases the cables are frequently driven at a lower speed, whilst the permanent ways used frequently present a lower tractive resistance. For example, at Newbattle Colliery, 68 per cent. of the engine power has been effectually utilised, but commonly the efficiency does not exceed 60 per cent. Similar good examples of endless cable haulage are to be seen at Cadzow and Clifton Collieries hereinbefore referred to, the plant being supplied by Messrs. Grant and Ritchie and Walker Brothers respectively.

When the first portion of the Chicago cable lines was opened, it has been published, that only about 45 per cent. of the engine power was utilised, and, again, that only $\frac{1}{5}$th horse-power was required for each ton of passengers, against 1 horse-power for each ton weight of machinery to be set in motion.

The wear and tear of the haulage cables are very important and expensive items in the operation of cable lines, the gripping appliances apparently producing a considerable proportion of the same. Good steel wire cables are the cheapest in the long run, a speciality to which Messrs. Bullivant and Co., of London, and Cradock and Co., of

Wakefield, have devoted much attention with considerable success. The quality and manufacture of the cables are of prime importance, and upon these the success of the system largely depends. Doubtless, the experience and inventive genius of the present age will give us the right cable the system demands. As before mentioned, the cables, if properly attended to, do not strand or break, and thus cause dangers and delays in the operation of the system. A type of rope should be used that will splice neatly, in order to work smoothly through the grippers, &c. The average lives of good cables, if properly treated, should certainly attain twelve months—if not longer—but this will necessarily vary according to the conditions of the line to be operated. In the concluding chapter, the question of the manufacture, &c., and further uses of cables will be considered at greater length.

Driving drums, pulleys, and apparatus, by which the cables are set in action, are also worthy of some consideration. In America the usual methods of driving by clip pulleys, or by numerous half-turns round grooved pulleys, appear, in some cases, open to improvement. The less the cables are bent or subjected to compressive strains the better, but in some cases more than one half-turn upon a drum is necessary in order to obtain the requisite adhesion to overcome the resistance of the cables and cars connected thereto. Upon some short lines with comparatively easy gradients, drums or pulleys constructed to drive cables with only 180 deg. of contact may be found advantageous. Such a type of driving apparatus has been adopted upon the Highgate Hill line and has given satisfaction. This drum or pulley was supplied by Messrs. Grant and Ritchie, the hauling power being tested to 7 tons resistance; a larger pulley can be constructed to haul 15 tons without slipping. This type of apparatus has been used in mines for some years past with success. There are numerous other types of driving appliances worthy of some attention, *e.g.*, Walker's, Fowler's, Barraclough's, Wilders', &c., pulleys. The first cost of these appliances are all moderate.

The type of clip pulley used at Highgate appears to possess the following combined advantages :—it is cheap, simple, and of reliable construction ; it occupies little space ; admits of an entire system being worked from one set of engines and shafting ; reduces the bending stresses on the cables ; admits of the employment of lighter tension weights upon the terminal carriages, and consequently a lower grade of tension on the cable.

Differences of opinion will always exist amongst engineers as to the best means of driving (as well as other details) to be adopted, and varying conditions likewise prevent any particular method being universally advocated. Hauling appliances, that succeed well in the mining industries, may in some cases be quite unsuitable for cable tramway purposes, on account, perhaps, of inflicting excessive wear upon the cables when driven at a higher speed, or from not affording sufficiently high tractive adhesion to haul comparatively heavy loads, &c. Again, such drums or pulleys should accomplish their efficiency within limited dimensions, otherwise high peripheral velocities may necessitate the employment of objectionable intermediate gearing, &c.

In some cases, systems of driving the cables by "lacing" and "reduplication," have been pronounced injurious to both the cables and drums, whilst in others the simple V-type pulley as above referred to, has been considered by some to objectionably bite and crush the former. However, so far as the latter system is concerned, we have evidence from mining haulage records, that it has done good service where suitably applied. For example, at the summer meeting of the Mining Institution of Scotland, of 1885, Mr. D. Ferguson, of the Cadzow Colliery, stated that he had found from practical experience with the employment of such V-type of hauling pulleys, that : "The arrangement is compact and simple, whilst its efficiency cannot be denied. . . . . We shall endeavour to show, that the insuperable obstacle and objection to some, from a wedging action of the ropes in the pulleys, may be dismissed, and are entirely without foundation in practice. There is no record, so far as we have been able to investigate, of a failure of a rope through injury done to it by a clip pulley worked in the same manner as those at Cadzow." This gentleman then went on to cite practical examples in which cables have been driven by these pulleys, for from $3\frac{1}{2}$ to $4\frac{1}{2}$ years in continual service, without injury, and after running 18,500 to 25,550 miles, and drawing 174,926 to 226,990 tons of coal. Thus cases were mentioned, in which cables had done useful work without excessive wear over distances exceeding the circumference of the world. However, on the other hand, it should not be lost sight of that these cables were driven at about half the speed of a cable tramway. The speed of endless colliery hauling cables is commonly about 4 ft. per second, whilst on cable tramways it is about 9 ft. to 10 ft. per second, and in cases of transmission of power by cables, about 70 ft. to 80 ft. per second.

Whatever system of driving be adopted, high speeds must prove comparatively injurious to the lives of the cables. Cables of extremely high tensile resistances appear unadvisable, as such degrees of strength must be attained at some sacrifice of toughness and elasticity. Any continual sharp bending of the cables must prove to some degree injurious, but there appears no data in support of making the diameters of pulleys around which cables have to pass, more than 100 times the diameter of the latter.

Referring to the cable-gripping appliances, practice seems to mainly advocate the employment of the L form or type, but there appears little if any data in support of the advisability of using small grip pulleys, which must occasionally run at very high velocities, and thus tend to wear themselves or the cables out. The grip shanks should be calculated to withstand maximum lateral and torsional strains, exerted at curved portions of any line, and which are proportional to the deflection of the cable or the distances of the pulleys apart. Such strains can be readily ascertained by setting out a diagram of the parallelogram of forces, and in which the diagonal resultant thereof represents the magnitude and direction of the same. In practice the versed sine of the arc of deflection is seldom arranged so as to exceed $1\frac{1}{2}$ in.

Respecting engines which appear to be suitable for operating systems of cable haulage, horizontal types, having comparatively long strokes and fitted with reasonably sensitive valve gear, seem to be well adapted, a speciality to which Messrs. Grafton and Co., of Bedford, have devoted successful attention. In some such systems of traction, compound-condensing engines may be employed to advantage, especially where water can be obtained free of cost or at a small charge. The close observance of the economical employment of steam power, as applied to the operation of the system at issue, cannot be too highly recommended. Comparatively high-working steam pressures will be generally found conducive to satisfactory and economical results. In estimating the requisite power of engines to be applied to any system, the following points must be carefully considered and computed, *i.e.*, the loads or resistance upon the cables due to the maximum load of cars to be hauled upon the lines—which will present variable tractive resistances in cases of fluctuating gradients : the dissipation of power, from friction of the cables, pulleys, and machinery—a variable resistance dependent upon the conditions and arrangements of a system ; frictional resistance due to the degree of tension under which the cables are to be driven, caused by the terminal tension, appliances, &c. Having determined the maximum tractive resistance of a system in question, the approximate power required is ascertainable, *e.g.*, by the product in foot-pounds (or work to be done at a given speed), having a desired piston velocity as a divisor, in order to compute the capacity or diameter of the cylinder, D, in inches for a given working pressure ; then the piston speed in feet per minute divided by twice the number of required revolutions equals the stroke S of engines in feet. Thus,

$$\frac{D^2 \sqrt[3]{S}}{15.6} = \text{nominal horse-power, for high pressure engines.}$$

Due allowance should then be made for friction in the engine itself.

The variable frictional resistance to traction upon gradients, as above referred to, may be computed as follows : Let,

a = angle of gradient or inclination of line.

ϕ =   „   friction.

p = power required to move a load up the grade.

w = weight of load.   Thus,

$$p = w\,\frac{\sin\,(a + \phi)}{\cos\,\phi} = w\,(\sin\,a + \tan\,\phi\,\cos\,a) =$$

$$w\,\left(\frac{\mathrm{B\,C}}{\mathrm{A\,B}} + \tan\,\phi\,\frac{\mathrm{A\,C}}{\mathrm{A\,B}}\right)$$

The section of a road, being assumed as a triangle, in which A is the starting point of grade or angle of inclination a; B, acute angle formed at the top or opposite end of the hypothenuse, and C, the right angle, formed at the base and vertical side thereof.   In practice, however, when the angle of friction is small $\dfrac{\mathrm{A\,C}}{\mathrm{A\,B}}$ = is nearly unity.

Readverting to the question of the permanent-ways of cable tramways—cast-iron tube frames, such as described upon the Clay-street, Geary-street, and Highgate lines, &c., may be frequently employed with the requisite efficiency and economy desired.   The elastic and fibrous nature of wrought-iron frames may make their employment appear advisable, but the cost is frequently against their adoption, besides the difficulty which is encountered in constructing a large number of duplicate compound wrought structures of exactly similar proportions, sizes, and clearances, &c.   Mechanically, the Chicago type of frame appears amongst the most unscientific designs, whether for cost or strength for a given amount of metal.   Concrete used in combination with such frames for forming a cable tube, constitutes a suitable and durable construction, but designs and materials to be adopted should be varied according to circumstances and places.   Fixing the pulley bearings in the concrete walls is not a satisfactory arrangement.   The foundations of these structures should be well studied, as any subsequent "settling" may cause much trouble and expense.   The designs and nature of such constructions should be modified to suit local conditions and the weights of street traffic to be withstood.   In fact, to do justice to the system, considerable care and experience is required in designing a line, and much room exists for injudicious and unnecessary expenditure of capital.

We will now investigate the approximate cost of working a suitable tramway according to the "cable system of traction."   Continuing the basis of a three-mile line, we will assume that it is so located as to support about a five minutes service of cars, or say, that fifteen cars are provided for actual service and that each performs about seventy car miles per working day of say about sixteen hours, and thus giving about 400,000 aggregate car miles, run in the course of a year.   The necessary expenses for working such traffic and maintaining the system should be about as follows :

	Per Annum.
	£
General superintendent	300
Engine driver and mechanical superintendent ...	150
Timekeeper or inspector	120
Cable splicer and assistant	104
3 boiler or firemen at 30s. per week ... ⎫	
2 mechanics at 35s. per week ... ... ⎪	
2 road boys at 10s. ,, ... ⎬	520
1 labourer at 20s. per week ... ... ⎭	
2 clerks (office) at 30s. per week	156
15 car drivers at 40s. ,, ...	1560
15 ,, conductors at 22s. ,, ...	860
Labour account	3770
Coals or fuel (say, 4 tons per day at 16s.), say ...	1180
Cable maintenance and renewals (average life assumed, one year)	900
Maintenance of engines, boilers, and machinery, &c., at 8 per cent.	500
Sundry repairing materials	100
Oil and tar, &c.	250
Water	90
Gas	30
Rates and taxes, &c.	350
Depreciation in buildings and way, &c.	1000
Total per annum	8170

Equivalent to about 4.9d. per car mile.

The above estimate is rather a liberal approximation, as an average cost of working. The rope account should be less, and in some parts the fuel cheaper, than above allowed for. The various items are deductions from practice. From the foregoing basis of 400,000 car miles run in twelve months, the inclusive working expenses according to the system in question should be about 5d. per car mile. The mileage assumed per car, is not excessive, when the facilities of the system for running a quick service are taken into consideration.

The approximate cost of establishing such an installation has been previously given as nearly 50,000*l*., but we will assume (from sundry extraneous expenses referred to) that the total capital account attains 60,000*l*., or 20,000*l*. per mile of double track. Then it follows, with reference to the working expenses above set forth, that if the gross traffic receipts per car mile amounted to only 10d. (whereas such receipts average about 1s. throughout the tramways of the kingdom), the 50 per cent. nett profit would be sufficient to pay about 14 per cent. upon the capital per annum. This is a very reasonable example, as the receipts assumed are low and the working expenses equitable. Some of our tramways earn 15d. to 18d. per car mile, whilst the Highgate Hill cable tramway has frequently earned from 2s. to 3s. per car mile.

Now it will be appreciated that if the above assumed system were extended to five miles, or that the traffic would allow about twenty cars being profitably run upon the same, then the car mileage could be raised to, say, 600,000 miles per annum, whilst the working expenses would conversely fall to about 4d. or 4½d. per car mile. In this manner it has been practically demonstrated, that it is quite feasible, under very favourable circumstances, to reduce the working expenses to 3d. or 3½d. per car mile. The main requirement is to have a line of reasonable length, and so located as to be able to support a frequent service of cars.

The merits of the system in question should be now recognised, and especially so, when we reflect that by working tramways by animal traction about 77 per cent. of the gross earnings are consumed in working expenses, out of which about 42 per cent. is absorbed for the animal power.

CHAPTER VII.

FINANCIAL AND OTHER CONSIDERATIONS OF TRAMWAY WORKING, &c.

It is now proposed to briefly refer to some recent publications in which the economy and utility of the cable system of traction has been called into question, and which have given rise to instructive discussions and opinions.

Mr. W. Morris (M.I.C.E.) appears to have first called the attention of the members of the Institution of Civil Engineers to the importance of the system at issue, in a paper, No. 1913, vol. lxxii., of the Minutes of the Proceedings of this Institution, relating to cable traction then being developed in the United States. The author therein states, that after visiting the San Francisco cable lines and carefully considering the subject, he considered that tramways could be worked by this system for 45 per cent. of the gross receipts, and consequently that many of our tramways could, by its adoption, realise something like 25 per cent. upon their share capital. He then mentioned that even our North Staffordshire tramways, worked by locomotives, consume about 65 per cent. of the gross revenue, and subsequently estimated the cost of working by the cable system at about 4.5d. per car mile, thus effecting (in many cases) a saving of about 50 per cent. over horse traction, and 25 per cent. over locomotives. Mr. Morris also expressed his opinion that the complete cost of construction could be reduced to about 9000*l*. per mile of single track, and further that in most cases the employment of so-called "dummy cars" was unnecessary, if not unadvisable. This gentleman's views have already been substantially corroborated by subsequent practice.

In the annual report of the American Street Railway Association of 1884, Mr. Holmes (of the Chicago tramways) is represented as stating, that after considerable practical experience with both horse and cable traction, his company find that working by the latter system costs about one-half as compared with the former. In the same report the following statement by the Honourable Drury Melone (formerly Secretary of State for California) is published. "We have a cable road running parallel with us (horse line) for four miles; they started it a year ago. It is now taking from 75 dols. to 100 dols. a day of our profits. We must quit horses and hitch on the cable; we have waited for electricity to be developed to help us out of this dilemma, but it has not yet come," &c.

In December, 1884, the Honourable R. C. Parsons, B.A., M.I.C.E., &c., read a paper upon "The Working of Tramways by Steam" before the Institution of Civil Engineers, and discussions upon the subject brought forth some interesting statements and opinions of various competent men respecting the practical utility, &c., of the Cable system, &c.—*vide* vol. lxxix. Minutes of the Proceedings of the Institution of Civil Engineers. During the discussion, Mr. Joseph Kincaid (M.I.C.E.) stated : "As to the cable system, of which he had some practical knowledge. . . . . he thought it could be economically used in many places where the locomotive was not suitable. Not one of the systems, however, was of universal application. The cable system could not be economically successful if there was only a very small amount of traffic, and on the other hand, steam locomotives would not be of service in the case of severe gradients," &c. Mr. Morris then referred to his previous communication to the Institution, after his tour through America in 1882, and concluded by stating : "He was much impressed with the way in which the cable system overcame such very steep gradients as 1 in 6, &c., and also the success which attended the brakes adopted to guard against accidents. By the cable system, as compared with working by steam locomotives (on a line as exemplified by Mr. Parsons), there could be a saving of sixty men, which at 4s. per day, would amount to about 4380*l.* per annum. A saving in the cost of fuel, repairs, and stores, would be about 1½d. per car mile as against 3.28d., giving a further saving of 3250*l.* There was another saving, on account of depreciation, which he had taken at ¾d. per car mile, and which would amount to about 1625*l.*; the total of the three items came to 9255*l.*, to which must be added the 6500*l.* placed to dividends by Mr. Parsons, thus giving a total net revenue of 15,756*l.* The result of the increased revenue being 9¾ per cent. dividend as against 6.6 per cent., or an increase of 50 per cent., in favour of the cable system of working, notwithstanding its extra first cost." In making these calculations Mr. Morris allowed 10,000*l.* per mile of single track, as the average cost of constructing and equipping a cable tramway. On the same occasion, Mr. N. Scott-Russell remarked, "The 'rope' or cable had been worked with great success in America and very well in this country ;" . . . . . For steep gradients, "he thought there could be no doubt that it was the best, and, in fact, the only means of locomotion." Mr. H. G. Harris said, "He himself was interested in another mechanical system, (viz., compressed air motors), but he did not think that this system, or steam, or anything else, would compare with the cable system for working over gradients like those of 1 in 15," &c. This gentleman then mentioned that the cost of sand for preventing cars slipping upon gradients was sometimes very heavy, *e.g.*, " On one line in London, where the steepest gradient is 1 in 25, it happened during one week last winter, that the cost of sand for a single car amounted to two guineas; six loads being used at 7s." Such expense is saved by the cable system of traction.

Mr. Norman Selfe considered that San Francisco had probably about the best tramway system in the world, *i.e.*, with regard to their entire system of cable, locomotive, and horse lines. " For connecting together important points within a city itself, through crowded streets, between lofty buildings, and where service was desirable every two to five minutes, large cars attached to locomotives would be a great hindrance to general traffic, and also there might be reasonable objections by passengers and residents to having the atmosphere further polluted by the products of combustion and steam. Admitting it to be true that even 50 per cent. of the (stationary) engine power provided was employed to move the cables alone, and that the wear and tear was heavy, still these lines were so successful that they were being copied in other cities, and as they fulfilled the conditions of being clean and noiseless, with the advantages of running a frequent service with single cars or short trains, and offered the minimum obstruction to ordinary street traffic, no real comparison could be made between the cable system and locomotives for city use."

In the *Birmingham Daily Mail* of June 22 last, may be read that Mr. E. Pritchard had returned from a tour through the United States of America, where he had been investigating the merits of the cable system with a view to its application to the streets of Birmingham, and it may be gathered he is well satisfied with its practical utility. The *Mail* stated that " Mr. Pritchard went out to the States somewhat prejudiced against the system, but he has returned thoroughly convinced, not only that cable trams are perfectly feasible, but that they are (all things considered) the most economical and desirable form of street locomotion yet put into practice."

The Hon. E. Coombes, C.E., one of the accredited representatives of the recent Colonial Exhibition, whilst speaking after a luncheon given at Messrs. Bullivant and Co.'s works, on the occasion of completing the cable for the Richmond line, Australia, stated, " he believed that the cable system of traction for tramways was the system of the future, alike for economy and efficiency, and that he had studied the system in America before its adoption in the Colonies, and that he spoke upon the subject as an engineer and not as an 'outsider,'" &c.

In a previous chapter, attention was directed to cases in which the system was fully supported by Sir Frederick Bramwell and Sir John Fowler, past-presidents of the Institution of Civil Engineers, as also by Mr. Greathead and Mr. B. Baker, members of the Institution of Civil Engineers, &c.

The foregoing statements and opinions concerning the system at issue appear very satisfactory, and especially so when it is remembered that the authors are competent and impartial men, *i.e.*, not strictly interested in cable tramway enterprises, but as a matter of fact, if anything, more generally associated with applications of locomotives or compressed air, &c.

In the *Melbourne Age* of the 13th of January, 1887, we may read the following : " The working of the Richmond and Collins streets cable tramways is generally regarded as valuable proof that the cable system is the best that could possibly have been adopted for the requirements of Melbourne and its suburbs. So far the running of the cable cars has resulted very satisfactorily. . . . At the present date there are ten miles of double line in running order, serving a population of something like 80,000 persons. The next line to be opened, is that which runs up Bourke-street, Nicholson-street, Gertrude-street and Smith-street. Simultaneously will also be opened, one running along Nicholson-street for serving North Carlton and Fitzroy. . . . St. Hilda, Yarra, Prahran, and Toorak, have given their voice in favour of the cable, and accordingly plans and specifications are being prepared. . . . The cable as a tractional power has proved applicable to all localities, and is the system which is being everywhere adopted," &c. . . .

The axiom, however, that no known system of tramway traction is capable of universal successful application should be carefully observed, for much harm is not unfrequently inflicted by those who advocate a general application of any one system in which they may be particularly interested. Such broad advocation or statements were pithily hinted at by a Mr. Johnson, of Cleveland, at a recent meeting of the American Street Railway Association, U.S.A., when he stated with reference to the question of modern tramway traction : " We are told by some that the cable system is the proper one to use, but to others we know it acts like a red flag to a bull. We are told, that there is great economy in it, that they can run the engines with the sweepings of the stables and floors, &c. ; whilst we were told by others that it is a fallacy, that it takes a thousand horses to make manure enough to keep the engines going," &c.

Note 44

Adverting to opinions in the United States, respecting the comparative efficiency of electric motors and the cable system, we may read in the last annual report of the American Tramways Association a statement by Mr. Cyrus Field as follows : " If you ask me, if cars can be run by electricity, I will answer 'yes, without doubt.' . . . but if you ask me whether they can be run as cheaply as by horses I will say ' no, without question of doubt.' Amongst objections to electricity,

Note 45

there is one, that with slippery rails you lose power; with the cable system, a slippery condition does not affect the power. In the cable system the power is separate and independent of the track. The objections made to starting and stopping cars run by electricity, are overcome in the cable system."

According to the researches of the Tramway Investigating Committee of Birmingham, who advised the borough authorities as to the best method of tramway traction to be employed, we may likewise gather their conclusions to be, that both compressed air and electricity can only at present be regarded as experimental applications. This Committee devoted attention to such electrical systems as installed at Brighton, Portrush, Blackpool, Newry, and Berlin, &c., but they were not satisfied as to their practicability, but considered them "generally, unsuitable for street purposes." According to some of these systems, considerable structural alterations have to be made in the ordinary permanent ways, &c. According to other systems, electrical accumulators or batteries are carried upon the cars, thus considerably increasing their weight with doubtful efficiency.

As little, if anything, appears practically known about the employment of gas motors and so-called fireless engines, &c., for tramway purposes, we may pass them over without comment.

The employment of compressed air appears to be in the same elementary stage as electricity. In the case of high-pressure air motors it appears that only about 23 per cent. of their absorbed power is commonly utilised.

From careful experiments carried out by leading engineers, it has been comparatively recently recorded, that in cases where compressing engines have indicated about 70 horse-power in charging locomotive reservoirs, the actual effective duty of the latter realised, has been only about 14 horse-power, thus showing a dissipation of 80 per cent. of the original power.

It is obviously a great disadvantage to such systems to have to derive their power second handed, whereas in steam locomotives the power required is generated and utilised in one machine at the same time. Another weak point is, when compressed air motors break down from any leakage of the reservoirs, &c., they must be drawn helplessly back to their charging stations to be repaired or re-enforced.

Returning to the cable system, we know that it has been practically worked with both mechanical and financial success for the past thirteen years, and that about 100 miles of line are in daily operation in the United States and our colonies, &c. About 20 more miles are now to be built in the States, 15 miles in Great Britain, and 30 miles in Australia, &c. The cost of construction and equipment can now be reduced to nearly that of a first-class horse tramway, such as laid and equipped within our metropolis, whilst the cost of working by the system at issue is only about one-half that of the latter. The comparative average costs of working tramways by horses, locomotives, and cables under suitable conditions appear to be about the following :

Cable traction	4d. to 5d. per car mile	
Locomotive traction	7d. to 8d.	,,
Horse or animal traction ...	9d. to 11d.	,,

We will now pause to consider the chief points or features that may be reasonably alleged in favour or support of the cable system of traction.

1. General efficiency and economical working.

2. The steepest gradients may be easily and economically surmounted.

3. Heavy or a fluctuating traffic can be dealt with promptly, efficiently, and economically.

4. Safety and convenience, greater than offered by locomotive traction and equal to animal traction, are secured, whilst a more uniform speed and service can be attained at less cost.

5. Cheaper administration and more punctual service of cars at any required intervals.

6. Practical noiselessness and freedom from evolution of products of combustion, gases, steam or sparks, and dirt, &c.

7. The tractive efficiency of the system is independent of the weights of rolling stock.

8. The power exerted by cars upon descending gradients is in a measure utilised for assisting the ascending cars, instead of being dissipated.

9. The stationary motive power is arranged so as to be automatically varied to meet the fluctuating working requirements of a traffic to be served.

10. A car service may be permanently or periodically increased with small additional cost, and in some cases the increased consumption of fuel is almost inappreciable.

11. The cars can be started, stopped, or controlled with efficiency and promptitude.

12. The system can be worked in (practically) any climate.

Note 46

13. The wear and tear of the permanent way is less than in cases of horse or locomotive traction.

14. The thoroughfares are not dirtied nor the air polluted.

15. Veterinary, stable, shoeing and harnessing expenditures, &c., are avoided.

16. Fewer cars are required to serve a given traffic on account of greater speed and carrying capacity.

17. Slippery condition of rails is no impediment to tractive efficiency.

18. The cruelty and inefficiency of animal traction is avoided.

Amongst the foregoing clauses, 1 to 10 inclusive, 13, 14, 16, and 17 are more or less peculiar to the system in question, the remainder are comparative. Some of the clauses might be satisfactorily met by compressed air or electric motors, when in a sufficient advanced stage of practice.

On the other hand, any alleged objections or defects in the system appear to be :—

1. The heavier cost of construction and equipment.

2. More ironwork is introduced upon the surface of the streets; occasional interferences with gas, water, and sewage services.

3. Any breakdown of the principal machinery or cables causes a temporary stoppage of the entire system.

It appears, however, that in most cases these objections would be more than counterbalanced by the advantages of the system. The third allegation appears of no great importance, as breakdowns should be of very rare occurrence if the system be reasonably well designed, constructed, worked, and attended to.

It has been before mentioned, that no known system of tramway traction can be universally applied with uniform success, but that all cases require knowledge and discrimination to guide their useful or judicious application. We will, therefore, now consider the general conditions which appear more or less necessary for a successful mechanical and financial application of the cable system of traction to tramway purposes, and which appear to be :—

1. Approximately straight lines or streets throughout.

2. Double lines throughout.

3. A district or locality capable of developing sufficient traffic to support a comparatively frequent service of cars.

Severe curvatures of line or single lines with passing places, should be avoided as much as possible. The sites for the engine-houses should be located upon level ground, or in valleys, and preferably at one terminus, in cases where the length of a system is not excessive. The termini should be located on level ground or on slight falling gradients.

Working round sharp curves on a main cable driven at a comparatively high speed, cannot be considered a safe practice, independent of the question of wear and tear; in cases, however, where auxiliary cables can be introduced and operated at a lower speed, this objection may be more or less overcome.

Authentic information received from the United States, shows that notwithstanding the past high cost of construction and equipment, average dividends of about 15 per cent. per annum have been realised upon such expenditures. The Mayor of San Francisco, U.S.A., in a recent communication to the Mayor of Birmingham, states with reference to the cable lines in this city : " These roads pay dividends from 8 to 24 per cent. per annum. The Market Street Cable Railroad Company, issued bonds for 3,000,000 dols. bearing interest at the rate of 6 per cent. per annum. They are now selling at 12 per cent. premium ; after paying interest on these bonds, there is left a handsome dividend," &c.

In Chicago about the same amount of money has been spent upon cable roads, as in the example last mentioned, and we may gather from the official stock exchange quotations, that the original stock since stands at from 285 dols. to 300 dols. Further we learn from the president of these lines that " The increase in the value of the real estate along the streets where the system operates, and on parallel and cross streets (for several blocks each way) is many times the cost of its construction, being from 50 to 200 per cent. in a single year." Recent information supplied from the New Zealand cable tramways tends to show that cable traction can be worked at about $3\frac{1}{2}$d. per car mile as against 9d. and 12d. by horses.

The question may be reasonably raised as to whether there are not some peculiar conditions common to the States which render the application of this system so advantageous ? In a measure the answer appears in the affirmative ; the breadth and straightness of the streets common to the cities of the United States are unquestionably highly favourable to the successful mechanical application of the system, but sufficiently similar or suitable conditions can be found to exist in many (if not most) leading cities throughout the world, to recommend its judicious adoption. Again it has been previously pointed out that the tramway travelling community in the States is exceptionally large, and as especially exemplified by the number of passengers carried by the Market-street cable line (San Francisco) and the Chicago cable lines, which have attained a traffic of 60,000 and 100,000 persons per day respectively. Two to five minutes' services of cars commonly find good support in the big cities of the States, and, as before mentioned, the proportion of the population that travel daily on these tramways has in some parts exceeded 25 per cent.

In this country some of our streets are very narrow, irregular, and tortuous ; further, in cases of contemplated conversions of ordinary tramways to the cable system, the effect of the increased capital cost (already high) should be carefully considered.

Reverting to the cable and locomotive methods of working tramways, the former has unquestionably an economical advantage over the latter as an application of steam power. Take an example of a tramway locomotive, say hauling a 40-passenger car at a speed of about seven miles per hour, with a consumption of about 50 lbs. of fuel per hour, whereas an economical arrangement of stationary hauling engines, *e.g.* —as required in the first system—could be provided to develop similar power for about one-third the consumption of fuel. Assume the consumption of the tramway engine in question to be about 8 lbs. per horse-power per hour, then stationary expansion engines—compound or condensing—could be worked for from about $2\frac{1}{2}$ lbs. to 4 lbs. per horse-power per hour. The weight of tramway locomotives may be from, say, 6 to 9 tons each, and therefore a strong permanent way is required for their satisfactory employment. There are, however, undoubtedly several types of serviceable tramway locomotives now in the market, *e.g.*, Scott Russell's, Kitson's, Merryweather's, &c., engines, and which are being used to advantage under suitable conditions.

The Board of Trade regulations respecting the employment of steam locomotives for tramway purposes are still severe, although ameliorated since 1883. Amongst the present rules is one of a more or less uncertain character, viz. :—" The Board of Trade and their officers may from time to time, and shall on the application of local authorities of any of the districts through which the said tramways pass, inspect such engines, &c. . . . . and may, whenever they think fit, prohibit the use of any of them, which in their opinion are not safe for use." In some instances, therefore, local authorities, &c., only permit a trial of locomotives on, say, a three months' lease, thus leaving an uncertainty as to whether the lease will be renewed. Such restrictions are not, however, extended to the use of the cable system of traction, and thus its application may be regarded as a permanent and not limited or conditional character, as in the former example.

That horse or animal power for tramway traction purposes will ultimately be superseded by some form of mechanical power appears evident, but as to what system should be adopted much difference of opinion will always exist. That no mechanical system of haulage or propulsion yet known, will judiciously bear universal application, seems generally admitted, but it certainly appears reasonable to admit that cable traction has a large scope for its successful employment. Animal power has been long recognised by engineers to be unsuitable for efficiently and profitably working tramways, and in the preface of Mr. Kinnear Clark's well-known book on " Tramways" we may read : " Tramways will not take their fitting place in the systems of transport of the kingdom until mechanical power is established in substitution for animal power."

The tramway systems of the United Kingdom are now no bagatelle, having involved an expenditure of over $12\frac{1}{2}$ millions sterling, and costing per mile about half as much as our railways with a greater earning capacity, and yet upon examination we find their working expenses much heavier. Although our horse tramways earn gross receipts equivalent to about an average of 20 per cent. upon the capital, yet the working and maintaining expenses are so exorbitantly high, that about 77 per cent. of such receipts are consumed before a net profit can be realised. The earning capacity of tramways is something extra-ordinary, but animal power is quite incapable of developing and serving anything like a maximum traffic. It will now be interesting and instructive to take a glance at some recent statistics, relating to the operation of our and other countries' tramway systems.

According to the Tramway Returns, ordered by the House of Commons, to be printed for the year ending June, 1886, we may learn :— The total authorised capital for tramways in the United Kingdom up to this date was 17,640,488*l.*, whilst the total capital expended attained 12,573,041*l.* The length of lines opened for public traffic was 865 miles ; the number of horses belonging to the various companies, 24,535 ; the total number of passengers carried during the year was 384,157,524 ; and the gross receipts derived from the twelve months' working, 2,630,338*l.* ; whilst the nett revenue was only 608,782*l.* These returns show, that there are about eight horses for each car, or about twenty-nine horses per mile of tramway—including the locomotive lines. The nett receipts available for dividends upon the above expended capital averages scarcely 5 per cent. per annum, whilst the average working expenses have been about 77 per cent. of the gross revenue. On some individual systems in which gradients are prevalent, the working expenses are still higher, *e.g.,* the Bristol tramways consume about 80 per cent. of their revenue ; Nottingham tramways, similarly, about 85 per cent., &c. The tramways of our kingdom carry daily about 3 per cent. of the entire gross population, whilst our metropolitan tramways convey daily over 8 per cent. of the population of London, notwithstand-ing the competition of railways, omnibuses, cabs, &c. The above facts graphically illustrate the good service done by tramways and at cheap fares—the average being less than 1¾d. per passenger carried. The capital expended per mile of line opened is about 14,500*l.* In some parts and countries the daily percentages of populations conveyed by tramways are largely above the examples already cited. For example, in Edin-burgh, an average of over 12 per cent. has been carried daily. Similarly, in Berlin, about 20 per cent.; in Bordeaux about 20 per cent.; in Buenos Ayres about 10 per cent. ; in Lisbon about 10 per cent., &c.

As some may consider that an average capital cost of about 14,000*l.* per mile, for an ordinary tramway is very heavy, it may be mentioned that many foreign tramways have cost as much and some more, whilst such constructions and equipments are mostly inferior. A marked example of this lavish—if not to say unjustifiable—expenditure, is given in the Constantinople tramways, where the capital cost has exceeded 30,000*l.* per mile, for one of the most primitive forms of construction and equipment.

Returning to the main considerations of this treatise, it may be reasonably inquired, whether cable traction as at present advocated, and applied to the working of street tramways, is not capable of being improved? A rational reply to any such questions appears to be, that it is probable that real improvements in details will be made and by which the cost of construction may be reduced, and even the general efficiency of the system still enhanced. On the other hand, it should be observed that numerous alleged improvements have from time to time been brought out, the bulk of which, however, appear so trivial, impractical, or old, that many are rather to be carefully avoided than observed. Amongst those which have engrossed some attention may be mentioned, a duplex system, in which two tunnels are to be provided to receive the tram-rails, and in which a pair of cables is also arranged to simultaneously operate. The wheels of the cars are to travel in these subways, being connected with the bodies of the cars by means of plates or shanks. The cars are to be propelled by means of double grippers, mounted between the wheels, so that they may simultaneously grip or release the two running haulage cables. The advantage presumed to be in view is not, however, clear, whilst the cost of such a construction would be very heavy.

Other devices have claimed attention, in which the gripper slot has been proposed to be arranged in the rails and the haulage cable beneath the same, so as to draw the car from the one side instead of centrally, as at present in practice. Such a construction would evidently reduce the amount of ironwork exposed upon the street surfaces, by dispensing with the central slot beams, but it appears that nobody has cared to try the experiment of building such a line, not knowing what the tractive results might be. A similar system of haulage has been tried in colliery practice without apparently satisfactory issues, as it was demonstrated that the lateral friction and wear upon the rails and wheels was considerably increased, such resistance being augmented in proportion to the tangent of the angle formed by the coupling or grip with the haulage cable. In this manner it was discovered that the tractive efficiency was impaired, whilst the wear of the rolling stock was increased.

Any system which tends to reduce the tractive efficiency of tramways is bad, as such resistance is already high, *e.g.*, to maintain the running of cars on a level road it may be from about 20 lbs. to 30 lbs. per car ton, whilst upon railways it is only about half this amount.

According to another method, it has been proposed to dispense with fixed cable supporting pulleys and mount the rope upon small trucks or trollies arranged to travel on rails provided within the slotted street tube. This device emanated from the desire to avoid inspection manholes in the streets, but the solution in question appears impracticable.

Assuming the linear velocity of a haulage cable to be six miles per hour, it appears that the truck wheels would have to make something like 300 revolutions per minute, and allowing, say, some 650 of such cable supporting trucks to the mile, the wear and tear, independently of the noise, may be appreciated. Further, the sectional area of the cable tubes should be as small as consistently possible, in order to obtain the requisite strength at as low a cost as possible.

There are also some comparatively recent specifications which may be consulted, wherein alleged novelties and claims are stated for matter known to those initiated in the subject, to consist largely in worthless, or evasive imitations, and in some cases incorporating actual reproductions or importations of American designs and details, which have been previously described in this country. It may be remembered by some, that such American practices have been copiously described in ENGINEERING at various periods from 1875 to the present date, and further, there are a number of U.S.A. patent specifications on the subject published quarterly at the public library of our Patent Office, a large proportion of which are not patented in this country.

Such practices can scarcely improve the system in question, nor enhance its popularity.

On the other hand, room may exist for studied and *bonâ fide* inventions or improvements which have for their object to provide more efficient, simple, and cheap constructions than those used or known.

Gripping appliances and subsidiary mechanical contrivances are already numerous, and can be almost indefinitely varied or modified, and which after all are only of minor importance, as they form but small items in the total cost. The principal requirement appears to be, some cheaper arrangement of permanent way and devices relating thereto.

A large amount of practical and valuable information may be found in colliery or mining haulage practices and records, but which too commonly appear ignored or unrecognised by engineers connected with the system.

By diligent study and observance of past practices better results may be reasonably expected with this comparatively new application of cable or rope traction. The manufacture of wire ropes is now better understood and greatly improved, so that their durability is consequently increased. Examples have already been given of applications of wire ropes to various purposes, and which under very trying conditions and circumstances have lasted for several years in reliable working order. In the concluding chapter of this treatise further particulars are given concerning the manufacture and employment of wire ropes.

In closing our inquiries and deliberations respecting the application of cable or rope traction to street railroad purposes, it is hoped that from the information herein given and investigations pursued, sufficient valid grounds have been established to justify giving the "system" fair and serious consideration as a practical and comparatively economical method of public locomotion. "Tramways" are now a widely sanctioned and approved means of public transport throughout the entire civilised world, and are further recognised as substantial factors of social and hygienic progress, therefore any new, improved, or rational methods for more efficiently or economically working the same appear entitled to claim some attention, if only of a technical nature.

CHAPTER VIII.

THE MANUFACTURE OF WIRE AND WIRE ROPES AND THEIR APPLICATIONS.

CONSIDERABLE progress has been made of late years in the manufacture of wire ropes, although but little practical information has been published upon this industry. Records concerning the manufacture may be found extending back over a period of more than half a century, but they are of a more or less meagre character.

In 1862, a paper upon wire ropemaking was read before the Institution of Mechanical Engineers by C. Shelley, and subsequently wire rope manufacturers were invited to contribute information relating to the subject ; nearly a quarter of a century has, however, passed away without this invitation being responded to in anything like a substantial manner.

Note 47

The manufacture and use of wire ropes appear to have originated in Germany, and were first practically introduced into England about the time of the construction of the old Blackwall rope railway, *i.e.*, about 1838.

In about 1824 wire supporting ropes were employed in connection with the Geneva and Freiburg suspension bridges, but these consisted of wires laid parallel to each other and externally bound together by fine wire "serving," and known as "selvagee" ropes. This is the strongest form of rope that can be made, and, some may be aware, is the type adopted for the suspension ropes of the great New York and Brooklyn Bridge, opened in May, 1883.

"Formed or stranded" wire ropes were not introduced until some time afterwards, and were first manufactured on "rope-walks" and then on hemp rope machines, with which the name of Cartwright was associated as an original inventor at the close of last century, and subsequently improved by Captain Huddart, of Deptford Dockyard. Attention was given later to the design of special machines for the manufacture of wire ropes, and amongst the earliest inventors in this branch the name of Archibald Smith will be familiar to many.

At first, only iron wires were used in the manufacture (*e.g.*, charcoal or B B iron), but within the last fifteen years, or so, steel has almost entirely superseded its employment. Wire ropes are now produced of great strength and flexibility, and consequently the scope for their employment has become very extensive, *e.g.*, for marine, mining, railway, and agricultural purposes, as well as for hoists, cranes, and analogous uses.   The applications of wire ropes to towing, rigging, and running gear of vessels, is familiar to many of our readers.   The field of application in the mining industries is also no less important, as is shown in the winding and hauling arrangements of our collieries, the extent of which may be in some measure appreciated when we reflect that about 160,000,000 tons of coal alone have been raised annually from our coal pits by means of wire ropes.   The uses of wire ropes for aërial trans-portation, mountain or inclined railways, and street tramways, as also for the transmission of power—the last application being largely due to the Brothers Hirn, of Switzerland—are some further examples of their applications, and which have already been more or less described.

We will now turn our attention to the process of manufacturing wire and wire ropes, and with such view, will refer later on to some of the leading works of the trade.   The metal rods from which wires are drawn are usually of about 2 to 5 S.W.G., and are commonly rolled at Sheffield and elsewhere from ingots of about 80 lbs. each.   These rolled rods may be about 130 to 150 yards in length, and after drawing through perforated plates, with tapering holes of decreasing diameters —to say a 14 W. gauge—are elongated to about 1200 yards in length. It should be understood, however, that this is not effected by one process, but by a dozen or more separate " drawing" operations during which the wire may have to be several times annealed or tempered, for, as the process of " drawing" proceeds, the metal becomes proportionally hardened.   In practice, the wire is sometimes returned about a half a dozen times to the annealing pots, during the process of drawing down to a small gauge.   The metallic rods may be of iron, " Bessemer, crucible, or plough steel," &c., and these are sometimes again subdivided into elastic and conventional trade names or classes.   The first two are comparatively "mild steel," whilst the last is richer in carbon ; the distinguishing names simply refer to the process by which the steel is manufactured or the purpose to which deemed peculiarly applicable.

Most of our readers must be aware, that the general principle of making wire ropes, consists in spinning or twisting cylindrical iron or steel wires, as above referred to, around hempen or metallic cores to form strands, and which are subsequently similarly twisted or closed around a central heart, thus forming the completed rope.   The manufacture, in fact, is very similar to the old process of spinning hemp cordage, &c.

We will now proceed to take a glance at the practice of wire rope making, as illustrated or carried out by some of our leading firms, and with such object will first describe the salient features of Messrs. Bullivant and Co.'s extensive and important works at Millwall, E.

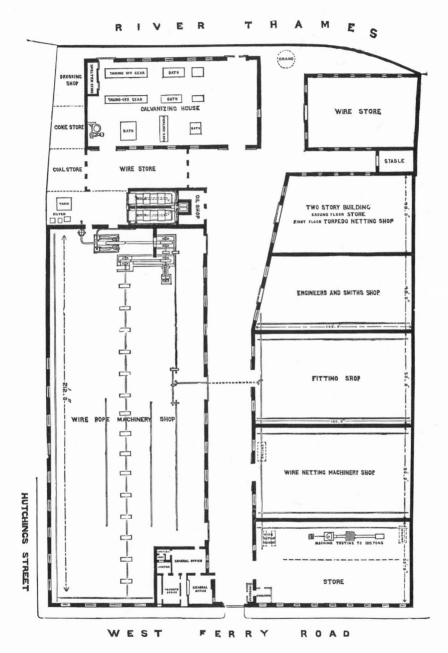

PLAN OF MESSRS. BULLIVANT'S WORKS.

These works stand on an eligible site of about three acres, situated on the north bank of the Thames, with a frontage of 310 ft., and the accompanying sectional plan illustrates the general arrangement of the different manufacturing departments contained therein.

Upon reference to this plan, the disposition and spacious nature of the various shops will be apparent, *i.e.*, the provisions for wire pickling, galvanising, and reeling ; the strand-making and rope-forming departments ; as also the fitting and smiths' shops, stores, wire netting, and torpedo net factories, &c.   The principal machinery shop has an area of about 25,000 square feet.   Wire ropes of different constructions are extensively manufactured at these works for marine, mining, tramway, crane, and other analogous purposes, according to modern improvements. The strand-making and rope-closing machinery provided upon these premises are chiefly according to recent approved designs, and derive their motion from suitably arranged shafting, pulleys, and belting, driven from the main engines in a manner that will be understood upon reference to the illustration.   Amongst these appliances are three, six, eight, ten, twelve, eighteen, and twenty-four bobbin strand-making machines, and some of the largest "rope-closing" machinery in existence, *i.e.*, capable of making a rope up to about 21 in. in circumference, and closing about 30 tons of wire in one length.

Iron or steel wires used at these works, in different manufactures, vary from 0.012 in. to .212 in. S. W. gauge.   Steel wire ropes can be manufactured to a considerable degree of flexibility and strength, some having a breaking strain of about 150 tons per square inch of sectional area. The wire strands are usually formed round hemp cores, previously soaked in tar or oil according to requirements.   Hawsers and fixed wire ropes are usually composed of galvanised wire strands, whilst haulage or running ropes are made of black wires, subsequently tarred.

In another part of the rope factory is provided modern submarine cable plant and machinery, &c.

The wire of which the ropes are composed is taken to that part of the premises which adjoins the water side, and here it goes through a preliminary testing.   It is then formed into coils, and cleaned, either in strong potash liquor or in acid.   The galvanising shop (shown on the plan) contains several baths, and is especially arranged for treating wire. It should be mentioned, that great care is required in galvanising steel wire, such as used in ropemaking, as it may easily become crystallised in the process if not properly treated.   The arrangement is simple, the wire being unwound from bobbins by a machine, and drawn (first through a bath of potash in the case of steel wire) through the galvanising bath consisting of molten " spelter metal."   On emerging from the latter it passes through a bed of sand, and is then wound again on reels.

The wire is then tested again for requisite strength and elasticity, when it is ready to be taken to the large building, which forms the main part of the premises, in order that it may be twisted into strands. Before describing the latter process, however, it may be advisable to give a few particulars of the composition or construction of various kinds of ropes.

A "laid rope" comprises a heart, consisting either of a strand of wires or a hemp rope ; this forms the axis of the rope, and round it are laid—or twisted—six strands, each being composed of a core, either of hemp or metal, around which six wires are similarly laid. A "formed rope," on the other hand, is composed of six strands laid round a heart as before, but each strand contains a greater number of wires. Thus the six wires will be laid round the core, and outside these another layer, consisting of twelve wires, will be twisted. Besides these two there is yet another recognised in the trade, viz., that of a "cable laid rope," which is composed (as in ordinary hemp ropes) of six ropes closed together. The latter form is often adopted for large sizes, but some are of opinion that it is the worst form in which wires can be put together, and is a construction Messrs. Bullivant do not believe in.

The strand and rope-forming machinery is of various approved descriptions. The bobbins containing the wires are placed on "flyers" carried by the rotary frames of the machines. These machines are now common to the trade, and as a matter of convenience will be more fully described in a following account of another firm's works.

The wires to form the strands, or the strands to form the ropes—the process being similar in each case—are unwound from the bobbins as the action of twisting proceeds. The bobbins are controlled by an eccentric motion so as to prevent them revolving or putting a turn in the wires, and the strands are closed by means of the revolving frame and a fixed lay plate or tube, the wires being drawn off and closed by drums actuated by gearing driven by the revolving portion of the machine. In another class of machine the whole of the bobbins are mounted round the periphery of a wheel or frame of large diameter, its axis being horizontal as before. In this apparatus the bobbins are caused to revolve on their spindles by means of an ingenious arrangement of eccentric gearing. After the wires leave the bobbins they converge towards a cone-shaped "nozzle," which has grooves cut in it, and is bored through for the passage of the core. The grooves guide the strands or wires, as the case may be, in the necessary direction for forming the rope, and after emerging from the grooves, the strands pass through a stationary die known as the "lay plate." The distance between the "lay plate" and the nozzle determines, to a certain extent, the pitch of the strands, technically known as the "lay of the rope." The longer the lay the less injury is done to the texture of the metal when a heavy strain is put on the rope, but obviously there is a limit to the looseness with which the strands may be closed.

The principal machine in the shop is of the latest type, and will "throw off" a rope of 30 tons in one length. It is capable of making rope up to 21 in. in circumference, which would have a breaking strain of 1200 tons on the single part. This is in excess of any actual requirement up to the present time, but considering the increase in the size which has taken place during the last few years it is thought that such a rope may some day be called for. Messrs. Bullivant have made 14 in. steel ropes which present a breaking strain of 500 tons. About twelve years ago the largest steel rope that had been made was only 7 in. in circumference. The smallest rope now in general demand is ¾ in. in circumference, but smaller sizes are made for special purposes. There is also in the principal shop, a large machine used for "cabling or closing" very long ropes. It is 150 ft. long, and is driven by spur gearing, actuated by a shaft below the floor. It will turn out three miles of 4 in. rope a day, and is principally employed in making telegraph cables and other long ropes.

The machines are operated by a pair of horizontal engines, to which steam is supplied by a couple of Lancashire boilers.

The flexibility of wire ropes lies principally in the multiplication of the number of component wires of which they are made, and the manner the same are laid : such number ranging between 12 and 400. It is comparatively easy to make a rope of few parts, but the difficulties rise in proportion as such numbers are increased. Much skill is then required so as to arrange the wires in such a way that each will bear its due proportion of strain.

The cores are composed of either hemp or metal, the former material, however, producing a more flexible rope. Iron commonly used for centres is selected on account of its softness and ductility. The hemp employed is formed into a rope of special make, hardness being a desirable feature, and is treated by a process which consists principally in boiling the rope in linseed or other oil, care having to be taken that there shall be no acid or water present, otherwise an internal source of decay will exist, especially with steel wire, which crystallises by the agency of acids. The ropes when complete are tested in a 100-ton machine ; and when the tensile strength is above this limit each strand is tested separately.

Careful attention is bestowed at these works upon all materials and workmanship employed in the various manufactures. The ropes, &c., made of such passed or accepted wires, are tested for any required aggregate strength and efficiency, as just mentioned, by submitting lengths of the same to practical trials in an hydraulic testing machine of an ingenious character. A side elevation of this hydraulic direct-acting lever machine is shown here, and consists of an arrangement of

compound levers, to which a desired load can be applied, in combination with a hydraulic ram.

The horizontal lever of the first part of the apparatus is mounted upon a suitable fulcrum, the short end thereof being fitted with an adjustable counterweight, whilst the opposite extremity thereof—or long arm—is provided with means of attaching weights, capable of exerting from 1 cwt. to 100 tons upon the terminal or testing shackle of the apparatus. The various weights that may be applied to exert any desired or requisite resistance are indicated in the illustration. A scale of 1 to 5 tons is also provided upon the horizontal lever, and upon which a travelling weight—actuated by appropriate gearing—may be caused to traverse and exert a force in proportion to the compass of such scale. The terminal shackle of this portion of the contrivance is connected with the horizontal lever by means of links, a bent or bell-crank lever and vertical connecting-rod, mounted on suitable fulcra. The ram or plunger of the hydraulic apparatus is provided with a crosshead to which rods are attached, and terminating at their other ends with a holding shackle.

It will now be understood, that when it is desired to ascertain the strength of any rope, a convenient section or length thereof is fastened between the said securing shackles of the ram and lever arrangement, when the approximate expected breaking load (acquired or known by experience) is brought into connection with the long arm of the said horizontal lever and hydraulic pressure is then applied. The requisite pressure is raised and maintained in the cylinder of the latter part of the apparatus by means of an ordinary pump, worked by hand for a certain limited force, and subsequently by a gas motor, and by which the ram and its connections are forced outwards and away from the lever mechanism, thus exerting a corresponding straining force upon the connecting piece of rope subjected to testing. Such force and strain are continued until the said portion of rope breaks or the resisting loads are overcome, and the horizontal lever raised against a stop controlling its movement. Thus by increasing the weights or resistance of the levers, the breaking strain of any rope may be accurately ascertained. The hydraulic cylinder is fitted with a pressure gauge, which indicates the force exerted when a rope is thus ruptured or parted. The auxiliary loading of the horizontal lever from 1 to 5 tons, or integral parts of same, is effected by moving the travelling weight along the same, as before mentioned. It is obvious that other manufactures and materials than ropes or wires may be tested in this machine.

As previously stated, the adoption of steel wire ropes, instead of chains and hemp ropes, has given great facilities during the last few years, the following being a few typical examples of applications of wire ropes supplied by this firm.

The 100-ton sheer legs (at Cronstadt) lately erected for the Russian Government by Messrs. Day, Summers, and Co., of Southampton, is worked by six parts of a 6-in. rope.

The 100-ton sheer legs of Messrs. Wm. Denny Brothers, Dumbarton, is operated by eight parts of a 5-in. rope.

The new floating derrick " Leviathan," designed and built by Messrs. Hunter and English for the East and West India Dock Company, is fitted.with six parts of a 6-in. rope.

Further exemplifications of the value of these specialities may be mentioned in connection with Messrs. Day, Summers, and Co.'s slipway at Southampton, where a rope 9 in. in circumference is worked from a barrel 4 ft. 6 in. in diameter, and also at the slipway at Ayr, where a 12-in. rope is used (taking a breaking strain of over 400 tons) and worked from a barrel 6 ft. in diameter.

This firm has also supplied traction ropes for the Highgate Hill Cable Tramway, and for similar mechanical tramways at Melbourne, Sydney, Mornington, San Francisco, and other parts.

Messrs. Bullivant and Co. have recently supplied the erection plans (that is, ropes, pulleys, and running gear) for the Sukkur Bridge about to be erected over the Indus, a clear span of 790 ft., and connecting the Karrachi and Quetta Railways.

At a shareholders' meeting of the St. Paulo Railway Company, Brazil, held at Cannon-steet Hotel in April, 1885, the chairman stated, " The Serra wire rope supplied by Messrs. Bullivant and Co., had run about 33,000 miles, and showed an increase of service of 23 per cent. more than any other rope used before on this incline."

The following Table shows the corresponding weights and strengths, &c., of different wire ropes made by this firm, and as compared with hemp ropes :—

Flexible Steel Wire Hawsers and Cables.				Tarred Hemp Rope.		
Size. Circumference.	Weight per Fathom.	Guaranteed Breaking Strain.	Diameter of Barrel or Sheave round which it may be Worked.*	Size.	Weight per Fathom.	Breaking Strain.
in.	lb.	tons.	in.	in.	lb.	tons
12	115	320	72			
11	97	270	66			
10	80	220	60			
9	65	180	54			
8	53	150	48	25	146	125
7	41	116	42	23	123	106
6	33	88	36	19	84	72
5	23½	64	30	15	56	50
4½	15	39	27	13	39	34
4	12	33	24	12	33	29
3½	9	26	21	11	28	24½
3	7	18	18	9	19	16½
2½	4½	12	15	7½	13	11½
2¼	3¾	9	13½	6½	11¼	10
2	2¾	7	12	5¾	9	8
1¾	2	5½	10½	5	6½	6
1½	1¾	4	9	4	4	4
1¼	1	2½	7½	3½	3¼	2¾
1	¾	1¾	6	2¾	2	1¾

* Where the rope only passes over a sheave, the diameter of the sheave may be one-sixth less than where the rope takes an entire turn round.

The following are some examples of the construction of different ropes as manufactured at Messrs. Bullivant's works.

A 2-in. to 3-in. circumference "laid rope," suitable for haulage purposes, &c., would be made of 6 strands, each of 7 wires, of 16 and 12 gauge respectively.

A 4-in. circumference winding rope, would be made either as a "laid rope" having 6 strands each of 7 wires of 8 gauge or as a "formed rope" having 6 strands each of 19 wires of 14 gauge.

A 6-in. circumference rope, of a standing type, could be composed of 6 strands each of 19 wires of 9 gauge, but on their system of making flexible ropes it would be made of 6 strands each of 30 wires, that is, each strand would have a hemp centre covered by 12 wires and then again by a layer of 18 wires all of 13 gauge.

A 12-in. rope is usually made at these works of 6 strands each of 61 wires, that is, each strand would be composed first of 7 wires; which would then be coated with 12 wires, this again with 18 wires, and finally with 24 wires.

It may be casually mentioned as a matter of general interest, that a special department is here set aside for the manufacture of torpedo nets—a speciality to which this firm has devoted much attention with considerable success; the principal vessels of most of the British and European navies being now provided with such protective appliances. In practice, such provisions have been found to be effectual. These nets are composed of a combination of woven steel wire grummets, secured by small welded rings, capable of resisting an impact of about 6 to 8 tons, each complete net measuring about 15 ft. by 20 ft. In practice two of such nets are supported between light steel booms, capable of being swung in vertical and horizontal planes and projecting over the vessel's side. Each of these booms is fitted with runners and tackle gear, so that the nets may be hauled out and set in position in a few minutes. Intermediate guys are also provided, so as to prevent boats effectually charging the nets.

We will now take a glance at Messrs. George Cradock and Co.'s wire and wire rope works at Wakefield. The general arrangement and equipment of this factory affords another good example of a modern and efficient wire rope works. Here the entire process, from wire-drawing, testing, and strand spinning, to closing the finished rope, may be seen in daily operation.

These works occupy an area of about three acres, and are situated on a convenient and accessible site, the buildings being chiefly composed of red brickwork with ornamental iron roofing supported upon light columns, &c.

Fig. 1 of these illustrations, on page 149, represents a plan of the works, and from it the general arrangement and situation of the various manufacturing departments will be understood.

It will be seen that there are two engine-houses marked Nos. 1 and 2 on the plan, which contain engines of the horizontal Corliss type of 150 horse-power each, the former operating the machinery in the core carding, spinning, rope-stranding and closing departments, and the latter driving the wire-drawing mill, &c. The engines are supplied with steam by two steel boilers, 7 ft. 6 in. in diameter and 28 ft. long, constructed with corrugated flues and fitted with Green's fuel economisers. The machines are actuated chiefly by overhead shafting and pulleys, motion being imparted to the shafting by cotton-rope belting driven by the engine. The strand and rope-making shop has an area of about 16,000 square feet, and in it the strand-forming and rope-closing machines are located ; in this shop a powerful overhead travelling crane is provided.

Portions of the rolled rods are here first submitted to chemical examination in the laboratory, in order to determine by analyses their exact composition, *e.g.*, the presence of the requisite amount of carbon, and, conversely, the requisite reduction or elimination of sulphur, phosphorus, and silicon, &c.

All rods not rejected are passed on for tempering, a process regarded as a trade secret, and upon it the excellence of the wire largely depends.

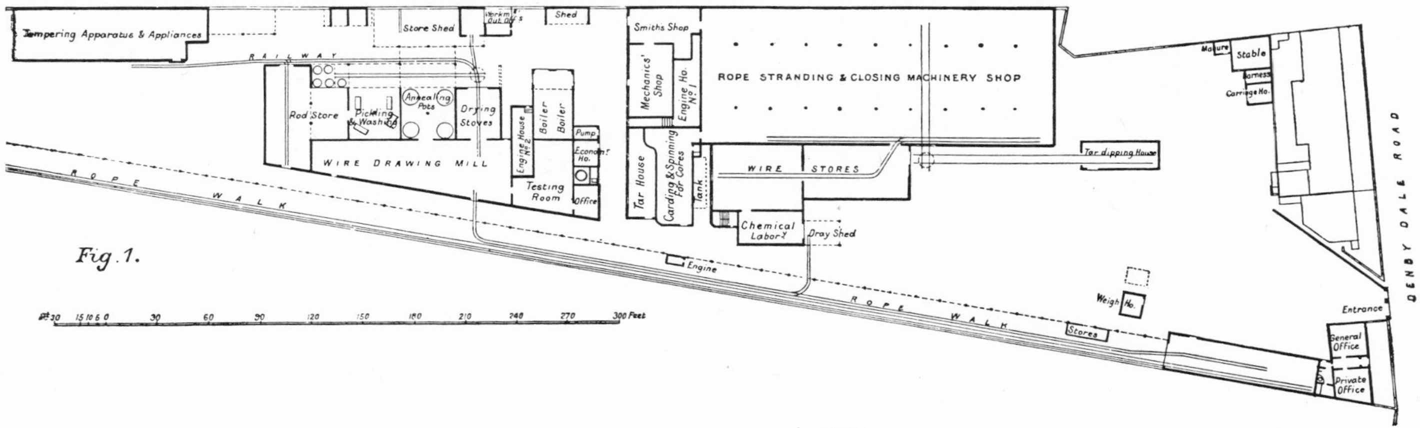
Tempering Apparatus & Appliances
RAILWAY
Store Shed
Workm Out Off's
Shed
Smiths Shop
Rod Store
Pickling & Washing
Annealing Pots
Drying Stoves
Engine House No 2
Boiler
Boiler
Pump
Econom.r Ho.
Testing Room
Office
WIRE DRAWING MILL
Mechanics' Shop
Engine Ho. No 1
ROPE STRANDING & CLOSING MACHINERY SHOP
Tar House
Carding & Spinning For Cores
Tank
WIRE STORES
Chemical Labor.y
Dray Shed
Tar dipping House
Manure
Stable
Harness
Carriage Ho.
ROPE WALK
Engine
ROPE WALK
Weigh Ho.
Stores
Entrance
General Office
Private Office
DENBY DALE ROAD
Ft 30 15 10 6 0 30 60 90 120 150 180 210 240 270 300 Feet

Fig. 1.

PLAN OF MESSRS. CRADOCK'S WORKS.

After tempering, the rods are taken to the smiths' shop, where one end is heated in a forge and "pointed" on an anvil, so as to present a tapering point capable of being introduced into the holes in the "draw-plates." The rods are then taken to the pickling and washing departments, where they are thoroughly bathed in a dilute acid solution, and subsequently washed with water to remove external grease, dirt, or

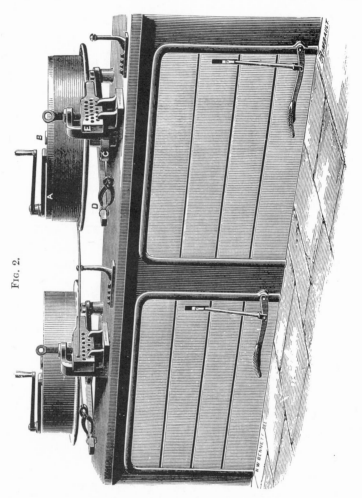

Fig. 2.

impurities. These cleansed rods are then dipped into lime water to assist the process of "drawing," and are afterwards removed to the stove or drying chamber for desiccation. These rods are now ready for the process of "wire-drawing," and accordingly are removed to this department.

The wire-drawing mill consists of a number of horizontal drums—

termed in the trade " blocks "—arranged to revolve on vertical axes upon a long counter or table, and by them the rods are drawn through perforated plates held in vices or clamping frames fixed to the counter, as will be readily understood by reference to Fig. 2, which represents a portion of the mill, with its requisite subsidiary appliances. The drawing pulleys are shown at A, arranged on vertical spindles B, capable of being put into motion or stopped by convenient known means, and C are cams fixed on the spindles ; E the draw-plates held by the vices, and D the pincers for starting the drawing operations.

It will be understood that the " pointed end of a rod" is introduced into one of the holes in a " draw-plate," and the portion projecting on the opposite side is laid hold of and pulled by a pair of the pincers. A pulley is then set in motion, and the rod drawn through the plate, by the pincer lever or draw-bar being forced back by the revolving cam for a distance equal to its throw, when the rod is released and caught hold of again nearer the draw-plate, this operation being continued until a sufficient length has been drawn in order to obtain a turn round the revolving pulley. When this is done, the turning of the pulley draws the whole rod through, thereby increasing its length, and of course reducing its diameter, and this process is repeated over a series of drawing pulleys, and through plates with decreasing apertures until the wire is drawn to the required gauge, the process being facilitated by the application of lubricants known as "wire-drawer's soap or grease." As before mentioned, after drawing the wire a certain number of times, the properties of the metal become altered, and consequently it has to be frequently annealed.

The successive draw-plates are formed with a number of tapering holes of decreasing diameters, the accuracy of which is frequently tried by the insertion of gauge punches. When the holes have increased in size by wear, the plates are heated and hammered up, and the holes partially repunched. It should be understood that the rods or wires are not cut, but simply drawn down, so that there is no appreciable diminution in quantity or weight of metal. The wires having been thus drawn to the required gauges, the bundles are transferred to the testing-room, where they are proved for torsional and flexible efficiency and degrees of tensile resistance by a weighted lever testing machine. The bundles which pass the wire-drawers' standard tests are now sent to the wire store of the strand and ropemaking department, all of which are shown on the plan.

Here, however, the wire-drawers' tests are not finally accepted, but the bundles are subjected to a similar ordeal by the ropemakers, thus affording a means of insuring the introduction of only approved wires into the manufacture. This firm conducts its departments upon thorough and scientific bases, combined with requisite care to insure that only the best materials shall be used.

It has been found that wires of extremely high tensile resistance are not necessary or desirable in the manufacture of ropes, and that some of the best results have been obtained with crucible steel wires having a tensile resistance of about 80 or 85 tons per square inch of sectional area. Such wires possess a proper proportion of elasticity and toughness. Before describing the actual manufacture of wire strands and ropes, we may refer to the subject of making the cores or centres, which are composed of hemp or wires according to requirements, in either a simple or compound form, but it is to the former class that we shall now refer. The best Russian hemp, which is here commonly used for this class of cores, is first " carded " by machinery to extract dirt and extraneous substances, and afterwards the fibres are drawn, spun, and warped, in a somewhat similar manner to the process of cotton and flax spinning. The fibres after being spun into yarns are thoroughly saturated with tar and subsequently formed into an ordinary hemp rope upon the " rope walk " in the usual primitive fashion. It will be understood that in making wire strands or ropes with hempen cores, the latter are " fed in " centrally, whilst the wires are twisted or closed around the same, but they are not supposed to contribute any useful strength to a rope.

The method of forming wire strands will now be explained with reference to Fig. 3, which represents one type of strand-making machine employed at these works. The selected wires of a requisite gauge—dependent upon the class of strands to be formed—are wound upon the bobbins A and placed in the "flyers" of the revolving frame B of the machine. The type selected for illustration has six bobbins or wires to the strand, and is a size largely used in the trade. The outer ends of the wires coiled upon the bobbins are passed through apertures provided in the rotary framing to the perforated revolving nozzle-piece C, and thence through the fixed closing block or tube D to the " drawoff drums" E. The hempen or wire core is drawn into the centre of the wires through the hollow shaft F of the rotary portion of the machine.

Attention is directed to the " tandem " arrangement of the wire bobbins, and consequently the easy angle at which the wires are drawn through the nozzle C to the closing contrivance D, which also serves to lay the wires compactly without materially bending or straining them, and further serving to push back any slack which may arise from difference of tension on the bobbins, &c. The bobbins A are mounted in flyers controlled by an eccentric motion at the back of the machine, so that whilst the framing B revolves they are always maintained in a vertical position, and thus any individual twisting of the wires is prevented. Each bobbin is mounted on an independent axis and provided

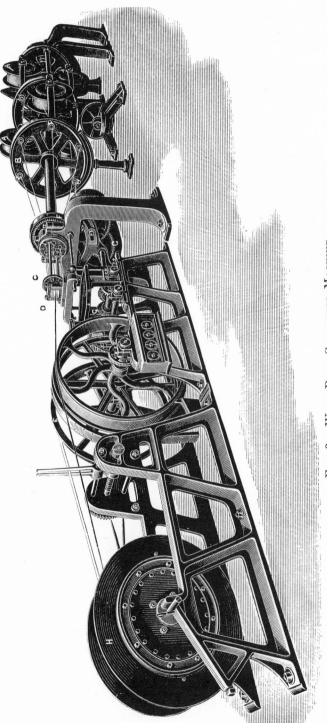

FIG. 3. WIRE ROPE STRANDING MACHINE.

with a tension cord and set screw so that the wires may be paid out uniformly.

The drawing-off drum E, is driven by a train of gearing G actuated by a spurwheel on the revolving portion of the machine, and which is proportioned to drive the drum E at a certain speed to obtain a required length of lay in the strand, or in other words, whilst the bobbins and frame are making one complete revolution, the periphery of the draw-off drum is arranged to receive an angular movement pro-portional to the lay required. When it is desired to change the lay of a strand, a different arrangement of gearing is substituted by means of " change wheels." The completed portion of a strand is wound upon a bobbin H, which is afterwards removed and placed in the flyer of a rope-closing machine of a similar construction to the strand machine already described. When it is required to form strands in long lengths, the wires are separately united by brazing a tucking, and in this manner a practically continuous strand of almost any length can be produced.

The example above given, represents the manufacture of a simple or six-wire strand, but it will be understood that strands of twelve, eighteen, or twenty-four wires can be produced by using similar but larger machines, *i.e.*, a machine with a corresponding number of flyers and bobbins to the class of strand to be manufactured, or number of wires required to form the same.

The wire strands formed in the manner just described—and wound upon the terminal bobbins—are afterwards removed to the " rope-closing " machines, which are very similar in construction and opera-tion to the "strand-forming machine" already explained, but are driven at a lower speed. For example, whereas the velocity of the former-named machines may be from, say, fifteen to thirty revolutions per minute, the latter may attain a speed of about one hundred and ten revolutions, and in some types of stranding machines it may exceed two hundred revolutions per minute.

Fig. 4 of the illustrations shows one type of " rope-closing machine" used at these works, and represents a large class of machine designed for closing about 30 tons of strands in one continuous length, and which has recently been employed in making ropes for the Melbourne cable tramways. These ropes were constructed of patent crucible steel wires, presenting a circumference of $3\frac{5}{8}$ in., and mostly of about 8300 yards in length, weighing 24 tons 13 cwt., and formed in one continuous piece, without a " tuck or splice." There are six bobbins and " flyers " in this machine, each capable of holding from 4 to 5 tons of strand. A, represents the bobbin frames carried by the shaft *a*, and in which the " flyers " *b* are arranged for carrying the strand bobbins B. The action of the flyers is controlled by the crank and eccentric motion D, so that as the

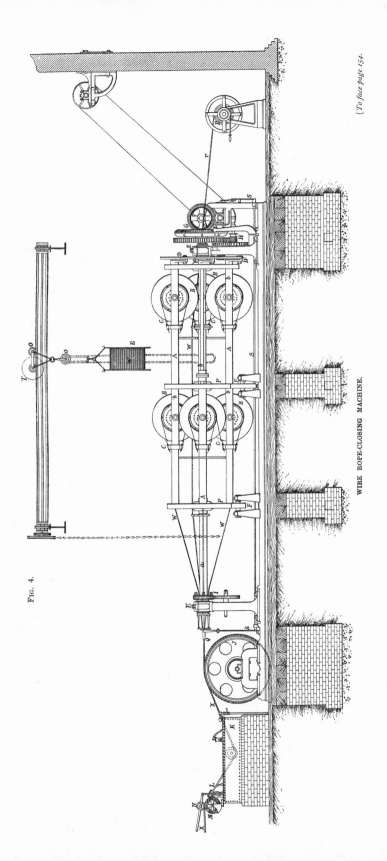

Fig. 4.

WIRE ROPE-CLOSING MACHINE.

frame revolves the bobbins are always maintained in their normal or vertical attitude.

The revolving portion of the machine—which, as before stated, may weigh about 40 tons—is carried in bearings E and upon friction rollers F. The main shaft a is $8\frac{1}{2}$ in. in diameter, and composed of the best " Lowmoor iron." The supporting rollers have axles of " Whitworth " steel, mounted in phosphor-bronze bearings, the weight, friction, and strains—produced by centrifugal force when the machine is in motion —being something considerable. The bobbins weigh about 8 cwt. each, and are mounted on independent axes, with tension cords and screws C, so as to insure them running with a desired speed and uniform resist- ance, otherwise the strands would be irregularly paid out. Motion is imparted to the revolving portion of the machine by a train of gearing G, operated by a separate engine having cylinders 12 in. in diameter by 24 in. stroke.

I, represents the " draw-off motion" actuated by a spurwheel on the shaft a for driving the " draw-off " drum J. The train of gearing, as also the fixed " closing " tube or rollers, are, however, omitted in this illustration, as they are practically similar to the arrangements pro- vided in the strand machine shown in Fig. 3 already described. K is the tarring tank ; L are brushes for removing superfluous tar ; M a traction pulley, and N a weighted or tension roller. The pulley M is driven from the shaft of the drum J.

It is obvious that a machine of this size and construction cannot be handled by direct manual power, and therefore the hand gearing H is provided for turning the same during the process of placing or remov- ing the bobbins, but which is thrown out of gear when the machine is put into operation.

The bobbins B are lifted into or out of position by an overhead travelling crane O, capable of being moved at right angles, so as to accommodate the machine ; T indicating the motion for moving it axially over same.

When the loaded bobbins are placed in position on the flyers, the outer ends of the strands are passed through holes in the annular framings P to the rotary nozzle piece Q, and as the framing A revolves, the strands are drawn forward from the bobbins by the drum J of the stationary part of the machine, and in this manner the strands W are twisted round a core r into a rope X between the nozzle Q and a fixed tube or roller device.

The hemp or wire heart r is simultaneously drawn forward (centrally to the strands) from a reel R through a part of the shaft a, terminating with the nozzle pieces Q. S represents an ordinary contrivance for throwing the driving strap, &c., out of gear, when a brake can be applied to the machine. At the commencement, the machine is driven at a speed of about seven revolutions per minute, and this is gradually increased as the strands run out and the weight consequently reduced, until a maximum speed of about twenty revolutions per minute is attained.

Ropes manufactured at these works for running purposes, or un-galvanised wire ropes, are boiled in, or thoroughly impregnated with, distilled Stockholm tar.

It should now be pointed out, that the usual practice of making wire ropes, is to twist or lay the wires of the strands to the left hand, and the strands forming the rope to the right hand or in opposite directions, and which was once thought absolutely necessary in order to keep the rope together and render it capable of being spliced, &c.

Messrs. Cradock and Co., however, manufacture now comparatively few ropes of this old construction, as they have introduced and established a new type of construction known as the "Lang" patent wire rope.

The peculiar feature of this type of rope as compared with those of

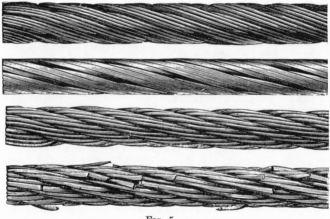

Fig. 5.

the ordinary construction, is that both the wires forming the strands, and the strands constituting the rope, are laid in the same instead of opposite directions, and whereby the component wires are subjected to more uniform work and wear. The appearance of the "Lang rope" when new and after wear, and as compared with similar conditions of the old style of rope, is shown in Fig. 5, and from which it may be seen that the new construction does not usually "break out" at the crown of the strands as in the old form. Ordinary ropes used for winding or hauling purposes are commonly "broken out," and not worn out, that is to say, simply rendered useless at a premature period of their employment from local wear confined to the crown of the strands.

At first, the idea of making a rope, in which the wires and strands were laid in the same direction, was deemed by some as ridiculously impractical, as it was considered impossible for such a construction to hold together, and much less be spliced. Later, some of the leading ropemakers in the country sought licenses of this firm to manufacture the type of rope in question.

Presently some examples of the remarkable efficiency of these ropes will be given. Mr. Lang's ingenious construction of wire rope was first exhibited at the Royal Agricultural Society's Show at Derby in 1881. The eminent engineering firm, Messrs. J. Fowler and Co., of Leeds, at an early date, recognised the value of these ropes, and have availed themselves of this construction for steam ploughing.

Messrs. Cradock and Co., having acquired an exclusive license for the use of this invention, commenced manufacturing the same in 1879. The advantages claimed from the use of this construction are chiefly the avoidance of a large amount of local wear and the employment of a less number of wires for a given strength. The wires, it will be seen, are laid more axially in the rope, and consequently longer surfaces of the same are exposed to wear, whereby the cutting tendency of the wires is reduced and the durability of the rope increased.

From tests and experiments it appears demonstrated that the " Lang rope" usually presents about 10 per cent. more strength, 20 per cent. more flexibility, and 50 per cent. more durability than ropes of the ordinary or old construction. Ropes composed of six strands of seven or fifteen wires is a frequent construction employed, but the number of wires used varies according to the purposes for which they are required ; in cases where great flexibility is desired, numerous wires of a fine gauge are employed. This firm has manufactured the " Lang rope" up to lengths of about five miles in one continuous piece, and excellent results have been obtained from crucible-steel wires presenting an ultimate aggregate resistance of from 85 to 90 tons per square inch. The uniform wear of the wires in a " Lang rope" is well demonstrated by dissecting out the wires of a worn portion of rope, when it will be observed that their cylindrical character has been uniformly worn away and wires of semicircular sections remain.

In the manufacture of compound strands or ropes the lays of the outer wires have an increasing pitch, in order to obtain an equal distribution of the working strains, or to arrange that each wire shall receive a proportional amount of the aggregate strains or work.

The Table on the next page gives the circumferences, weights, and equivalent strengths of some round wire ropes of different useful sizes and materials as manufactured by Messrs. Cradock and Co.

The weights and strengths given are for round ropes made with wire cores in strands, and hemp cores in ropes, and refer to ropes composed of ungalvanised wires.

Cradock's Improved Plough Steel.		Patent Crucible Steel.		Bessemer Steel.		Equivalent Strength.		
Circumference.	Weight per Fathom.	Circumference.	Weight per Fathom.	Circumference.	Weight per Fathom.	Breaking Strains.	Working Load for Vertical Winding.	Working Load for Inclines, &c.
in.	lb.	in.	lb.	in.	lb.	tons	cwt.	cwt.
...	...	...	...	1⅛	1¼	2½	5	7
...	...	1⅛	1¼	1½	1¾	4	7	10
...	...	1½	1¾	1⅝	2½	5	10	15
1⅛	1¼	...	...	1¾	3	6	12	18
1½	1¾	1⅝	2½	1⅞	3½	7	14	21
...	...	1¾	3	2	4¼	8½	17	25
1⅝	2½	...	...	2⅛	4¾	10	19	28
...	...	1⅞	3½	2¼	5¼	11	21	31
...	...	...	...	2⅜	5¾	12	23	34
1¾	3	2	4¼	2½	6½	13	26	31
...	...	...	...	2⅝	7¼	14	28	42
1⅞	3½	2⅛	4¾	2¾	7¾	15	30	45
...	...	...	...	2⅞	8¼	17	32	48
2	4¼	2¼	5¼	3	8¾	18	34	51
...	...	...	...	3⅛	9¾	20	38	57
...	...	2⅜	5¾	3¼	10½	21	42	63
2⅛	4¾	2½	6½	3⅜	11½	23	46	69
2¼	5¼	2⅝	7¼	3½	12½	25	50	75
2⅜	5¾	2¾	7¾	3⅝	13	27	52	78
...	...	2⅞	8¼	3¾	14	29	56	84
2½	6½	3	8¾	3⅞	15	31	60	90
2⅝	7¼	3¼	10½	4	16	33	64	96
2¾	7¾	3⅜	11½	4¼	18	36	70	108
2⅞	8¼	3½	12½	4⅜	19	39	76	114
3	8¾	3⅝	13	4½	20	41	80	120
3⅛	9¾	...	...	4⅝	21	43	84	126
...	...	3¾	14	4¾	22	45	88	132
3¼	10½	...	...	4⅞	23½	47	94	141
3⅜	11½	3⅞	15	5	25	50	100	150
3½	12½	4	16	5½	29	56	115	172
3⅞	15	4½	20	6	36	70	140	210

The following are particulars of the constructions of some important sizes of wire ropes, as made at these works :—

Sizes. Circumference.	Number of Strands.	Number of Wires in Strands.	Number of Wires in Cores.	Gauge of Wires.	Lay of Strands.	Lay of Ropes.
in.				in.	in.	in.
2	6	6	1	.072	2¼	6
3	6	6	1	.105	3	7½
4	6	8	7	.116	3¾	9
6	6	10	7	.146	4¾	13

One hundred and thirty-four tons and twenty-four tons of this firm's ropes have recently been shipped to Australia and New Zealand respectively for the cable tramway enterprises in these colonies, and

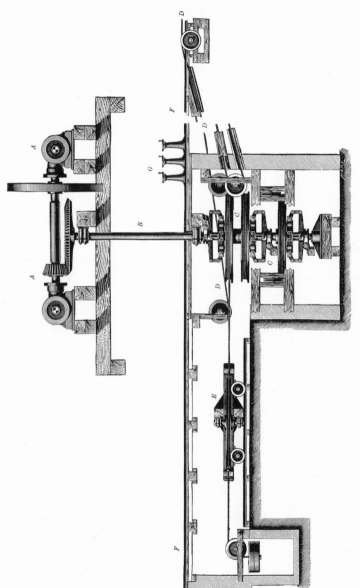

THE CLIFTON COLLIERY UNDERGROUND HAULAGE SYSTEM.

[*To face page* 159.

reports received of their performances are very satisfactory. These ropes were made of patent crucible steel wire.

We will now refer to some practical applications of these ropes which the author has inspected at work or examined after removal.

During a recent visit to the Clifton Colliery, Nottingham, the writer inspected with interest Mr. Fisher's system of underground haulage, and where a rope, by Messrs. Cradock and Co., may be seen at work which has been in constant operation for nearly seven years, also others for three and four years, without undergoing repairs. One of the ropes, $\frac{7}{8}$ in. in diameter, runs a distance of nearly 5000 yards and has been working daily for the past four years on one of the main roadways of the system. The speed of haulage is about $2\frac{1}{2}$ miles per hour, which is worked according to the "endless rope system," operated by Messrs. Fisher and Walker's ingenious friction clutch drums. Here there are several gradients varying from 1 in 4 to 1 in 6, and curves from one chain radius upwards. One of the longest ropes is 4000 yards in length. Two curved portions of line, of five chains radius, exists on a part of the system, on a grade of 1 in 10. Sometimes eighty tubes of 16 cwt. each are hauled upon this system, or about 64 tons. The rope-supporting pulleys are of cast steel, varying from 6 in. to 8 in. in diameter, and last for about three years in constant use. The driving pulleys are 6 ft. to 7 ft. in diameter, around which the ropes are coiled about three times for obtaining driving adhesion. These haulage ropes are of plough steel and chiefly composed of wires of 13 B.W.G. The calculated cost of the ropes per ton per mile is about .22d., and the total cost of haulage about 1.6d. per ton per mile. The machinery, appliances, and general arrangements at this colliery are of a first-rate character. No practical difficulties have been experienced here in splicing the "Lang rope."

On the Plate opposite is given an illustration of a portion of the machinery, &c., as used in the haulage system at Clifton Colliery, and which has been before referred to on page 8. A, represents the cylinders of the driving engines, supplied with compressed air, and from which the ropes are driven by the intervention of bevel gearing, actuating a shaft B, at the lower end of which the "Fisher and Walker friction clutch drums" C are fixed as shown. The haulage ropes D are wound round these drums a sufficient number of times to obtain the required driving adhesion, whilst a tension carriage E of the ordinary construction is arranged behind the same, for taking up slack in the manner as hereinbefore described. This portion of the machinery is arranged in a pit below the level of the gallery flooring F. G represents hand gear for releasing or securing the driving drums C, when it is desired to throw out or put in motion any particular haulage rope. Figs. 1 and 2 illustrate views of the ingenious arrange-

ment of friction clutch drums C.　　H represents a metallic disc, fixed
to the driving shaft, and round which a segmental belt of steel I is
arranged to work by means of the right and left-handed screw bolts
J, operated by the lever appendages K connected to the crossbar L
formed with a tubular boss, so as to be free to slide upon the main shaft.
The driving drum or pulley is secured to the friction disc H by bolts
or keys in any convenient manner.

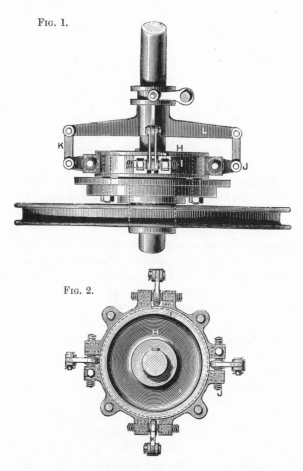

Fig. 1.

Fig. 2.

It will now be understood, that when it is desired to allow the shaft
to revolve without the driving drum (thus leaving the rope inoperative)
the crossbar L is moved axially, by means of convenient hand gear, so as
to turn the screw bolts J, and thus release the hold of the segmental belt
I upon the disc H.　By moving the crossbar in the opposite direction
the metal belt is made to again grasp the fixed disc, when the whole

contrivance is caused to revolve bodily as before. It will be further seen that in the event of any sudden or excessive strains being thrown upon the ropes or working parts, the clutch device will "slip or give," and thus prevent breakages or undue straining of the machinery, &c.

At Clifton Colliery the haulage is arranged on the endless rope system driven at a low speed, and which is a good and economical arrangement where double lines can be laid down and a practically uninterrupted supply of coal to the pit shaft can be maintained. Intermittent and high-speed deliveries of wagons present disadvantages, besides straining the engines, machinery, and ropes spasmodically.

In the example before us, the wagons are distributed along the entire lengths of the ropes, at intervals of about 15 to 20 yards apart, the "empties" going into and the "full ones" coming out of the mine.

The wagons are connected to the continually moving endless ropes by means of clip hooks, and in this manner a steady and uniform method of haulage is effected whilst only a comparatively small engine power is required to work the same.

The intermittent snatches, pulls, and jerks resulting from "tail rope working" are more or less injurious to the ropes and machinery, besides absorbing more driving power.

Records relating to the construction and working of the Clifton Colliery haulage system may be found amongst the Transactions of the North Staffordshire Mining Engineers and those of the Chesterfield and Derbyshire Institute of Engineers.

Mr. H. Fisher is the engineer and manager to this colliery, and the engines, air compressing and most of the other machinery, was manufactured by the well-known firm, Messrs. Walker Brothers, of Wigan.

At the Wollaton Colliery, near Nottingham, other haulage ropes, by Messrs. Cradock and Co., have been running for about four years. One rope, composed of crucible-steel wires, is run at a speed of about three miles per hour, by means of a Fowler clip pulley; the steepest gradient is 1 in 8. Steel pulleys and rollers are also used at this colliery with satisfactory results.

Here we will briefly pause, to make ourselves cursorily acquainted with the salient features of the "Fowler rope-driving clip pulley," and as shown in side elevation and plan by the accompanying illustrations.

This type of driving pulley was first patented by Messrs. Fowler and Co., in 1859, and therefore shows that the identical type of clip drums used on the Clay-street Cable Railway, U.S.A., previously described, was by no means a novelty. Since this date, Messrs. Fowler and Co. have much improved the contrivance and provided the same with a flange adjustment, so as to suit various sizes of ropes. The maximum recommended size for these pulleys is about 8 ft. in diameter, and which presents a tractive or hauling efficiency of about 9 tons. The flanges of the pulley are composed of a series of movable clips, so arranged as to form two continuous clipping faces, in fact, similar to the driving devices described upon the Clay-street, Union and Roslyn, &c., cable tramways. The radial pressure produced by a hauling rope causes the clips to grip the same, and therefore the tractive efficiency is proportional to the strain exerted upon the former. One flange carrying its clips is capable of adjustment (like a large nut), so that the apparatus may be conveniently adjusted to suit the diameter of any rope.

These pulleys have been largely used by this firm for ploughing purposes—being usually about 5 ft. in diameter, and driven at a speed of about three miles per hour and exerting a haulage power of about 3 tons.

They have likewise been much used for mining haulage, transmission of power, travelling cranes and towing boats, &c. Their use is not, however, generally advocated for purposes where high speeds are required. These pulleys can be fitted in a vertical or horizontal attitude, and will haul the ropes with only a half-turn.

At Messrs. Pope and Pearson's Colliery, Normanton, the author has inspected " Lang's ropes," as employed for winding purposes. These ropes, of plough steel, were making forty winds per hour and running nine hours per day; one rope $1\frac{1}{2}$ in. diameter and 500 yards long had been in operation for thirty-five months and still looked in good condition. This rope was raising 8 tons per wind, or 500 tons of coal in eight

COLLIERY WINDING ENGINES.

To face page 163.

hours, or 1500 tons per day, if taking into consideration the dead weight of cages and rope, &c. The maximum speed of the winding drum (of about 18 ft. in diameter) was something like 25 miles per hour, and ran a peripheral distance equal to some 18,000 miles per annum. The usual average lives of the under ropes was stated to be seventeen months, and the over ropes about twenty months.

At the Monk Bretton Colliery, Barnsley, the writer has examined winding and haulage ropes supplied by this firm, which had been working for two years and seven months and two years and three months respectively. The winding ropes were $4\frac{3}{4}$ in. in circumference, and one 350 yards long, all composed of plough-steel wires. A bottom or underside rope had worked for two years and four months. About 1500 tons per day were being raised from this shaft, and the lift of 300 yards was effected in about thirty seconds. During the year 1886 about 250,000 tons of coal were raised at this colliery.

This firm's plough-steel ropes have a breaking strain of about 110 to 120 tons per square inch.

A haulage rope was at work here, 1700 yards in length and $\frac{5}{8}$ in. in diameter, which had been in operation for two years and three months, running at a speed of ten to twelve miles per hour. A load of about 18 tons is run in each set. There are further some sharp curves and gradients on this system.

Attention has been directed to the difference of durability between " top and bottom ropes " used for winding purposes, it therefore seems appropriate to now offer some further explanation of the causes producing such results.

As previously pointed out, the top ropes appear to commonly last in good working condition for about 15 per cent. longer time than the under ropes. A common arrangement of winding ropes as used for colliery purposes, &c., is shown on the folding plate opposite, and which represents a pair of engines driving a winding drum to which an over and under rope is attached.

The type of machinery here illustrated, is that according to one of the designs of Messrs. Walker Brothers, of Wigan, a well-known firm of Engineers, who have devoted much attention to mining specialities, and to whom the author is indebted for the illustration referred to.

It will be noticed that one rope passes from the top and the other from the bottom of the drum, out of the engine-house, on their way to the usual head pulleys arranged or mounted over the mouth of the pit-shaft, so that whilst the engines are raising one cage they are simultaneously lowering another.

This arrangement, however, puts an ∽ bend in the under rope, by which its component wires are continually subjected to alternate bending and compression, or strains of contraflexure, and in this manner the under ropes are usually worn more severely. Further, the angles that such ropes are worked at in relation to the shafts—dependent upon the height and distance of the head-gear in relation to the winding drums—is another point which affects the efficient services of the ropes. An average size of such drums is about 15 ft. to 20 ft. in diameter, and the average speed imparted to the cages may be about 2000 ft. or a maximum of 3000 ft. per minute.

Bending, winding, or haulage ropes in opposite directions, as above mentioned, must prove to some degree detrimental, and yet it has been previously pointed out that drums with cross lacing at sharp angles have been in some cases selected for driving the ropes of cable tramways.

On the Stanley self-acting surface incline of the North-Eastern Railway Company in Durham—which is 2350 yards in length—a crucible-steel " Lang rope" of this length and $3\frac{3}{4}$ in. in circumference, composed of six strands of six wires, formed round a wire core, had been in daily operation for the past three years and four months, lowering some 5000 tons of coal and coke daily, or about 1,000,000 tons per annum. The total weight lowered by this rope, when the author was present, exceeded the remarkable aggregate of about 3,400,000 tons. This rope was exposed to all kinds of weather, and was continually flagging upon the ballasted road. Other types of ropes used upon this incline have mostly worked only for about ten months, while some have been rendered useless after six months' use. The working hours of this incline are sometimes from 6 a.m to 9 p.m. There are a great number of similar rope inclines working in the county of Durham, and also in South Wales, &c.

At the Houghton-le-Spring Colliery, Durham, the author examined a similar rope, used for driving a pump, $2\frac{1}{4}$ in. in circumference and 5600 yards long, of plough steel, which was run for about eleven hours every night or after raising coal has ceased. This is an endless rope and had been working for five years on the 6th of April last ; it had pumped about 1,400,000 tons of water and run a distance of over 220,000 miles ; the pumping gear is about 38 fathoms below the surface ; the rope was expected to run another eighteen months or so. At the same colliery, some similar ropes contained in a system of about ten miles of haulage were provided for serving workings about three miles from the shaft; the speed of hauling being about twelve miles per hour. The longest " Lang rope" was 3000 yards, with a circumference of $2\frac{1}{4}$ in., and one main rope had worked for two years and eleven months without repairing, and after hauling about 900 tons per day. Ropes employed for underground haulage in collieries are frequently roughly treated besides working in an atmosphere of coal dust, and further, sometimes in wet places. At the Houghton Colliery, one of the ropes had run for thirty-three months and travelled 27,146 miles, and hauled 488,600 tons of coal. It was afterwards used as a tail rope at the Herrington pit for about $2\frac{1}{2}$ years and hauled 357,500 tons ; thus the total amount hauled, or work done, equalled 846,100 tons.   At Messrs. Cradock's works the writer inspected a rope which had recently been removed from the main winning of the Upleatham Ironstone Mines, put on in April, 1881, and removed December, 1886 ; the number of working days being 1638, and amount of ironstone hauled 820,000 tons.

Attention may be directed to a recent performance of one of this firm's ropes at Meir Hay Colliery, Staffordshire.   On February 9, 1883, a galvanised plough-steel rope 340 yards long, and $3\frac{3}{4}$ in. in circumference, was put in one of the shafts of this colliery, and which ran day and night until February 9, 1887, raising on an average 1800 tons during the twenty-four working hours.   The proprietors felt it would be a risk to run it any longer after such a performance, although the rope to external view did not appear badly worn, it having raised during its period of employment 2,630,000 tons, and the shaft in which it worked was a wet one.

Upon examining the construction of ordinary wire ropes, it will be seen that whilst the cores serve as supports upon which the wires and strands are laid in position, they do not add tensile strength to the rope. This will be apparent when it is remembered that the outside wires of the strands, and the strands themselves, are, owing to their varying circumferential turns, necessarily longer than the cores.   It is also apparent that the open structure of an ordinary rope leaves interstices for absorbing water and dirt, whilst the external configuration causes uneven, or local, wear at the crowns of the strands.

A novel and ingenious type of wire rope has been recently introduced by Sir George Elliot and Co., and as patented by Messrs. Latch and Batchelor in 1884 and succeeding year.   This rope is composed of specially shaped wires, so formed that when closed together they inter-lock, and thus whilst reducing the defects before mentioned, present a structure with a more uniform wearing surface, and in which each wire is firmly locked in its proper position.

Note 48

This ingenious arrangement was introduced in 1884, and some samples were shown at the Inventions Exhibition, the following year.   At the present date it would be premature to express any definite opinion as

Fig. 4.

to the probable ultimate value of the invention ; the ropes in practical use are, however, doing well, and the rest remains for time to prove.

The manufacturers produce two distinct types of ropes, viz., the "locked coil" and the "locked stranded" ropes, which are represented in Figs. 4 and 5 respectively of the illustrations. The former type is

Fig. 5.

further illustrated in the accompanying sectional diagrams, where A represents a transverse section taken through one of the "locked coil ropes," composed of a simple wire core, around which are laid a series of radial wire and two layers of locking wires of special form as indicated in the illustration. In the second example, B, the section represents a locked coil rope, composed of a compound wire heart, around which a suitable number of radial locking wires are closed. The manner in which "the locking" of the external wires is effected in both examples, appears to require no further explanation, as the arrangement is clearly shown in the diagrams.

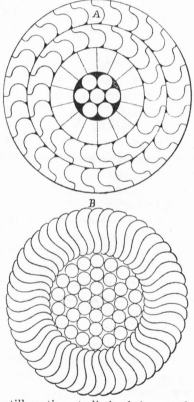

It will be evident that in this manner a dense and compact metallic rope is formed, with an external surface, composed of wires locked in position, and presenting a uniform and smooth wearing surface, like a round bar or rod. These ropes can be made highly flexible, and should any wires become broken they will still continue to lie in their normal positions, whereas, in the ordinary construction of wire ropes, broken wires commonly turn outwards, thus causing obstructions and wear, and sometimes stripping of strands.

The first cost of the ropes is at present rather higher than those of the ordinary construction, but this should not be an important objection if the ropes prove more durable and safe. It is not considered that the "lock coil rope" is capable of being well spliced, but there exists a wide demand for unspliced ropes, and "socketting" is now frequently adopted as a means of connecting ropes which are even capable of being spliced. For example, in colliery endless haulage systems the ropes are sometimes united by sockets instead of splicing, as a quicker or more economical method; while for winding ropes and main or tail rope haulage, splicing is not necessary.

This method of connecting the rope is represented in Figs. 1, 2, and 3,

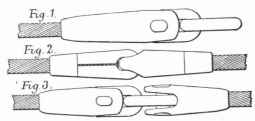

which show a suitable arrangement of winding or tail end socket, and two types of coupling sockets respectively, the ends of the ropes being plugged, brazed, or wedged therein, as may be convenient.

In cases where it is found advisable to adopt a rope which may be easily spliced the "lock principle" can be modified into what is known as a "locked stranded rope," and which practically consists in forming a rope of the ordinary type, composed of locked wires. This rope is capable of being spliced in the usual manner.

The manufacture of the "locked coil rope" is effected in one operation, this new type being "closed" direct in one apparatus, into the finished rope, the machinery employed for the purpose being ingenious and effectual.

Although only two sections of lock ropes are shown, it will be understood, that numerous types of sectional wires may be employed with similar results. The advantages claimed for the system are as follows :

With ropes constructed according to this system, there results great durability, as the inside layers, which furnish half the strength of the rope, are not exposed to wear. The wearing surface is quite uniform, and therefore its smoothness reduces the friction to a minimum. The ropes may be made very flexible, and as they have no hemp within them there is no tendency to corrosion. The wires are securely locked in their places and all bear an equal strain, hence the strength of the rope is greater than with the usual construction, and there is no tendency to spin. Further, there is a saving of weight and wear upon pulleys, as also less room occupied upon drums.

The efficiency and strength of these ropes as compared with others of ordinary construction appears demonstrated by the following data obtained from Lloyd's testing-house at Cardiff. A crucible-steel wire "lock rope," 2.18 in. in circumference, gave an ultimate tensile breaking strain of 101.7 per cent. of the aggregate breaking strains of the wires contained and previously tested.   An aggregate efficiency of from 85 to 90 per cent. of the actual breaking strains of the separate component wires, is the usual average results in ropes of ordinary construction. The breaking strain of the new rope was 21 tons, whereas an ordinary wire rope of the same circumference would only stand 13 tons before breaking; further, the weight of the lock rope was 6 lbs. per fathom, whereas an ordinary rope of equal strength weighs about 8 lbs. per fathom.

Referring to some practical applications of the ropes which the author has had the opportunity of recently inspecting, the following particulars may be found of interest.   At the Kimblesworth Colliery, Durham, two crucible steel locked coil winding ropes, forty-five fathoms long and $2\frac{3}{4}$ in. in circumference, are raising about 500 tons of coal per day under severe conditions.   The lift is effected in about ten seconds, the overhead pulleys are only 9 ft. in diameter, and the winding drum is of the same size, yet at present the ropes exhibit no signs of wear or elongation. The position and work was admitted to be severe.

At the same colliery, in an underground main and tail rope system of haulage, locked coil ropes have been running in satisfactory daily operation for about a year, and show no appreciable sign of wear.   One rope thus employed is about 1100 yards in length and $2\frac{1}{4}$ in. in circumference, the speed of hauling being about ten miles per hour.   The rope worked very silently over the pulleys, and was smooth and bright like a polished rod.

At the Pelton Gravitation Incline, Durham, about 900 yards in length, the writer examined a "locked stranded" rope which had been continuously working for the past thirteen months, and yet showed no external signs of depreciation; 800 tons of coal are let down this incline daily.   This is a surface incline, so that the ropes used upon it are fully exposed to all kinds of weather.

At the Holmside Colliery, Durham a (S or under) locked coil winding rope, had been working successfully for the past nine months.   This rope was $2\frac{3}{4}$in. in circumference and 132 fathoms in length; it appeared from inspection to be practically as good as when new.

At the Hilda Colliery, South Shields, a small underground winding rope, 2 in. in circumference, had been in daily operation for about thirteen months, in a position said to be very trying, owing to repeated severe deflections and bending around a $3\frac{1}{2}$ ft. winch barrel, &c.

An average life for ropes similarly used at this colliery, is stated to be about 140 days.

At the Boldon Colliery, near Tyne Docks, an underground locked coil haulage rope, 2 in. in circumference, was working round a sharp curve and on an incline of 1 in 3, at the bottom of which the sets had to be promptly detached or the rope was seriously jerked.   This was

unquestionably a severe test position.   The rope had, however, been at
work for about six months, hauling some 800 tons of coal per day with
every satisfaction.   It was stated that previous ropes used in the same
place and of the common construction, only lasted about half the time
this rope had already run.   The length of this rope was 150 yards, and
the speeed of haulage about ten miles per hour.

A locked coil winding rope $2\frac{7}{8}$ in. in circumference and 370 yards
long, has been working for the past fourteen months at the Powell
Duffryn Colliery, Aberdare, during which time it has not perceptibly
reduced in circumference, which is considered a remarkable result after
such a period of work.   Similar cables have recently been supplied to
the Bridgewater Trustees, near Manchester, of $4\frac{9}{16}$ in. in circumference
and 760 yards in length.

In 1885, Messrs. W. and T. Laidler obtained a patent for constructing
ropes of radial wires of sectoral section.

F. W. Scott, of the Atlas Wire Rope Works, Reddish, towards
the close of last year patented a novel construction of wire rope, which
has for its object to provide a simple form of "locking," and at
the same time present a better wearing surface than by the old
construction.   According to Mr. Scott's invention, two or more wires
of the outer series of the strands or rope are held together by thin
strips of steel, which have their edges turned up, so as to partially
embrace the wires and hold them in position.   The pairs, or convenient
number of wires thus secured by the metallic strips, are then twisted into
strands or ropes, and in this manner the external wires are locked or
held down, so that they cannot spring out if any of them become
broken.

Amongst other wire ropes that have recently furnished favourable
records of work and efficiency, some supplied by the old-established firm
of Messrs. Haggie Brothers, of Gateshead, are worthy of notice.   At
the Newstead Colliery, Nottingham, 2500 yards of 3 in. plough-steel
rope, made by this firm, was put on an underground haulage system
on November 22, 1878, and which is still in use, after hauling about
1,325,750 tons of coal.   The speed at which this rope is driven is about
two and a half miles per hour, and is operated by a pulley 7 ft. in
diameter, around which it is coiled three and a half times.   At the
Eastwood Colliery, in the same locality, 440 yards of this firm's 4 in.
patent steel winding rope has been at work for three and a half years,
and where the cost of raising coal has been under one penny per 100 tons
delivered at the surface.   At the Bickershaw Colliery, Leigh, 600 yards
of their $4\frac{3}{4}$ in. winding rope has been similarly worked for the past
six and a half years, but the amount of coal raised has only been
230,000 tons. This rope was used in conjunction with sinking the shaft,
and is still in use.   Similarly, at the Silksworth Colliery, Sunderland,

one of Messrs. Haggie's plough-steel winding ropes, 690 yards long and 5¼ in. circumference, has raised 479,195 tons of coal, the working load being 14 tons, and the speed of winding thirty-eight seconds. The breaking strain of this rope is about 125 tons.

As an example of this firm's iron-wire ropes, it may be mentioned that they supply such class of construction for the Cowlairs Incline of the North British Railway Company, which is about 4560 yards in length. The iron-wire ropes supplied for this purpose are 5 in. in circumference, and weigh about 23 tons. These ropes work the passenger and goods traffic, which is of a very heavy character, over a gradient of about 1 in 18, their average lives being about twelve months.

Messrs. Haggie Brothers also manufacture slipway ropes to about 9 in. circumference, and presenting a breaking strain of about 250 tons. The largest closing machine at their works will make up a rope containing about 27 tons of strand in one continuous length.

It may be remembered by some, that it was Mr. P. Haggie, of this firm, that gave some valuable information upon wire ropemaking, &c., at the Institute of Mechanical Engineers in 1862, during the discussion upon Mr. Shelley's paper on the subject, and which has been previously referred to.

Messrs. J. and E. Wright, of Birmingham, have supplied numerous wire ropes for working inclines upon the L. and N. W. Railway, &c., and some similar ropes furnished by this firm for haulage systems in Spain are stated to have given good results.

At the Boldon Colliery, Durham, about 1400 tons of coal are raised up one shaft in eleven hours by means of their ropes.

At Hilda Colliery, in the same district, the longest train of sets in the county, viz., of 100 tubs, and weighing about 80 tons, may be seen being hauled by the agency of wire ropes.

Some wire rope manufacturers design and build their own machines, but amongst Engineers who have made a speciality of the manufacture of such machinery and appliances, the firm of Messrs. T. Barraclough and Co., of Manchester, holds a leading position. This firm has devoted much attention to the details of construction involved in this class of machinery, and consequently their productions are creditable.

Messrs. Barraclough and Co. supply a large number of these machines to the home and foreign markets, and at present are manufacturing the largest rope-closing machine in the world, *i.e.*, a machine constructed to carry six-strand bobbins, each capable of containing 8 tons of strands, or an aggregate of 48 tons of wire. The machine will produce a rope weighing from 52 to 56 tons in one length, dependent upon whether a hemp or a wire core is used. The construc-

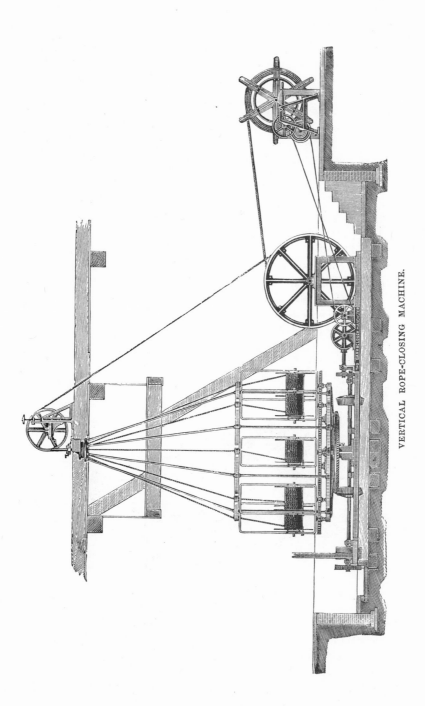

VERTICAL ROPE-CLOSING MACHINE.

tion adopted is "the vertical system," that is, the bobbins are arranged in wrought-iron frames which revolve round a vertical shaft. The bottom ring of the machine runs on a series of steel balls arranged in a circular path so as to reduce the power required to drive the machine, and to do away with the troublesome footstep of the centre shaft. The flanges of the strand bobbins are 7 ft. diameter. The machine is so designed that these colossal bobbins can be rolled by hand into their proper positions in the frames or flyers. A machine of such dimensions could not be practically arranged on "the horizontal system;" in fact, the only practical mode of carrying such an enormous weight of strand is the vertical system. This machine is being constructed for a rope-making firm in the United States.

A somewhat similar class of closing machine, but of smaller capacity, is shown on the preceding page.

These machines are constructed with six, seven, eight, or nine flyers for the strand bobbins, and one central flyer for carrying the core bobbin. The flyers are controlled by "sun and planet" gearing, whilst the stationary lay or closing die is arranged above the machine, as shown. The "draw-off" motion is similar to the other examples already described.

The reel which is provided for winding on the finished rope is appropriately geared to allow for the increasing diameter of the coil, and each machine is fitted with an indicator to record the length of rope made. The "draw-off" motion can be varied by "change wheels," as before explained.

The illustration below represents a special core-making machine

designed by the same firm, for manufacturing hempen hearts of uniform density and size. The bobbins, filled with yarns, are mounted on a wall or floor creel, from which the yarns are suitably conducted to the adjustable rose-plate of the machine, whence they pass into a tube or die placed in a metal box, heated by gas or steam. The yarns, twisted together by

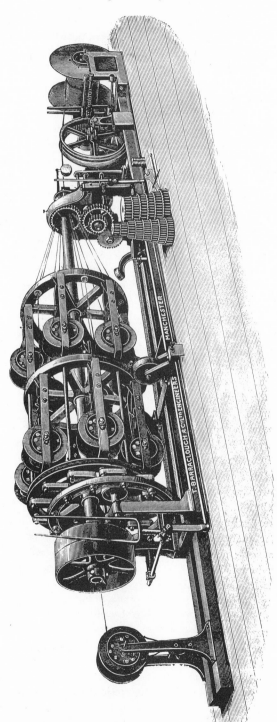

TWELVE-BOBBIN STRANDING MACHINE.

the revolving part of the machine, are drawn through the tube or die in the heated chamber, then pass around the grooved draw rollers, and are finally wound upon the take-up bobbin provided with a suitable tension appliance. This bobbin when full is placed in the centre of the rope-closing machine.

On page 173 is given an illustration of one of Messrs. Barraclough and Co.'s horizontal 12-bobbin wire-stranding machines. The principles of construction and operation are similar to those embodied in machines already described, and therefore it is only necessary to direct brief attention to some special details peculiar to this firm's designs, *e.g.* : The spindle bearings in the flyers of this machine are formed of malleable iron bushes, easily replaced when they become oval through wear ; the supporting rollers of the revolving portion of the machine are provided with transverse adjustments ; the wrought-iron cranks of the flyer motion are secured by keys as well as by pins ; the front end or head of the horizontal-bored steel shaft is arranged to bear and run upon anti-friction rollers ; a novel arrangement of compound gearing for actuating the terminal reel ; a metal belt brake fitted to the annular framing of the revolving part of the machine, &c. As a whole, it appears a convenient self-contained machine, and thoughtfully designed, whilst the materials and workmanship employed at this company's works are very good. The bobbins of this machine are 14 in. in diameter, and hold about 140 lbs. of wire each. Nearly all Messsrs. Barraclough's standing machines are constructed to close ropes as well as to make strands, and the maximum size rope that this machine will close is $2\frac{3}{4}$ in. in circumference.

There appears a considerable demand now for 19-wire stranding machines, whereby highly flexible strands can be made in one operation.

Strands made of seven wires are considered unsuitable for forming many descriptions of cables, and therefore strands made with nineteen wires and upwards are largely used. It is evident that of two strands, each having the same diameter, the one composed of nineteen fine wires must be more flexible than the one composed of seven thicker wires. Until quite recently a wire rope weighing 10 tons was considered something unusual ; now, however, cables are manufactured up to 8000 yards long, and even longer, without a splice, and weighing from 25 tons to 30 tons each. In the United States and in some of our colonies, where the advantages of rope haulage for tramways are being realised, these long unspliced cables have become most desirable.

The above-named firm of engineers have recently acquired the sole right to manufacture a compound machine in which the wire strands are formed and the rope closed in one continuous operation.

This compound wire ropemaking machine has recently been patented in this and other countries, and in its construction it is claimed that several important features have been introduced with success. These machines are not only capable of making wire cables of any practical lengths and weight without splice or joint, but they cause the individual wires to pass from the bobbins into the strands without injury, thus retaining to a full extent the quality and strength of the wires. The machines are stated to be easy to manage, take little power to drive, and produce cables at a small cost.

These machines are of horizontal construction, and are made in various sizes, the difference in size being caused by the varying sizes of the bobbins containing the wires, and also by the varying number of wires which the machines are adapted to treat.

The body of the machine is carried by a revolving central tube of steel or iron, supported at each end in strong frames. Affixed to this tube are the stranding contrivances, of identical construction, each containing the bobbins of wire. The central tube which carries the stranding apparatus being set in motion causes the wire strands to issue from the stranding apparatus and to combine together. In the centre is placed the core, which, having been previously saturated with tar or oil, passes along the middle of the tube and takes its place centrally at the point where the strands combine around it and thus form the finished rope.

The stranding apparatus has a motion of its own, in order to enable it to form the wires into a strand. This motion is conveyed by means of suitable gearing from the centre of the machine to each driving apparatus.

The machine has, therefore, two distinct but simultaneous motions : firstly, the stranding devices revolve with the central tube ; and secondly, each of the same has an independent simultaneous revolving motion of its own, in order to form its strand.

Each strand is carried forward to a central point of meeting by means of suitable mechanism, care being taken in the construction of the machine that all strands are drawn forward with great regularity. This is an important point, as any differences in the lengths of strands would produce an imperfect rope. These machines are capable of making ropes in which the strands are each composed of any number of wires not exceeding nineteen.

After the strands have been united together round the central core or heart, they pass round a draw-drum, which is one of the chief points for insuring a sound rope ; this draws the strands forming the cable through powerful dies, and then passes the cable on to the tarring apparatus on the way to the reel on which the finished cable is wound automatically. It also shows, by means of an indicator, the exact length of cable made.

It may be understood, by the above rough description, that the wire need only be handled once ; that is to say, when the coils of wire arrive at the works the wire is wound on to the bobbin of the machine. These bobbins are placed in the cable-making machine at one end, and the finished rope leaves it at the other. The machines are stated to be capable of making wire cables of *any length or weight* without splicing.

The power required to drive these machines is said to be from six to eight horse, whilst the room occupied by a set of machines is small, and the mode of manufacture simple.

It may be worthy of mention, that the process of galvanising wire usually deteriorates its value about 2 or 3 per cent. ; in some instances it has been more, in others it may have been rather less. A circular section, or cylindrical form of wire, appears the cheapest, strongest, and generally most suitable description for the construction of ropes. Wires of fancy sections are usually difficult and costly " to draw," and further, are weaker than a circular section, and in·some cases cannot be drawn from metal of such suitable qualities and properties.

Ropes, composed of wires and strands laid in the same direction, are liable to elongate rather more than those of the old type, and are more subject to spin and kink, and therefore they appear not so suitable for crane or hawser purposes ; but a construction well adapted for winding, hauling, or running ropes.

Ropes composed of separate or independent layers of wires or coils cannot usually be well spliced, and appear liable " to creeping," *i.e.*, a tendency of the outer coils to work axially and independently over the inner ones. Ropes composed of wires of fancy sections cannot be neatly spliced, whilst repairs to injured strands are rendered very difficult.

The tensile strength of wire ropes is usually about 10 to 15 per cent. below the aggregate strength of the wires separately considered.

The amount of stretching of wire ropes after use is dependent upon the degrees of angularity with which the wires are laid in relation to their axes, and which may vary from about .5 to 1.5 per cent. of their original lengths.

Cheap wire ropes will be found generally dearest in the end.

The high tensile strengths of round wire ropes will be appreciated when we remember that a steel wire rope of about 4 in. in circumference is as strong as a manilla rope 11 in. in circumference, or a hemp rope 13 in. in circumference.

At present, the average prices in this country for good wire ropes of so-termed crucible and plough steel, range between about 40*l.* to 45*l.*, and 60*l.* to 65*l.* per ton, respectively. In the United States similar ropes may cost from 70*l.* to 90*l.* per ton.

The following Table gives the new and only standard wire gauge :

DENOMINATIONS OF STANDARDS.

Descriptive Number.	Equivalents in Parts of an Inch.	Descriptive Number.	Equivalents in Parts of an Inch.	Descriptive Number.	Equivalents in Parts of an Inch.
No.	in.	No.	in.	No.	in.
7/0	.500	13	.092	32	.0108
6/0	.464	14	.080	33	.0100
5/0	.432	15	.072	34	.0092
4/0	.400	16	.064	35	.0084
3/0	.372	17	.056	36	.0076
2/0	.348	18	.048	37	.0068
0	.324	19	.040	38	.0060
1	.300	20	.036	39	.0052
2	.276	21	.032	40	.0048
3	.252	22	.028	41	.0044
4	.232	23	.024	42	.0040
5	.212	24	.022	43	.0036
6	.192	25	.020	44	.0032
7	.176	26	.018	45	.0028
8	.160	27	.0164	46	.0024
9	.144	28	.0148	47	.0020
10	.128	29	.0136	48	.0016
11	.116	30	.0124	49	.0012
12	.104	31	.0116	50	.0010

Since March 1, 1884, no other wire gauge has been allowed in this country, that is, no contracts or dealings can be legally enforced which are made according to any other standard or sizes than those above given.

It may be mentioned, that persons interested in the question of aërial rope transports, may find it repay them to inquire into the features and merits of Messrs. Jordan and Comman's and Messrs. Roe and Bedlington's systems of overhead ropeways. The former system has been much used on the Continent with apparent success, *e.g.*, at Giessen; Lueneburg; at Messrs. Krupp's mining establishment at Braunfels; Magdeburg, Luxemburg, Dresden, Hamburg, &c.

In principle, all such ropeways appear very analogous, varying only in matters of detail; and, therefore, after the description given on page 14, but little more need be stated. According to Messrs. Jordan and Comman's system, some special arrangements of disc grips and couplings, form prominent features of interest. According to Messrs. Roe and Bedlington's method of aërial transportation, similar attention has been bestowed upon special gripping devices, in order to prevent the buckets slipping on gradients. In this example, an automatic gripping action is effected upon the rope by the load itself, through the agency of suitable mechanism, and in this manner, high and expensive trestles or supports may be dispensed with, and practically any gradient worked.

There certainly appears a wide field for the judicious application of this class of transports, *e.g.*, for colliery purposes, granaries, mineral transportation, tipping grounds, quarries, cement works, brickfields, and for works and warehouses of numerous descriptions.

Attention has been previously directed to the employment of cast-steel pulleys for supporting, guiding, or controlling haulage ropes—as a substitution for pulleys composed of cast iron—and with which satisfactory results have been obtained. During a recent tour of colliery inspection, the author could not fail to observe the increasing applications of cast steel for such purposes, and when at the Houghton-le-Spring Colliery, already referred to, such pulleys were being similarly employed with satisfaction. Trials were conducted at this colliery to ascertain the comparative efficiency of cast-iron and cast-steel pulleys, and with this object, pulleys of both materials were placed in severe positions for wear, and further pulleys were tried in inter-changed positions, but with similar results in favour of those of steel. In some instances the cast-iron pulleys were worn to a useless condition in about one month, whilst the steel pulleys after running for nine months appeared very little the worse for wear, the speed of the haulage ropes being about ten miles per hour. The hardness of steel pulleys does not appear to appreciably shorten the lives of the ropes, if light, properly mounted, lubricated, and attended to. It has been before mentioned that steel pulleys only 6 in. in diameter are used on the Clifton Colliery haulage system with success, and that some of the ropes have attained working lives of about four years, whilst the pulleys have run for about three years in continual daily service. Similar examples have been referred to at the Wollaton Colliery, &c., where both the ropes and steel pulleys have run for long periods with satisfactory results.

Cast-iron pulleys, as employed upon cable tramways, have been also found to frequently cut out very rapidly, and thus cause occasional delays and annoyances, besides presenting a considerable item in the working cost of the system. On the Highgate Hill line, some of the cast-iron point-pulleys have been cut through after a month's work. Some more durable and reliable material appears evidently desirable. The present appears an era of steel for the mechanical community, and practice seems to point to its application being judiciously extended to the construction of street and other rope railway pulleys.

The process and manufacture of steel and steel castings are surrounded with technical difficulties, which only study and experience can render subordinate. Steel castings are now, however, much better understood, and many improvements have been made.

Amongst the manufacturers who have devoted special attention to this branch of the steel industry, "The Hadfield Steel Foundry Company," Sheffield, has attained an eminent position. In the busy centre of the steel trades, where all descriptions of this material are manufactured and fashioned into articles of utility (from a needle to an armour plate), this firm has established its well-appointed works and reputation. The thorough and scientific principles upon which the departments are conducted, combined with study and experience, has resulted in the production of a quality and class of manufacture which is highly creditable.

Many must be aware that there is "steel and steel," and it is upon the genuine character of the materials used in such manufactures that chiefly contributes the soundness and durability so desirable.

At the " Hadfield Foundry," the materials are subjected to crucial chemical tests, so as to insure the presence and proper proportion of the requisite constituent elements, and further, the metal produced is afterwards mechanically tested for requisite cohesion combined with capacity for elongation, as also resistance to compression, flexion, or impact. Here, unhammered steel castings are manufactured so as to be capable of withstanding a tensile resistance of 40 tons to the square inch, with an elongation of about 20 per cent., and of a milder steel 30 per cent. of elongation. Their patent manganese steel has given the extraordinary tensile resistance of 65 tons per square inch, with 50 per cent. elongation. Some other steel castings have been made in these works, presenting a tensile resistance of about 60 tons to the square inch, but with some sacrifice of elasticity.

The hardness of steel chiefly depends upon the presence of the requisite percentage of carbon and the degree of heat to which subjected during its manufacture, which should be of a uniform character.

The better the iron used in the process of manufacture, the better the steel produced. Cheap or inferior cast steel may prove highly objectionable in practice. Consumers should bear in mind, that the class of steel should be varied or specially manufactured to meet the purpose for which it is intended to be employed.

The steel castings used in the construction of the Highgate Hill cable tramways were supplied by the above-mentioned firm.

APPENDIX.

THE CITY OF LONDON AND SOUTHWARK SUBWAY.

ON the 1st of April, 1887, ENGINEERING published the following interesting statistics bearing upon the above enterprise, which has been previously briefly described on pages 108 and 109 of this volume :

Last year every man, woman, and child in London rode on an average more than ninety times in one of the four leading conveyances, viz.: the Metropolitan Railway, the District Railway, the General Omnibus Company's vehicles, and the tramways, not including the suburban railways, the London Road Cars, or the very numerous private omnibuses and vehicles. As high as this average appears, although spread over a population of more than four million souls, it is far less than obtained in the City of New York, where the traffic of the overhead railways and the street lines alone shows an annual average of more than two hundred journeys per individual, and which is increasing much more rapidly than the population. The difference these figures exhibit in the habits of the two cities does not depend entirely upon the topographical conditions or climate, but is an illustration that proper " facilities create traffic." If any one doubts that London could provide double or treble the number of passengers which now throng its public vehicles, provided there were cheap and rapid means of carrying them, he has only to look back a few years and note the changes which have been wrought by the extensions of underground railways and tramways, and by the better paving of roads. For the purposes of comparison we will take the three years 1864, 1874, and 1884, and trace the increase of the metropolitan circulation during that time, and the change of character which it has experienced. At the first date the two great local carrying agencies were the Metropolitan Railway Company and the General Omnibus Company. The former carried 42 million passengers per annum and the latter 11 millions, the population being 2,940,000, or one-eighteenth of the total passengers on these lines. The average fare for the omnibuses was 3.4d. and for the railway 2.4d. Between 1864 and 1874 two new means of conveyance, the District Railway and the trams, came into operation, stimulating travel, both by opening up new districts for residence and by fostering the habit of riding. At the end of the decade the annual total of passengers had risen to 155 millions, made up of the following items :—

General Omnibus Company	...	...	..	48,000,000
Metropolitan Railway ...	...	...	...	44,000,000
District Railway...	...	...	...	...	21,000,000
Tramways...	,..	...	...	...	...	42,000,000
				155,000,000

The population had risen to 3,420,000, the average journeys per individual being 45.3. Thus in the brief space of ten years the frequency of travel had increased two and a half times ; the better means of communication had also taught men to use the public vehicles for shorter journeys than formerly, evidence of this being found in the reduction of the average fare, which was at this time as follows :—

Line.						Average Fare.
						d.
General Omnibus Company	...	...	...	...	...	2.6
Metropolitan Railway	...	...	...	...	...	2.4
District Railway	...	...	...	...	...	2.3
Tramways ...	...	...	...	...	...	2

Part of this reduction in the case of the first company was due to the competition of the tramways, but this would not apply to the Metropolitan Railway, which was out of the scope of their influence.

We now come to the period 1874-84, during which there was great activity in the building of tramways. The railways, too, spread out their arms into the suburbs, and even beyond, going to Putney, Ealing, Richmond, and Harrow, but the passengers they gathered on these extensions added only a small fraction to the total. At the end of the period the passengers had risen to the immense total of 308,000,000, and this with a population of 4,010,000 gives an average per individual of seventy-seven annual journeys.

Line.	Passengers.	Average Fare.	Average Cost per Passenger.
		d.	d.
General Omnibus Co.	75,000,000	2	1¾
Metropolitan Railway	76,000,000	2	¾
District Railway ...	38,500,000	2.4	¾
Tramways	119,000,000	1.55	1¼
Total	308,500,000		

During twenty years the population had increased 36 per cent., the average number of journeys per individual 330 per cent., and the general travelling 500 per cent. This growth is calculated, it must be remembered, on an incomplete basis, omitting as it does the vast number of season ticket holders, each with an average of probably 600 annual journeys, who emerge every morning from the fourteen great railway stations of the metropolis. Formerly many of these used to travel backwards and forwards by omnibuses.

If we had space to follow the rise of the traffic year by year, it would be seen that it was quite steady in the aggregate, and that each of the companies had its rate of progress which remained fairly uniform. With the experience of the past as our guide we may venture to explore the future, and to forecast the annual movement of the population of

the metropolis in the year 1895. The truth of our estimate is dependent on the past rate of increase being maintained, and this again
depends upon fresh facilities for travel being provided. More trains,
omnibuses, and trams must be available, and no doubt will be, but the
capacity of the streets and the existing lines will not provide for all the
vehicular traffic which London could and would support eight years
hence if the means were offered to it. At that time the annual movement will have risen to the enormous total of over 800 million journeys,
if engineers will devise the methods and capitalists will provide them.
It must be remembered, however, that the essential feature of modern
city travelling is cheapness, and that the penny fare rules the day.
There are engineers in plenty capable and ready to build railways under
every street, but the investor, taught by experience, will not provide
the money, for he has learned that the carrying power of even a three-
minute railway service is limited, while its fares are regulated by
the competition of omnibuses running over streets maintained at the
expense of the ratepayers. It may be confidently affirmed that the
piece of railway from the Mansion House to the Tower Station will be
the last of the kind built in the metropolis for many years to come, and
that no statistics, such as we have given above, will float a scheme
while the cost is computed in millions per mile. At the first glance
it is difficult to understand how a railway, such as the Metropolitan
with its immense capital, can pay at all when we remember that
it only carries the same number of passengers as the General Omnibus Company's omnibuses, and does it at the same rate. The
reason of its success is shown, however, when we turn to the cost of
transport, for there we learn that while it costs the omnibus company
1¾d. to carry the average passenger, the railway does the same work for
three farthings, leaving a penny to pay interest on its immense capital.
If the railway had to be built now, and to pay present prices for land
and compensation, it is very probable that one penny per passenger
would only pay a very meagre return on the outlay.

As matters stand, the omnibuses, the trams, and the Metropolitan
trains represent three kinds of successful enterprises, each, however,
having grave defects and inconveniences, which would prevent their
expansion from meeting the enormous traffic we have laid down as possible in 1895.

In devising a new means of transport, the ends to be kept in view are
that the line should follow the thoroughfares, and that it should be
carried right into the centre of the business activity of the town. The
method of haulage and management should approximate to that of a
railway, while the original cost must be far less. If a system of transport embodying these features perfected be exploited on a scale
large enough to carry demonstration, then the Londoner of 1895 will

find no difficulty in making his 180 annual journeys or more if he desires it.

Twenty years ago we should have scoffed if told that travelling would increase 500 per cent., and even now it is difficult to believe it can see an equal rise during the coming twenty years.

ENGINEERING was thus induced to deal at some length with the question of the traffic of London, when about to describe the ingenious undertaking referred to, which is designed to provide means of communication between London Bridge and Stockwell, passing in its course through the Borough High-street, Newington Causeway, Kennington Park-road, and Clapham-road, as already mentioned in this treatise.

The first portion of the route is shown on the following page illustration.

The line is laid with due consideration for existing structures, and which the railway engineer would not observe. This subway will take a course below all foundations, pipes, and sewers, &c., and is being laid by a method which prevents settlement.

The economy of construction obtained by keeping the subway low, entails the disadvantage of having the stations at a considerable depth below the street. The experience of the Mersey tunnel (opened since this Act was passed), however, shows that passengers may be lifted by hydraulic hoist from deep stations without any difficulty, and that the public learns to use the same as a matter of course.

It is, therefore, proposed to place two lifts at each station, each capable of carrying fifty people, and that each shall make its journey in about 15 seconds. If this arrangement be followed, egress would be obtained more quickly than at present from stations where the progress of the crowd is regulated by the speed at which the tickets can be collected. At Liverpool the hoists at the James-street Station have a lift of 76.6 ft., and at the Hamilton-street Station of 87.7 ft., and carry each 100 passengers, so that the proposed lifts on the subway do not attain the limits of experience. The pressure will be obtained from pipes laid within the subway from a pumping station near the Elephant and Castle.

The route, as already stated, extends from the City to the Swan at Stockwell. This distance is $3\frac{1}{6}$ miles, and for which Parliamentary powers have been obtained.

The up and down lines of the subway are separate, each being carried in an iron tunnel. These two tubes do not necessarily run side by side, but as shown in the plan they commence together at the terminal station in King William-street, then the down line falls more rapidly than the other, and before Swan-lane is reached, it has taken up a position exactly below the upper tunnel, and removed from it by some 5 ft. This arrangement is adopted because Swan-lane is too narrow to allow

THE CITY AND SOUTHWARK SUBWAY.

the two tubes to run down it side by side without encroaching on the adjacent private property.   At the bottom of Swan-lane the one enters the river bed, about 15 ft. below the surface, and the lower deviates a little to the right until the two are side by side.   At the opposite bank of the river there is no convenient road for the subway to follow, and it therefore crosses under Hibernia Wharf into Borough High-street, after which the tubes maintain their relative positions.   In plan they are side by side with about 5 ft. intervening between them, but in section one is at a lower level than the other, in order to reduce the standing expenses at the station, by rendering it possible to work them entirely from one side.   The passengers from the lower platform will pass under the other, and will ascend by a short ramp to the waiting-room from which the lifts and staircases start.   Thus the premises will be confined to one side of the street.

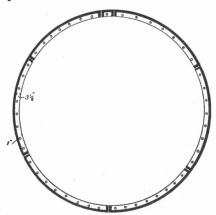

Each tunnel has an internal diameter of 10 ft. and is formed of metallic rings in segments bolted together by internal flanges.   Each ring is 1 ft. 7 in. long, and is composed of six equal segments, and a short key segment with parallel ends as shown in the accompanying illustration.   The flanges are $3\frac{1}{2}$ in. deep by $1\frac{1}{4}$ in. thick, and are bolted together by $\frac{3}{4}$ in. bolts.   The circumferential joints are made by tarred rope and cement, and the longitudinal joints by pine strips. The method of erection is almost as simple as the tunnel itself.

Supposing a short length of tunnel to be already in place in the clay, there is a steel shield consisting of a cylinder 6 ft. long and of sufficient diameter to slide easily over the portion of the subway already bolted together.   The forward end of this cylinder has a cutting edge, while about midway of its length there is a bulkhead having a door in it.   Through this aperture the workmen remove a part of the clay in front, cutting out a small chamber considerably less in diameter than the shield.   When this has been done the shield is forced forward by six hydraulic rams fed by two hand pumps. The hydraulic cylinders are bolted to the shield, while the ram heads abut against the last ring of the completed tunnel. The cutting edge clears out an exact circle in the clay, forcing the material into the space prepared for its reception, from which it is dug out and removed. As the shield moves forward it leaves at its rear an annular space, of about an inch, between the iron and the surrounding clay, and this is immediately filled with grouting to prevent any subsidence either of the tunnel or of the ground.

The grouting, which is made of blue lias lime and water, is mixed in a wrought-iron vessel provided with paddles which can be worked from the outside. The vessel is closed, and compressed air, at a pressure of 30 lb. to 40 lb. per square inch, is admitted to it, while the paddles are kept revolving. By means of a hose pipe terminating with a nozzle, the grouting is forced through holes provided in the iron lining into the space between it and the clay, until the entire cavity is filled with a shell of cement which forms an impermeable coat round the subway, and protecting it from oxidation. After the shield has been moved forward a ring of segments is bolted in, the rate of progress being about 10 ft. in twenty-four hours.

The works are being actively pushed on, and already one tunnel is completed from the north to the south side of the Thames, and the second is following it.

The company disclaim the use of steam locomotives on their lines. It is their intention to use rope traction, a method of haulage which is peculiarly well suited to a subway, as it is practically independent of gradients, and enables a uniform speed to be maintained at all parts of the line. The trains will be drawn by endless wire ropes running up one tunnel and down the other from a central motive power station near the Elephant and Castle. There will be two wire ropes; one will start from the engine house, proceed to the City along the " up " and return along the " down " line, while the other will make a similar circuit in the opposite direction to and from Stockwell. The leading carriage of each train will be connected to the rope by a gripper, that is, by a jaw which can be closed upon the ropes by a screw or lever when it is desired to start, and can be relaxed as a station is approached. The ropes will travel in the first instance at the rate of ten miles an hour, and the average speed of the trains will be about nine miles per hour, including stoppages at four intermediate stations. The vehicles will resemble tramcars, but will have more head room, while their width, which will exceed by 18 in. that of the second-class carriages on the Metropolitan Railway, will render them very comfortable and convenient.

The following illustrations represent the relative sizes of the subway cars, the General Omnibus Company's vehicles, and the second-class carriages of the Metropolitan and London, Chatham, and Dover Railways.

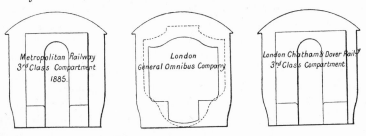

The outside lines indicate the capacity of the Subway Cars.

There is only one spot on the line where the gradients are steep enough to be of importance, that is, between the City station and the river, where the up line rises at 1 in 30, and the down line falls at 1 in 15. The cars will be fitted with efficient brake appliances.

A train of loaded cars will weigh about 20 tons gross, against 165 on the Metropolitan Railway, and of this 7 tons, or 35 per cent., will be passengers, against 15 per cent. on the railway. Each carriage will have separate inlet and outlet doors ; thus the train will get away very rapidly, as the motive power will not have to start from a state of rest, but will be capable of exerting a greater tractive power, in proportion to the weight of the train, than ordinary locomotives. At the terminal stations both lines will converge on to a single track. The driver will move from one end of the train to the other at terminals, and will engage the leading gripper with the return rope. He will then be ready to start out again without the delay which would be entailed if a locomotive had to be moved out of a siding and coupled to the train, and without causing a temporary block to the service.

As there are to be no locomotives used, the greatest cause of foul air will be absent, while the constant direction of the traffic in each tunnel will convert the trains into a series of pistons which will maintain an active circulation of air.

The cost of this new subway from London Bridge to Stockwell is estimated at 550,000*l.*, including land, buildings, stations, and rolling stock. To pay 5 per cent. on the capital, there will be required, after recouping expenses, the sum of 27,000*l.* per annum, to be raised by fares of 1d. and 2d., according to the distance travelled. A part of the route traversed by the subway is already covered with a system of tram lines, and from their published accounts we may find that the average annual earnings per mile are about 14,000*l.* Consequently if the subway is no more successful than its competitors overhead it will take 46,500*l.* per annum. One need not be very sanguine, however, to believe that the underground traffic will greatly exceed that of the tramways.

The advancement made in practical engineering science of recent years is well demonstrated by this enterprise, when we appreciate, that according to Mr. Greathead's method and designs, the bed of the Thames has just been tunnelled in about as many weeks, as years occupied in constructing the first Thames Tunnel.

Note 50

A subway, in which the traffic is worked by rope traction, is about to be built in Glasgow; but in some points the designs or solutions appear of a retrogressive character, and in some respects similar to the old Blackwall Railway. Seven equi-distant stations, some 700 yards apart, are to be provided on the system, which will be constructed with double lines throughout, but only arranged to leave passing room at the stations. An endless rope, mounted outside the rails, will be provided for hauling the cars, and which is to be intermittently driven. The passing of the carriages will be effected at the stations. The internal clearance of the tunnel will be about 144 square feet, and the carriages will be about 7 ft. 6 in. wide. The total distance of this line will be about 5000 yards. All the cars will be started and stopped simultaneously throughout the line, and the maximum speed of progression will be about fifteen miles per hour. The tunnel will be constructed at depths varying from about 15 ft. to 50 ft. below the surface, passing under the City Railway at Buchanan-street, and over the River Kelvin at the bridge.

The estimated cost of the construction and equipment is about 200,000*l.*

INDEX.

NOTES.

1. William Munton Bullivant — Proprietor of Messrs. Bullivant & Co.'s Wire and Wire Rope Works, Millwall, London. See below, pages 140-148. Bullivant died at the age of 80 at Bromley in 1908.

2. The characterization of compressed air and electric motors as "expensive or unreliable" is unchanged from the serial text of 1884.

3. The serial version includes at this point:

> The practical introduction of this valuable system into Europe must mainly be attributed to the ability and incessant labours of Captain H.F. Mills, R.A., although Messrs. Parish and Eppelsheimer some years previously had unquestionably devoted considerable time and energy in endeavouring to introduce it into Liverpool, Edinburgh, and Bristol. The above gentlemen are still actively identified with the scheme which now promises to produce a popular, efficient, and remunerative system of public locomotion.

4. Mr. Brooks — Benjamin H. Brooks, who in July 1870 received a franchise from the City of San Francisco for "steep grade endless rope" traction. Unable to finance construction, he sold his franchise to Hallidie.

5. The serial version concludes this paragraph with the sentence:

> The preparation of the necessary plans and details, as also the superintendence of the construction of this inaugural cable tramway, were carried out by a Mr. W. Eppelsheimer, who from that time has been much associated with the introduction and development of the cable system generally.

6. Recent newspaper research indicates that the trial trip was held on August 2, 1873.

7. The serial version at this point contains the sentence:

> However, the trial trip had to be made, so that Mssrs. Hallidie and Eppelsheimer at once succeeded to the charge of the "dummy car," accompanied by some of their financial co-operatives and employees.

8. In a major change, the last sentence in this paragraph drops some

important historical information. The serial version reads:

> This gripping apparatus, was designed by Mr. Eppelsheimer, but the principle involved in its construction for clearing the pulleys was described by Beauregard in 1869, as already stated.

This passage in the original version strengthens the case that the mechanical novelty in Hallidie's installation was largely Eppelsheimer's. The passage also indicates that Beauregard's grip is better described as a bottom grip than as a side grip, reversing my judgment of *The Cable Car in America*, pages 18, 54.

9. The serial version reads:

> The amount of wear and tear inflicted upon the cables by the nipping action of the car grippers is also not of a serious nature.

See discussion in the preface to the second edition of this reversal in view.

10. The serial version described the control of cable cars as "perfect," rather than "excellent." See the preface to the second edition for comments on this judgment.

11. The serial version mentions Henry Casebolt as designer of the Sutter Street line, and Henry Root as superintendent of the California Street Cable Railroad.

12. The final sentence of the paragraph describing Figure 29 does not appear in the serial edition; Smith had presumably discovered recently the undesirability of the winding method being described.

13. Mephitic = malodorous, noxious, or pestilential.

14. Smith apparently failed to recognize that the method of traversing the curve (at the present intersection of Union and Columbus Streets) in full release represented a major advance in the technology of cable traction. At the outset cable cars had been thought incapable of traversing curves at all. Rather than being an inferior method, the "let-go curve," as such an arrangement was called, was in certain respects superior to the "pull curve" in which the car held the cable throughout. On a pull curve it was necessary to hold the cable as tightly as possible to avoid the risk of dropping the cable onto a non-revolving portion of the conduit. This, in turn, entailed turning curves at the speed of the cable. A gripman could slow down on a let-go curve without this risky practice. The Union Street line on a later extension rigged a curve as a pull curve upbound and as a let-go curve downbound, indicating that a let-go curve was the preferred alternative when possible.

15. In the serial version "probable result" reads "certain result."

16. In the serial version "a few feet" reads "twelve feet."

17. The Honourable W. Morrow — William W. Morrow, in 1889 attorney for the State Board of Harbor Commissioners and chairman of

the Republican State Central Committee, subsequently, Member of Congress 1885-91, and Federal judge for the Northern District of California 1891-97.

18. The tramway in Los Angeles is the Second Street Cable Railroad, notable for the steepest grade on any American endless cable line. See *The Cable Car in America*, pages 323-324.

19. The serial version states the minimum temperature to be 15 to 20 degrees below zero. The serial text identifies Asa Hovey as the chief engineer of the Chicago City Railway.

20. Though the characterization of the Cottage Grove cable as "amongst the longest in use" is correct, cables of such lengths became reasonably common. The record was 43,700 feet, laid on the Lexington Avenue line of the Metropolitan Street Railway of New York in 1895.

21. Mr. Wharton — S.D. Wharton, Superintendent of the Decatur (Alabama) Street Railway.

22. Mr. Richardson — William Richardson, President of the Atlantic Avenue Railroad in Brooklyn. The response to his question overstates the future building of the Chicago City Railway. The Cottage Grove Avenue line was extended south to 71st Street with a branch to Jackson Park, and the State Street line was extended to 63rd Street. Of the additional lines shown on the map and powerhouse diagram on the accompanying plate, the Calumet Avenue line was never built, and the rest were constructed as electric lines.

23. Gripping wheels or rollers — The reference is to the roller grip, in which a brake stopped four wheels on the grip to propel the car. Such a grip was used on the Brooklyn Bridge rapid transit line until 1885, although the idea had been rejected by Hallidie and Hovey in San Francisco previously.

24. The Philadelphia top grip was, as Smith indicates, thoroughly unsatisfactory in making ejection of the cable difficult, but also in requiring long distances for retaking the rope at cable crossings, and being hard on the cable in its gripping action. The attraction of top grips was relative freedom from the risk of dropping the rope on pull curves.

25. In the serial version the sentence ending in "trouble and anxiety" continues "by repeatedly causing and allowing the closing up of the grip slots at places." The change appears to indicate that Smith knew slot closure was a more serious problem than the book would lead a reader to believe.

26. Multibular — a typographical error for "multitubular."

27. Mr. Miller — D.J. Miller, chief engineer of the Third Avenue Railway. His duplicate system was also known as "the American system."

28. The blank space immediately under figure 54 should contain "if."

29. The serial version continues to describe British patents on the duplicate system, and to observe that the costs of the system make its general deployment unlikely.

30. The Kansas City Cable Railway found the duplicate system unsatisfactory and removed it in 1885. The line in St. Louis referred to is the St. Louis Cable & Western Railroad, and the Omaha line the Cable Tramway Company of Omaha, neither of which used the duplicate system. See *The Cable Car in America*, pages 257, 341-342, 366-368.

31. The Cincinnati Line described is the Mount Adams & Eden Park Railway. The projected extension to Fountain Square and Walnut Hills was made in October 1886. See *The Cable Car in America*, pages 289-291.

32. Elevated cable railway — The North Hudson County Railway. See *The Cable Car in America*, pages 336-339. The serial version continues with an account of the New York Cable Railroad, a vast project covering Manhattan, projected by the patent trust. Failure to mention it in the book may indicate Smith correctly anticipated the railway would not be built.

33. The serial version at this point gives an expanded account of the engineering history of the Highgate Hill line:

> Mr. [W.W.] Hanscom, of San Francisco, was first engaged upon the design of the Highgate tramway line, but after some months of work he abandoned the undertaking. Mr. W. Eppelsheimer then became responsible for the designs to be employed, and his views differed considerably from those of his predecessor. The entire works are substantially and well carried out, but many of the arrangements designed have turned out to be unsatisfactory, and, in some instances, almost impractical. The execution of these works was left to the charge of the present writer.

34. The principal updating of the serial version is the passage beginning here and extending through the first three lines of page 110.

35. The Edinburgh system proved to be the only comprehensive cable installation serving any city in Britain. See D.L.G. Hunter, *Edinburgh's Transport* (Huddersfield: The Advertiser Press, 1964), pages 67-113.

36. The Birmingham Central Tramways Company operated a single cable line on Soho Road from 1888 to 1911. No specific history of the line has yet been written, but see W.A. Camwell, *ABC of Birmingham City Transport*, Part I (London: Ian Allen, 1950), p.12.

37. As mentioned in the preface to the second edition, the City & Southwark Subway was projected as a cable line, but in August 1888 the directors decided upon conversion to electricity. The line was opened as an electric subway on December 18, 1890. See T.S. Lascelles, *The City & South London Railway* (Lingfield, Surrey: The Oakwood Press, 1955), pp. 3-8.

38. The map shows the Melbourne system short of its full extent. See John D. Keating, *Mind the Curve!* (Melbourne: Melbourne University Press, 1970) for a thorough history of the Melbourne system to its ultimate conversion in 1940. The map on page 57 of Keating's volume shows the full network.

39. The two Sydney lines were North Sydney and King Street. For their history see *Australian Railway Historical Society Bulletin* No. 441, XXV (July 1974).

40. The Lisbon lines described are funiculars, though the city did subsequently have two endless cable lines: Estrela and Largo de Graca.

41. The underground line in Constantinople was a funicular. Known locally as the "Tunel," it is still in operation.

42. The serial version reads "10 to 15 per cent above that of our good horse lines." Even with the change, the estimate is an understatement of the costs of cable traction.

43. G.B. Kerper — George B. Kerper, president of the Mount Adams & Eden Park Railway in Cincinnati.

44. Mr. Johnson — Tom Johnson, the major street railway operator of Cleveland and sometime mayor of the city.

45. Cyrus Field — Principal engineer of the Atlantic cable.

46. Entry 12 in the serial version reads:
The system can be practically worked in any climate.

47. C.P.B. Shelley, "Manufacture of Hemp and Wire Rope," *Proceedings of the Institution of Mechanical Engineers*, 1862, pp. 170-210, plus plates.

48. A locked coil cable of this character was used on the Brooklyn Heights Railroad but found unsuitable for endless-cable operation because of the difficulty of splicing.

49. See note 37, above.

50. The Glasgow Subway was completed as a cable operation, though it operated by cars gripping and ungripping off a continuously moving cable in the usual fashion rather than as described here. The line was converted to electricity in 1935, and is still in operation. A superb history of the enterprise is D. Thomson and D.E. Sinclair, *The Glasgow Subway* (Glasgow: Scottish Tramway Museum Society, 1964).

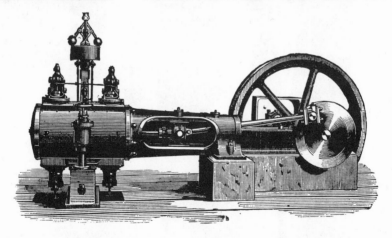

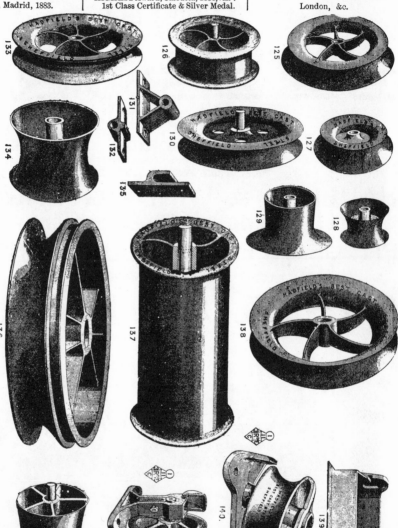

WIRE ROPEWAYS

(OTTO'S PATENT).

☞ Over 250 arrangements of these Ropeways are now at work and giving complete satisfaction. ☜

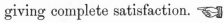

—:o:—

SEE

TESTIMONIALS

AND

CIRCULAR

SENT POST FREE.

—:o:—

SOLE MAKERS:

T. B. JORDAN, SON & COMMANS,

52, Gracechurch Street, LONDON, E.C.

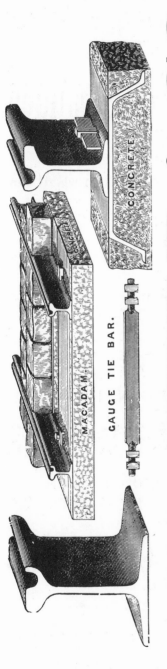

 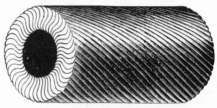